T0330030

Environmental Economics and Policy Making in Developing Countries

Environmental Economics and Policy Making in Developing Countries

Current Issues

Edited by

Ronaldo Seroa da Motta

Co-ordinator of Environmental Studies, Research Institute for Applied Economics (IPEA), Rio de Janeiro, Brazil

Edward Elgar

Cheltenham, UK • Northampton, MA, USA

Published by
Edward Elgar Publishing Limited
Glensanda House
Montpellier Parade
Cheltenham
Glos GL50 1UA

Edward Elgar Publishing, Inc.
136 West Street
Suite 202
Northampton
Massachusetts 01060
USA

A catalogue record for this book
is available from the British Library

Library of Congress Cataloguing in Publication Data
Environmental economics and policy making in developing countries / edited by Ronaldo Serôa da Motta.
     p. cm.
   Includes bibliographical references and index.
    1. Environmental economics—Developing countries.   2. Developing countries—Economic policy.   I. Motta, Ronaldo Serôa da.

HC59.72.E5 E584   2001
333.7'09172'4—dc21

                                  00–065452

ISBN 1 84064 602 0

Typeset by Manton Typesetters, Louth, Lincolnshire, UK.
Printed and bound in Great Britain by MPG Books Ltd, Bodmin, Cornwall.

Contents

Figures

Tables

Contributors

Denisard C.O. Alves University of São Paulo, Brazil

Edward B. Barbier University of Wyoming, USA

Cees van Beers Associate Professor of Economics, Delft University of Technology, The Netherlands

Robert E. Evenson Yale University, USA

Claudio Ferraz Co-ordinator of Environmental Studies at the Research Institute for Applied Economics (IPEA) and Pontifícia Universidade Católica, Brazil

Anil Markandya Department of Economics and International Development at the University of Bath, UK

André de Moor National Institute of Public Health and the Environment, The Netherlands

Hans Opschoor Professor of Environment and Development Economics and Rector of the Institute of Social Studies, The Hague and Vrije Universiteit, Amsterdam, The Netherlands

David Pearce Director of the Centre for Social and Economic Research on the Global Environment (CSERGE) and Professor at University College London, UK

Daiane Ely Sayago Research Assistant at the Research Institute of Applied Economics (IPEA), Brazil

Ronaldo Seroa da Motta Co-ordinator of Environmental Studies at the Research Institute for Applied Economics (IPEA) and Universidade Santa Úrsula, Brazil

Carlos Eduardo Frickmann Young Institute of Economics, Federal University of Rio de Janeiro, Brazil

Introduction

Environmental issues are growing in importance in the political agenda of developing countries with high industrial and urban levels and modern agricultural activities. However, growth expectations in these economies are still high, particularly to accommodate unsolved social problems, and consequently the introduction of environmental concerns in policymaking is becoming more complex.

As has been fully discussed elsewhere, environmental management deals with issues of inter- and intratemporal equity. When ecological degradation costs are not paid by those generating them, they are externalities to the economic system. Economic activities are then planned without taking into account these environmental externalities and so people's consumption patterns are forged without any internalisation of environmental costs. The result is a pattern of natural capital appropriation in which benefits accrue to some users of environmental services without compensating for the costs incurred by the excluded users. Moreover, future generations will be left with a degraded natural capital stock, bearing the costs that may result. In addition, sectoral and macro policymaking areas show very little concern about and knowledge of the economic aspects of ecological matters. Such a vacuum increases the difficulty of improving the allocation of natural resources in the economy.

In the presence of these externalities we have a good case for governmental intervention. This intervention may include distinct instruments, such as the assignment of property rights, the use of pattern standards, compensations and so on.

Although governmental intervention is legitimated, it is not trivial. First, our knowledge of ecological functions is still limited, which poses serious restrictions on environmental impact assessment. Secondly, since environmental management will affect production and consumption patterns it will reveal distinct costs and benefits across society. Governmental intervention, consequently, is inevitably faced with the challenge of balancing costs and benefits among contemporary and future generations to justify policy actions in a way which maximises social welfare. Although such an optimisation path is not easily identified, there are good opportunities to internalise environmental matters in a cost-effectiveness approach in which selected environmental targets can be achieved at the least social costs. To take this further, apart from physical, biological or geographical criteria, environmental policymaking could also rely on complementary economic criteria.

In the context of developing countries, where growth expectations are high, least-cost environmental policies are crucial since they reduce the conflict with environmental issues. Therefore, policymakers in the region must be very aware of the specific issues of the relationship between economic aspects and environmental phenomena to offer policy initiatives which can increase efficiency and improve equity.

The set of articles invited by the editor to make up this volume is an attempt to give guidance on these matters. They cover topics which vary from very general analysis of growth and conservation to specific issues such as environmental taxation, deforestation and climate change. The idea behind the order of the chapters is to offer policymakers in developing countries a comprehensive view of the challenges and legacies they have in order to convert environmental policymaking into an actual exercise of welfare improvement.

This set of articles was first published in a Brazilian periodical, *Planejamento e Politicas Publicas* (*Planning and Public Policy*) sponsored by the Research Institute for Applied Economics (IPEA) in Rio de Janeiro, Brazil. The authors are well known environmental economists who have considerable experience and expertise on developing issues. The Brazilian writers are those who have been working or collaborating with IPEA. I am extremely indebted to them for their valuable contributions.

We have made every effort to present these topics in an accessible language, without oversimplifying the economic issues. Such an approach can sometimes fail, with parts of the texts being thought of as either too simple for experts or too complex for non-specialists. We hope to have reached a fair balance. The following summarises the contributions to this volume.

CAN GROWTH AND TRADE BE COMPATIBLE WITH THE ENVIRONMENT?

The prime policy-related environmental issues are the links between economic growth and environmental impacts. We expect that the scale of production increases pressure levels on the natural resources basis. Does environmental degradation tend to reduce as the economy grows beyond certain income levels?

Each level of income gives rise to a certain level of degradation pressure. Higher income levels may create the desire for higher consumption of the clean environment, which induces an endogenous technological path that reduces degradation intensity. When this rate of decline exceeds the income growth rate, total degradation decreases despite consumption growth. If this happens, it is expected that when the average income exceeds a certain threshold level, economic activity may be separated from degradation. In other words, the income and environment relationship may follow an inverse U curve form.

This is the kind of relationship that the Nobel prizewinner Simon Kuznets first observed between income distribution and economic growth and, therefore, in the case of degradation it is called an environmental Kuznets curve (henceforth EKC). The existence of EKC is crucial for developing countries since it gives room for reducing the conflict between growth and the environment through technological advancement. If that is possible, the technological transfer from rich countries is paramount for accelerating delinking in emerging economies.

The first chapter by Hans Opschoor is aimed at these issues. It first sets the general framework for the discussion of the integration of environment and growth and welfare issues by discussing the sustainability of development policies. Next it presents a detailed analysis of EKC studies. The author suggests that they are far from being conclusive, and there is no strong empirical evidence to expect that rising average income alone will allow for the process of 'delinking' economic activity from environmental degradation.

Opschoor shows that data problems in capturing appropriated environmental indicators and limitations in econometric techniques cast doubts on the evidence presented in these studies. Moreover, most of them adopted cross-country analysis which does not capture developmental factors over time and, consequently, misleads the evidence. Although there is no strong evidence of EKCs, this chapter shows that the scale effects of growth on the environment have to be reduced by induced technological progress and demand-driven sectoral composition effects. Therefore, developing countries may pursue policies which alter consumption patterns to create cleaner outputs and improve technological performance at production and consumption levels.

However, can developing countries attain these policy improvements without jeopardizing their comparative advantages in the use of natural resources in the current globalization process? The relationship between international trade and environmental policy is carefully analysed in the following chapter by van Beers and de Moor. Although they show that the effects of trade on the environment can be both positive and negative, it is possible to confirm that perverse subsidies, which hide environmental externalities, affect trade patterns by increasing pressure on the natural resource base. This is a case of comparative advantage at the expense of environmental degradation.

Consumption subsidies which are usually found in developing countries (for example, in energy) may lead to overconsumption, aggravating both the environment and trade deficit in these economies. The authors go further, indicating that perverse subsidies in rich countries are mainly on the production side, particularly in agriculture. This is causing harmful implications by distorting the possible positive effects of the comparative advantages of developing countries which are then led to increase their reliance on natural resource exploitation.

The chapter emphasises that the reform of subsidies will require an internationally coordinated policy effort within the World Trade Organization (WTO) in which OECD countries would reduce their barriers against imports from developing countries, thus creating additional market access for exports in order to allow the latter to reduce domestic perverse subsidies.

WHAT ARE THE COSTS OF DEGRADATION?

As can be seen, the above policy strategies to reduce the impacts of growth and trade on the environment have to be based on a clear understanding of the economic costs caused by degradation which, in fact, would be the major incentives to carry out these initiatives. What is the economic importance of these environmental impacts and how much does society value them? In other words, without a proxy for environmental costs and benefits, how can society allocate its scarce resources? This is one of the key questions a policymaker has to deal with.

Cost–benefit analysis (CBA) is the most widely used technique to create economic indicators for the setting up of priorities in policy appraisal. Its objective is to compare the costs and benefits of impacts of alternative policy strategies, with distinct priorities, in terms of their monetary values. Note that benefits here are those ecological goods and services which will be recovered or maintained in society and which have impacts on people's welfare. Costs, on the other hand, are the foregone welfare, and flow of non-ecological goods and services due to the diversion of the economy's resources to ecological policies rather than to other economic activities. Benefits as well as costs should be also determined as to whom they accrue, that is, identifying beneficiaries and losers to properly address the resulting equity issues.

Ecological goods and services are measured by their total economic value in two parts, namely: (i) use values which are related to current and future environmental goods and services, and (ii) non-use (passive) values which are derived from existence or intrinsic values as a bequest and stewardship.

Use values are associated with direct and indirect uses currently undertaken by individuals or option values related to future uses. Non-use or passive values are those that individuals place on biological resources that they do not intend to use, and include cultural, religious and heritage values.

Ecological values can be estimated with economic valuation methods which rely on the same theoretical background of microeconomics. These methods can be classified in various ways and literature is prone to offer distinct proposals. We can, for example, classify them into production and demand approaches as follows:

Production Approach

This approach assumes that impacts are valued equal to the foregone income or avoided costs valued at market prices. If impacts from degradation affect production processes elsewhere in the economy by reducing the supply of ecological inputs, one may estimate how much these production losses are valued in the market. This market value reflects a use value, for example: (i) soil erosion costs which diminish agricultural yields, where production losses can be easily estimated from yield-declining rates by multiplying foregone output by respective market price; and (ii) deforestation for land conversion for agriculture and livestock generates income but it also eliminates a flow of income from sustainable logging and non-wood extracting activities, which offers a good indicator of environmental losses associated with other use values of the forest. Foregone output from these activities is estimated using their market prices.

Alternatively, if the increased benefits from conservation mean that costs are avoided elsewhere in the economy, these avoided costs are good estimates of use values. For example, health costs associated with a certain illness can be avoided with medicines developed from genetic resources prospecting. Use values can be estimated by hospital expenditures related to this illness which would be avoided with the new medicine.

Also, if impacts from conservation result in the substitution of ecological inputs for private goods, the market value of these private goods offer a good indicator of use values. For example, the investment costs incurred on habitat recreation due to dam flooding needed for hydropower generation can be assigned as use values for this habitat.

Demand Approach

This approach assumes that welfare changes are equal to the consumer surplus measured as the difference between the total willingness to pay for the environmental good or service minus what was actually paid. Surplus estimation, then, requires the identification of demand functions which can be done using the following methods:

a. *Property prices method* – Property prices vary according to the many attributes associated with them. House prices, for example, reflect size, commercial facilities, local infrastructure and other attributes including the environmental quality of the location of the house. Statistically analysing house prices, one can assess the contribution of environmental quality to house price variations and estimate how much people are willing to pay for changes in environmental quality. That measurement represents a use value for that environmental change from which the demand function can be estimated.

b. *Travel cost method* – Plotting visitation rates to a natural site against travel costs incurred by visitors, one can estimate a demand curve for the site where travel costs are use values. Travel costs will, in this case, also consider the costs of time spent travelling. However, any other purpose for the visit, which is not related to natural appreciation has to be included in the estimation procedures.

c. *Contingent valuation method* – Asking people directly how much they are willing to pay for a change in a provision of benefits from biological conservation, one can create a hypothetical market where a demand curve for ecological services can be estimated. This method is the only one which allows for the estimation of non-use values since hypothetical markets can be created for them. Based on associated preferences, and not on revealed preferences as in the other demand approaches, contingent valuation may incur various biases from strategic answers to lack of information. Such biases are currently well documented and techniques have been developed to avoid them.

Other methods vary according to their assumptions on market equilibrium, data availability and the benefit being measured. Therefore, the choice of method will also depend on these factors and the estimation of the monetary values of ecological impacts will be difficult due to: (i) reduced knowledge on ecological linkages to economic activities; (ii) lack of data and indicators; and (iii) methodological limitations on theoretical grounds.

Although one will always face many shortcomings on environmental valuation, the process of establishing economic values raises socioeconomic issues which ecological criteria alone cannot. It is worth mentioning that the valuation of a few of the environmental impacts of a given policy may be enough to show that they are already justifying a change in policy targeting.

Identifying how the costs and benefits are distributed across society (that is, who are paying the costs and who are getting the benefits), policymakers can also find ways to compromise other alternatives and build a consensus which facilitates policy implementation. This feature of CBA, very often disregarded, is vital in developing countries where equity issues usually constrain policy implementation due to the unequal distribution of income.

The use of CBA on this basis is an important step before society can implement a more sophisticated ecological–economic criteria approach.

The effects of pollution on human health is a dominant issue in environmental policy. In wealthy countries these negative health effects have been among the most applied indicators of environmental costs associated with pollution-related effects; that is, indicators associated with variation of risk levels of premature mortality and morbidity. This is still more appropriate in the case of developing countries where low income levels in the poorer classes warrant defensive expenditures against pollution effects. However, this poses an additional complexity to monetary valuation since it requires the valuation of health costs associated with people's life and sickness. Literature on the health costs of pollution suggest several methodological procedures to value health benefits.

Measures based on foregone output due to premature death and sick leave are estimated on the income of those affected and, consequently, have been strongly criticised since, in the context of low-income countries, it would reveal very low bounds for health costs. Literature has given alternative emphasis on methods based on people's willingness to pay (WTP) for risk reduction which, in turn, are costly to implement. Therefore, several studies of developing countries have applied back-of-the-envelope procedures to account for health costs associated with pollution. More recently, transfer functions have been seen as a promising methodological shortcut to apply WTP-based estimates, thus avoiding expensive willingness-to-pay direct surveys.

Chapter 3 by Pearce and Chapter 4 by Markandya cover this controversial issue. Pearce's chapter gives us a careful overview of the theoretical and methodological basis for measuring the statistical value of life. He emphasises that risk reduction is not a costless activity, since society has to choose among many sets of risks and other key activities such as education. In so doing, the value of mortality risk reduction has to be estimated to guide priorities in policymaking.

Pearce then brilliantly discusses the controversial concept of the statistical value of lives through the perspective of risk analysis and comparing its methodological alternatives. He offers us evidence to show the importance of the careful valuation of these estimates and how they tend to dominate overall damage estimates in environmental cost–benefit studies.

In many developing countries, however, this risk analysis is not practicable due to data and research constraints. Therefore, Markandya's chapter presents detailed methodological guidance on how to use functions and data from other countries to estimate health costs in developing countries. His analysis includes an interesting transference exercise for developing countries of the statistical values of lives based on the sophisticated research efforts in this field in the European Union context.

Understanding environmental costs and benefits is crucial for setting policy priorities and strategies. However, reductions in public budget requirements can allow government expenditure on more objective current needs, such as health and education, than on diffuse ones, such as environmental protection.

The current world financial crisis is imposing severe fiscal constraints on the emerging economies. Fiscal reforms are being urgently conceived to reduce public expenditure and increase fiscal capacity. In this context, charging for natural resources can be advocated as a more efficient way to shift the tax burden from positive things, such as capital and labour, to negative things, such as pollution and the depletion of natural resources.

Very few countries have experienced this shift on a macroeconomic basis. It is not a trivial matter. It depends on a solid fiscal system able to make adjustments, and also on a good environmental monitoring and regulation enforcement to make the shift viable.

The economic literature, however, is prone to proposing economic instruments (EIs) as a more efficient way to apply environmental policies than the emission/use and technological standards, commonly denominated as command-and-control mechanisms (CAC), usually adopted elsewhere. However, the choice of an appropriate economic instrument is not only theoretically complex but also the experience of its application is full of controversy about its effectiveness in accomplishing the proposed environmental targets.

The pricing procedures for natural resources can be summarised according to three distinct criteria:

1. Achievement of the optimal use level: pricing the full environmental costs of production and consumption activities to adjust output to optimal levels (Pigovian taxes).
2. Improvement of cost-effectiveness: pricing natural resource users in order to allow flexibility for producers and consumers to achieve environmental goals with lower costs (incentive taxes).
3. Generation of revenue: pricing natural resource users to generate revenue for financing investments or the costs of providing environmental goods and services (public prices).

The choice of one of these three criteria is also important and is not always recognised through the design, implementation and performance analysis of an economic instrument. Above all, it is important, particularly in developing countries, to consider the capacity for institutional enforcement capacity and public opinion awareness.

Very few cases are made for Pigovian and incentive taxes, although the use of EIs to raise revenue in order to fund environmental programmes and projects and/or to finance environmental management services is widely reported in the literature with several successful experiences, particularly in the OECD countries.

Chapter 5 by Seroa da Motta and Sayago discusses some of these issues and offers estimates of the social benefit of recycling in Brazil. After an introduction to the theoretical and conceptual issues on the application of economic instruments, they identify opportunities for the adoption of fiscal devices which are already in place and under discussion in recycling and package law bills in Brazil, in order to enhance the efficiency and equity performance of the package and recycling markets in the country. To accomplish this the authors have made some estimates of the social benefits of recycling and, based on these values, analyse the taxation levels of these bills. Results show that the choice and design of economic instruments are crucial and monetary valuation may be helpful in this process. However, analysis of the economic and social implications of the instruments can be constrained by data availability.

WHAT ARE THE CAUSES OF DEFORESTATION?

In developing countries, ecological distress is not only due to pollution damage from the intense process of industrialisation and urbanisation. Deforestation is another key issue which generates serious and irreversible ecological damage. Since developing countries control the last sources of native forests in the world, quite often deforestation issues receive higher priority by international agencies and organisations than urban problems.

One of the most important characteristics of tropical forests is their open access feature. It is very important to understand the peculiar characteristics that allow agricultural peasants and timber loggers to clear the forests without any concern about resource scarcity and its economic consequences.

Deforestation is driven mainly by agricultural and logging activities. The expansion of these activities into open access areas has been rapid despite legal restrictions. Apart from an institutional weakness in enforcing norms and rules in developing economies, the deforestation of important ecosystems is also a result of several economic factors, namely: (i) a highly concentrated personal income distribution and land tenure system which creates an immense surplus of low-income workers ready to seek occupations in frontier areas; and (ii) favourable credit and fiscal systems to agricultural activities with no regard to soil agroecological features and managerial practices which result in a mere replication of agricultural technologies already in place in areas with distinct ecological conditions.

In Latin America, deforestation is mainly related to agricultural frontier expansion rather than to timber extraction, as observed in Southeast Asian cases, although farming and logging activities show an interesting synergy in the region. First, the land titling of a property is based on the productive use of the land, such as the area allocated to farming which has to be separated from deforestation. Therefore, in an open access regime, land titling not only legalises clearing but encourages it. Secondly, timber which is taken from the clearing can then finance land conversion and titling.

How much is deforestation related to rural poverty and land conversion for agricultural activities? This is the topic addressed in Chapter 6 by Barbier when he reviews studies applying cross-country econometric analyses to identify the relationships of population, income, agricultural yields and timber production with forest clearance in Latin America. He acknowledges that results are affected by the problems of obtaining comparable and reliable data across countries. Despite this, he concludes that the alleviation of rural poverty would act to reduce forest clearance. This relationship, however, needs to be qualified since poverty, rather than being a direct cause of deforestation, may instead constrain poor rural households in their ability to mitigate rural degradation. If so, policy reform can no longer ignore these rural poverty–deforestation linkages and more targeted policies are required, such as rural extension and marketing programmes, improved access of the poor to fiscal and credit schemes and extended key infrastructure.

Looking at the same perspective, the deforestation process in Brazil is carefully analysed by Young in Chapter 7. His empirical analysis attempts to capture the contribution of sectoral and macro policy-related actions to forest clearance in Brazil in the period 1970–85. His focus is placed particularly on export promotion policies and regional development programmes and their fiscal and credit aspects and implications on labour and land markets. The chapter concludes that, apart from the appreciation of land and agricultural prices, the low opportunity cost of labour will also play a major role in the deforestation process in Brazil. Finally, it stresses the importance of property rights in order to prevent natural capital losses caused by the mining of the forest in open access basis.

The issue of forest management and climate change is inescapable. Apart from local environmental problems, either pollution or deforestation-related, there are also policy concerns on the so-called global issues, such as acid rain, the depletion of the ozone layer and climate change. The ozone problem is by far the most alarming global problem. It will not only alter earth temperature but also increase flood risks by causing rising sea levels and affecting dry seasons by the changing rainfall pattern.

Although the burden of controlling greenhouse gases was mainly assigned to developed countries in the emission caps set at the Kyoto Protocol, developing countries must be aware of the potential impacts of climate change.

Only by recognising them can policy be effective, particularly for adaptation strategies.

Most developing countries still rely heavily on the agriculture sector which is the economic activity most strongly affected by changes in climatic conditions. Chapter 8 by Evenson and Alves analyses the implications of climate change effects on the Brazilian agriculture due to variations on land productivity levels. Their results indicate that the least advantaged areas in the Northern and Northeastern regions and part of the Centre-Western region will suffer most, whereas some currently advantaged areas in the South, Southeast and Centre-East may, in fact, benefit from climate change effects. Conclusions emphasise the importance of mitigating these effects by enhancing agricultural technology policies and reducing forestland conversion.

Can we propose policies which increase forestland values for activities that do not lead to deforestation? In other words, can forests create values out of the slash-and-burn practices for agricultural conversion? How to make this change in the property right regime is the crucial challenge. Therefore, a policy alternative would be to promote sustainable logging as an option for agricultural expansion. One way to achieve this is through a system of public concessions where long-term leasing contracts of large tracts of forests are made to private corporations with clauses specifying accepted conditions on the use of land and natural resources. Non-compliance with sustainable practices defined in concession licensing would be subject to sanctions and concession termination. Supervision and monitoring of these concessions could be shared with NGOs.

Such a scheme is particularly feasible, for example, in the Amazon forest where there is still a large availability of unclaimed areas. However, apart from the serious technical procedures which need to be addressed (managerial practices, concession period, stumpage fees, and so on), such a change in property right assignments may face numerous political barriers, such as land concentration, international ownership and agricultural activity restrictions.

The final chapter, by Ferraz and Seroa da Motta, draws attention to some economic issues that are crucial for the attainment of the objective of promoting sustainable logging extraction in concessional terms in the Amazon. Departing from the failures which occurred in other countries with similar experiences, and accounting for institutional and economic barriers found in the region, they identify economic incentives to counteract deforestation trends and open room for making sustainable logging a viable alternative for the use of forestland in the Amazon.

As readers can see from this overview, the main topics of this edition are at the forefront of the environmental policy agenda and reflect a special selection of studies. I hope readers will benefit from their analysis, results and recommendations.

I wish to express again my gratitude to the authors for their prompt response to my request for collaboration and their ability to grasp the spirit of this policy issue in their very qualified articles, particularly considering their tight professional schedules. I also thank Edward Elgar Publishing Ltd for their initiative in dedicating this special edition to economic issues for environmental policymaking in developing countries.

Ronaldo Seroa da Motta, Editor
Rio de Janeiro

1. Economic growth, the environment and welfare: are they compatible?

Hans Opschoor

One major concern in the debate on human development and social change is related to the consistency of economic development goals and others, especially social and environmental objectives. Anand and Sen (1996) have argued that there is no basic difficulty in broadening the concept of human development to accommodate the claims of future generations on their rights to lead worthwhile lives. They show that their basic, '*universalist*', precept of human development includes such values as the need to ascertain the availability of sustainable development possibilities to future generations, whilst giving due attention to the urgency of addressing the needs of the deprived people of today. The UNDP definition of human development – which includes dimensions such as: empowerment to exercise choice, participation and, notably, sustainability (see below) – also brings together the needs of people now and future needs.

Compatible as sustainability and development may be conceptually, this does not entail that all factual manifestations of economic development are sustainable. This holds particularly for economic growth, taken to be a rise in the overall levels of production and consumption. The question is, where and when the forces of economic growth can be expected to be compatible with development and environment interests. Recent studies on the links between income growth and sustainability and between income growth and welfare in general, do give rise to such questions.

This chapter is organised as follows. First a framework is presented, linking the concepts mentioned above (Section 1.1). Subsequently, the main issue in front of us is addressed: the interrelationships between economic growth and environmental quality (the so-called '*Environmental Kuznets Curve*' – EKC); we approach that from a theoretical, as well as empirical perspective (Section 1.2). Finally, the main findings are restated and recommendations are made on what these conclusions may imply in terms of policy response (Section 1.3).

1.1 SUSTAINABLE HUMAN DEVELOPMENT

Concepts

Let us begin by clarifying some of the concepts involved in the issues we wish to address. One speaks of human development when: (i) the range of social, economic and political choice of groups and of individuals is expanded, and (ii) a decent standard of living is assured not only in terms of education, nutrition and health, but also in terms of freedom, democracy and human security (see UNDP, 1996, pp. 17, 49ff), as well as 'sustainability': meeting the needs of the present generation without jeopardising the ability of future generations to meet their needs (UNDP, 1996, p. 55ff).

This is compatible with the World Commission on Environment and Development's description of sustainable development as:

> a process of change in which the exploitation of resources, the direction of investments, the orientation of technological development, and institutional change are all compatible and enhance both current and future potential to meet human needs and aspirations. (after WCED, 1987, p. 46[1]).

Thus, the notion of 'sustainable human development' is broader than that of 'economic growth': it is dimensionally richer in capturing much of what social scientists refer to as well-being or welfare, and it is interested in structural and institutional aspects of development, in a time frame embracing generations to come. Yet, many analysts of development factually appear to accept a more reductionist approach in which economic growth is seen as a 'proxy' for development. And, when it comes to the sustainability side of development, it has been proposed that indeed this reductionism might be justified (as we shall explore in more detail).

In the contexts of development studies and policy, and particularly in economic development theory, development traditionally was defined as 'consciously, deliberately stimulated growth' (for example, Brenner, 1966), with growth or economic growth defined as non-negative changes in per capita income or gross domestic product (for example, Kuznets, 1965; Tinbergen, 1967). The most important driving forces behind growth and hence development were: an increase in capital per head and an improvement in the skill levels of a population and in the methods of production used. Anand and Sen (1996) relate this concept of development to the old 'opulence-oriented approach' or 'wealth maximization approach' within mainstream economics.

It has been thought for decades that it was not too unreasonable to assume that if economic growth occurred, this would enable development in a much broader sense. Pigou (1920) saw income as a proxy measure of economic welfare; and Tinbergen (1967) regarded growth of production or income as 'the most natural basis for a long-term increase in material wellbeing'. But as we saw, (human) development is more than economic development and even economic development is more than economic growth.

Sustainability is an old notion with roots in disciplines such as forestry and economics. In the latter case, sustained growth was regarded as non-negative change in per capita income over time, without deliberate outside intervention to support it (for example, Kuznets, 1965, pp. 6 and 110). Since the Brundtland report (WCED, 1987) sustainability has come to mean: the capacity to maintain a certain phenomenon such as growth or development, based on the potential of inherent or underlying social, economic and ecological processes. Economic sustainability focuses on the maintenance of a set of factors of production large enough to ensure future non-negative changes in income or welfare per capita; environmental sustainability implies concern for the maintenance of a life-supporting environment essential for production and the continued existence of humanity or life in general (see, for example, Goodland, 1995).

Welfare Measures

Economic growth in terms of per capita income, production or consumption, is expected to provide a proxy for economic aspects of development and hence to enhance options for human development. To what extent does GDP growth live up to this expectation? Past decades have shown widespread macroeconomic growth and in many regions more of it is needed as a precondition for alleviating poverty (UNDP, 1996; p. 27). But, on the whole, one cannot speak of strong compatibility between GDP growth and the other dimensions of human development, notably in the area of equity. In fact, as UNDP (1996) shows, we are living in a world that has become more polarised between countries as well as within them: the gap in per capita income between the industrial and the developing countries has almost tripled in the period 1960–93.

Human development is measured by UNDP as a composite index (the 'Human Development Index' or HDI) of life expectancy at birth, adult literacy and weighed enrolment ratios, and standard of living (real GDP/cap in PPP$). In fact, the correlation between HDI and per capita income is far from perfect: at the national level, the HDI rankings of countries may differ considerably from their GDP rankings (see, for example, Tables 2.10 and 2.11 in UNDP, 1997). Moreover, such average measures disguise sometimes severely aggravating distributional situations within countries. For development to occur it is not sufficient to trigger a process of economic growth in a society – even if that is a necessary condition. What these figures fail to capture, is the link with environmental trends. There are no reliable aggregate indicators yet of 'environmental quality' or 'natural capital', but perhaps we may take the United Nations' assessment of these trends as indicative of the dynamics on this interface: in assessing progress since the UNCED Conference (1992, Rio de Janeiro) it was observed that five years later 'all main environmental trends were negative' (UNGA, 1997) which might affect the future possibilities for economic development especially in the poorer countries. This 'political' assessment is backed up by a series of detailed scientific studies at the global level. For instance, UNDPCSD (1997) observe increasing environmental pressure due to energy use (with still rising levels of carbon emissions) and increased threats of damage to natural resources such as land and water and forest cover, declining per capita grain harvests, increasing water withdrawals as a proportion of water availability; it is expected that these trends may continue well into the twenty-first century. RIVM (1997) report a build-up of environmental pressures and a growing risk of depletion of renewable resources and increasing water scarcity. UNEP (1997) provide an assessment of environmental trends for seven world regions and for resources or environmental systems such as land, forests, biodiversity, freshwater, marine and coastal zones and the atmosphere: in almost all of these combinations the environmental situation had not improved and in more than half it had in fact deteriorated.

Indeed, it may be true that in the long run human development can be sustained only if supported by economic growth, but for growth to be sustainable it must be nurtured by human development and be ecologically viable. Progress towards a sustainable future has simply been too slow (UNEP, 1997). In conclusion of this section: GDP is not by itself an adequate measure of welfare, nor is it a 'smart' proxy for it by indirectly reflecting equity or sustainability.

Economic Growth and Alternative Measures of Welfare

One early attempt to capture more aspects of welfare than the production side of it, is by Nordhaus and Tobin (1972) who developed a 'measure of economic welfare' (MEW). A more recent and also more complete one is the Index of Sustainable Economic Welfare (ISEW) by Daly and Cobb (1994, see also Max-Neef, 1995).

Nordhaus and Tobin intended their measure to more broadly capture the value of consumption. They do so by: (i) subtracting from GNP conventionally valued depreciation, intermediate expenditures incorrectly considered as final consumption (for example, health expenditure), the capital component included in consumption of durables as well as a depreciation for these; and (ii) by adding components such as free time, non-market activities, disamenities of urbanisation, services from private and public capital, and a correction for hypothetical net investment required to maintain consumption per capita in a growing population. The resulting value of MEW was much higher than GNP or NNP especially because of the added dimensions of non-market activities and free time. Another interesting conclusion in view of what ISEW has to say is that between 1929 and 1965 MEW grew by 1.1 per cent pa against a GNP growth of 1.7 per cent; even though MEW grew less than GNP, yet the positive relationship between both remained beyond doubt.

Daly and Cobb's ISEW added several dimensions including environmental considerations. They started from personal consumption and adjusted for changes in the degree of equality of income distribution, depletion of (some) natural assets, defensive expenditures (for example, on health and environmental protection), non-market activities, the costs of unemployment, and so on. The main improvements *vis-à-vis* MEW are the inclusion of environmental protection expenditure, resource depletion, unemployment and distributional features. Of course from a methodological point of view valuing these aspects is far from being easy and any first attempt is bound to be open to much criticism – which has, indeed, been the fate of the authors. Yet, their results are interesting and hypothesis-provoking. Max-Neef (1995) presents the comparison with GNP for five countries (USA, UK, Germany, Austria, Netherlands) for the postwar period (1945–95). The main feature is that GNP and ISEW in all of these countries essentially ran parallel until some point (different for each country) between 1970 and 1980, after which ISEW levelled off or even started to drop.

What this suggests is, obviously, that the link between welfare and production may vanish beyond a certain level of per capita income – for whatever reason. Max-Neef (1995) regards this as confirmation of his 'threshold-hypothesis', on the deterioration of the quality of life beyond a certain level of economic welfare. He takes this as a pointer for the need for a qualitative change in the pattern of development in economically advanced countries.

What is the relevance of this for countries at lower levels of average income? Can one assume that there, too, welfare may be dropping as per capita income rises? The answer is probably not – at least not on environmental grounds and if we restrict our scope to the current generation. At low income levels environmental preferences other than those for some natural resources may be relatively low, so that economic factors predominate. On the equity side, rising incomes in regions of low average income may be associated with very divergent effects on the income distribution, so that the impact on welfare may be in any direction. Hence, one cannot, and should not, generalise.

1.2   ECONOMIC GROWTH AND SUSTAINABILITY

It is widely acknowledged that economic growth may give rise to environmental pressure. But the notion has been put forward that economic growth
may eventually result in environmental sustainability: environmental quality
may be a luxury good that societies will want more of as income levels rise,
and this will automatically generate a demand for new, cleaner and leaner
technology. If that is so, then economic growth may beyond some stage (in
terms of average income) induce an endogenous process of 'delinking' or
'decoupling' of economic activity from environmental degradation (see World
Bank, 1992). Hence, beyond that threshold, one would not really have to
worry both about growth and about sustainability – all that is needed (leaving
equity issues aside) is to make sure that the economy expands.

The relationship between environmental pressure (defined here as the aggregate of pollution, depletion and other human activity-related threats to
environmental quality) and per capita income is often assumed to take on an
inverted U shape (see, for example, Shafik and Bandyopadhyay, 1992; Selden
and Song, 1994; World Bank, 1992) referred to as the 'Environmental Kuznets
Curve'. This may be illustrated by data on emissions of CO_2 and per capita
income for a number of countries as in Figure 1.1: the parabola presented in
it indeed is an inverted U and is derived by imposing a quadratic regression
equation on the data as plotted along the axes.

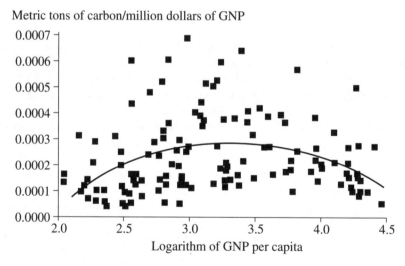

Source: World Bank (1995).

Figure 1.1   Kuznets-type curve for carbon emissions, 1989–91 average

Results like this have appeared to emerge from a rich collection of empirical studies (see below). And if they are pervasive, such findings would indicate that societies might perhaps simply 'grow out of' (to use a phrase introduced by Shafik and Bandyopadhyay) their environmental problems and that there is no incompatibility between economic development and the environment in the long run.

We shall take a closer look at the evidence on materials (and energy), on pollutants and – more generally – on 'throughput' as a proxy for overall environmental pressure. But first we will have a look at the theoretical underpinnings of such curves, and of alternatives.

Economic Theory and Environmental Kuznets Curves

The interactions between economic activity and the environment have been metaphorically labelled society's and 'industrial metabolism' (for example, Ayres 1994): the set of physico-chemical transformations that convert raw materials and energy, plus labour, into finished products and the wastes or residuals entailed by these transformations. The flows of matter and energy involved in this metabolism have been called 'throughput' by Daly (1991, p. 36). We will use the symbol S for it. Following Ayres (1994) we define metabolic efficiency as the economic output per unit of throughput. Economic output is often measured by the level of net production or income, Y, so metabolic efficiency is measured as Y/S. The inverse of this, S/Y, is the 'throughput intensity' s. A more efficient metabolism would be characterised by lower levels of materials and pollution intensities. These would induce a 'delinking', or decoupling of economic activity from environmental impacts. If $S = s \cdot Y$, then:

$$dS/dt = Y \cdot ds/dt + s \cdot dY/dt \qquad (1.1)$$

or environmental degradation changes over time as the weighed sum of the rate of change in the throughput intensity (ds/dt) and the rate of change of economic activity (dY/dt).

Delinking can be labelled 'absolute' when the level of throughput drops over time or at least does not increase, for any positive rate of economic growth. A sufficient condition for this is that $dS/dt < 0$. This implies (see equation (1.1) that:

$$(-ds/dt)/s > (dY/dt)/Y \qquad (1.2)$$

or that the rate of change in the throughput intensity must exceed the economic growth rate. This is equivalent to saying that the throughput–income elasticity must be negative with an absolute value exceeding 1. 'Relative delinking' would be the situation where there is delinking, that is, $ds/dt < 0$ but where the effect of this on S is overtaken by that of economic growth. So, S would increase despite an enhanced metabolistic efficiency.

There may be a point beyond which throughput rises again with per capita income. From that point onward, the economy and environmental pressure S will be relinked (Opschoor, 1990), at least until further breakthroughs in research and development occur, or a more intensive application of environmental policy checks is implemented.

Given the need to delink if economic growth is to be or become sustainable, one may wonder to what extent delinking may occur spontaneously in the economic process – or, to put this in economists' jargon: that delinking is 'endogenous' or inherent in economic growth.

In purely technical terms, delinking or enhanced metabolic efficiency may result from different sets of developments (or combinations thereof):

i.   changes in production processes and in product design;
ii.   changes in the structure of production and consumption;
iii.   reductions in the level of consumption and production.

How do these technical options relate to economic development?

Economic growth will lead to rising per capita income levels. These will trigger changes in the structure of demand for products and services, as the more urgent ones are increasingly being satisfied. In the past this has given rise to drastic changes in the sectoral composition of the national product. Economies have moved from resource-incentive agricultural and mining stages to more industrial ones, and seem to be moving towards a post-industrial, service and information-oriented stage, and it is often presumed that this in itself will lead to a reduction of S/Y. Furthermore, it is assumed by many economists that environmental quality is a good that will gain in priority as income levels rise so that increasingly environmental concerns will be manifest on the basis of pressures from within the economic process. This may show up in absolutely and relatively larger budgets for environmental policies and even in more effective implementation of these policies. Additionally, with rising environmental pressure knowledge of ecological functions may become larger and more widespread, and alter hitherto prevailing preference schemes and political priorities. This might accelerate the impact on S/Y from industrial development. Moreover, technological innovations have given rise to changes in relative scarcities and prices also inducing shifts in the structure of demand for goods and services leading to derived changes in the production structure. To a large degree the environmental features of innovation may be or may have been irrelevant to the innovators, and hence the overall environmental impact of it may have been unpredictable. But environmental considerations have triggered technological change where resource scarcities and deteriorating environmental qualities became matters of concern and even urgency. And to the degree that these became economically relevant they have given rise to spontaneous or endogenous rises in metabolistic efficiency. Sometimes these scarcities were induced or created by economic power (for example, the oil crises in the 1970s and 1980s) and the results were environmentally benign in that whatever the source of scarcity (absolute stock reductions or monopoly power) the result of it triggering price increases is likely to be a reduction in demand. Some refer to these processes as 'structural change' (Simonis, 1989; Jänicke et al., 1993) indicating that changes in pollution and materials consumption are not only or not primarily due to economic fluctuations, but to more structural changes underlying the economic process. To the extent that prices reflect environmental costs, markets may be assumed to generate signals (in the form of price changes) supporting the processes of substitution mentioned above, and providing incentives to innovate in terms of the development of new products, processes or inputs. If prices do adequately capture these costs and if market processes are flexible enough, then delinking may be a (near-) spontaneous, endogenous development within the economic process. In addition to being driven by endogenous forces, delinking may also be stimulated by exogenous influences (for example, induced by policy interventions, or new lifestyles as a result of shocks in awareness). Finally, changes in international specialisation may occur as income rises: poor countries may attract 'dirty' and material intensive production while richer countries specialise in 'clean' and material extensive production, without altering the overall consumption patterns.

Thus, economic factors explaining tendencies to delinking include (Jänicke et al., 1993; Opschoor, 1990; World Bank, 1992; Panayotou, 1993; Selden and Song, 1994; Stern et al., 1994): (i) structural change in production patterns with rising income; (ii) positive income elasticities for environmental quality given preferences and priorities; (iii) changing preferences and priorities due to increasing information about environmental degradation as production grows; and (iv) increased levels of trade as income rises.

Theoretically, continued delinking can go on only as long as the rates of reduction in environmental throughput or intensity per unit of income exceed production growth rates – and this is likely to come to an end and possibly even reverse. Along a prevailing technological paradigm technological efficiency improvements may show declining revenues and/or increasing costs that will eventually even suppress positive learning curve effects. Thus, ds/dt might fall in the long run, despite an ongoing need to decouple. On the side of changing patterns of consumption in relation to economic growth the same may be expected to occur: increasing diseconomies to consumers to further change their consumption patterns unless radical changes would take place at the level of their preference structures. Assuming economic growth tendencies to remain in force, even if we start from $|ds/dt| > dY/dt$, from some point onward economic activity and environmental pressure S may relink (Opschoor, 1990), at least until further breakthroughs in research and development occur, or more environmental awareness alters preference structures or a more intensive application of environmental policy checks is implemented. This prediction we call the 'relinking hypothesis'; empirical manifestations of $dS/dt > 0$ in specific areas of environmental concern are taken as validating it, at least in part.

The issue of relinking versus ongoing delinking is one that has direct relevance in the economically more advanced (in terms of per capita income) countries of the world, that is, in much of the OECD region. There, the endogenous forces would possibly have shown up and certainly since 1970 the impact of environmental policy interventions may have accelerated them. If anywhere, the EKC should manifest itself there and it would be of interest to other countries to know more about the magnitude of the effects, the turning points, the contributions of the various factors and the persistence of the phenomenon. Elsewhere, countries would still be expected to be in the upswing or linkage phase or at best in the beginning of the downswing. However, there are possibilities of OECD–non-OECD linkages that are relevant from a development perspective. To begin with, the downswing to a large degree may have been made possible by the relocation of dirty and wasteful industries to regions outside the OECD, thereby adding to the slope of the relationship between growth and environmental impact. Secondly, and more revelant from a development policy perspective, if the EKCs of countries are to be 'suppressed' to lower levels and if turning points are to be pulled forward in time, then technological cooperation and technology transfer might be very relevant. Environmentally-oriented innovations in the North may be transferred to developing countries, giving rise to accelerated relative delinking there. Empirically, both tendencies work in opposite directions and for that reason alone the links between growth and throughput, as well as the changes therein, need to be analysed empirically.

There is one last issue to mention before turning to the empirical work on EKCs. That is the issue of the economic value of environmental sustainability. As was said above, a short-run approach to the costs and benefits of preserving environmental assets at a certain level based on today's assessments of the current generation alone, may indicate that such assets could perhaps be run down. In a welfare maximisation approach the costs of maintaining sustainability may be higher than the benefits of doing so, and hence it seems optimal to sacrifice environmental assets until marginal costs and benefits match again. From a long-term perspective, however, and taking intertemporal interests into account, one could argue that certain losses of environmental sustainability may have serious long-term welfare implications. Taking into account intertemporal stakes, one might argue in favour of preserving a higher level of environmental assets than indicated by the welfare maximising approach, in order to keep a safe minimum or a 'satisficing' (rather than 'optimal') level of environmental stocks so as to ensure the physical potential for welfare generation in future. Analogously, there may be lack of knowledge or uncertainty of other forms, leading some policymakers to opt for a 'precautionary approach' (that is, to not accept certain environmental changes and to prevent these with cost-effective measures), or others to follow a 'no-regret' strategy of taking in any case measures that have positive benefit–cost ratios on other grounds. Choices between optimising and satisficing and no-regret versus precautionary are in the political domain.

We now leave these theoretical and policy issues aside and turn to reviewing empirical studies of the EKC.

Empirical results: materials and energy

Many studies have revealed decreasing material and energy intensities in a range of OECD countries, especially during the period 1950–80. We review them here, drawing on Moll (1993) and De Bruyn and Opschoor (1997).

Most materials (such as metals, cement, paper, chlorine and ethylene) show decreasing material intensities through time since 1950 and especially since 1970 in most OECD countries.

Because of materials substitution it is important to study more complete aggregates of materials consumption. Only a few empirical studies analyse such aggregates over time. Moll (1993), using an aggregate of materials (steel, cement, paper, aluminium, copper, zinc and plastics), finds that for the US economy the aggregated material intensity is decreasing since 1970. However, if volume (measured in m^3 materials) rather than weight is taken into account, no decreasing intensities can be found.

In the area of energy, most of the member countries of the International Energy Agency have experienced declining energy intensities (see, for example, Chesshire, 1986). Suri and Chapman (1996) have analysed (commercial) energy intensity changes in relation to shifts in the international division of labour. They show that after controlling for structural change effects, international trade has played an important role in the generation of intranational emissions. It appears that industrialising countries as well as industrialised ones have both added to their energy demands by exporting manufactured goods, albeit the former more than the latter; furthermore, on the importing side reductions in energy needs have been realised, particularly by the industrialised countries. The authors conclude that exports of manufactured goods by industrialising countries have contributed to these countries' upward-sloping EKCs whereas imports by industrialised countries have helped these to realise a downward slope.

Empirical results: pollutants

Data on pollution in relation to economic development often show reductions of pollution per unit of production or income, as income levels rise, and often even reductions in absolute levels of pollution. The World Bank has reported absolute delinking for sulphur oxides, lead and particulates for all OECD countries since 1970 and for NO_x since 1980 (World Bank, 1992). Several other references confirm such trends, at least for certain types of pollutants (for example, Shafik and Bandyopadhyay, 1992; Selden and Song, 1994).

Shafik and Bandyopadhyay (1992) correlate stages of economic development with several forms of environmental pollution as well as a time trend, for up to 149 countries for various time intervals in between 1960 and 1990. Their results do not confirm a general pattern between environmental pressure and income. Emissions of CO_2, water pollution (measured by the water quality indicator of dissolved oxygen in rivers) and the amount of municipal solid waste per capita show increases as income rises. Contrary to this, the level of income does not have significant effects on the annual rate of deforestation or total deforestation. They showed delinking in the cases of Dissolved Oxygen in rivers, Suspended Particular Matter (Dust) emissions and SO_2 emissions. An N-shaped form was found for faecal coliform in rivers, while inverted-U curves were found for urban air concentrations of SPM and SO_2. The turning points for these latter types of environmental pressure are respectively US$ (1985) 3280 and 3670.

Selden and Song have regressed per capita income (PPP-based) to aggregate per capita emissions of SO_2, NO_x, Suspended Particulate Matter (hereafter SPM) and CO for 30 countries over the periods 1973–75, 1979–81 and 1982–84. They add population density as an explanatory variable, as sparsely populated countries might be less concerned with reducing per capita emissions. Intercept dummies have been added to capture time effects. The regressions confirm an EKC for SPM, SO_2 and NO_x emissions with turning points at respectively US$ (1985) 9811, 10 681 and 12 041. The reason for the much lower turning points of urban air quality quoted above compared to the turning points calculated by Selden and Song for national emissions can be summarised as: (i) the political importance of urban air quality over national emissions; (ii) the lower cost of achieving improvements in urban air quality; and, (iii) the rise in land rents in urban cities which forced industry to move out (Selden and Song, p. 148). Studies by Panayatou (1993) and Grossman and Krueger (1996) found results similar to those reviewed so far.

Sengupta (1996) has investigated CO_2 emissions for a sample of 16 countries ranging from India to the USA excluding economies in transition (but including China) over 1971–88. He finds a best fit with a polynomial of third degree, suggesting the existence of an N-curve with an initial maximum close to (purchasing power parity) PPP$9000 per capita and a subsequent upswing beyond PPP$15 000. He ascribes the latter to lifestyle-related drastic changes in the patterns of consumption in high income countries such as the use of electricity and transport – both of which indeed have recently been reported to account for upswings or relinking in the Netherlands. He also finds that for CO_2 emissions from gas a continuous linkage with GDP per capita is to be expected, with a high GDP elasticity.

Empirical results: throughput
Some analysts of environmental degradation feel that energy consumption is a reasonable first proxy of throughput. To the extent that this is correct, we have already addressed some throughput analyses above. The Berlin Science Center (Jänicke et al., 1988, 1993) was one of the first to adopt a throughput-based approach making efforts to aggregate several types of environmental pressure into one environmental indicator: energy consumption, steel consumption, cement production and weight of freight transport on rail and road (as a general measure of the volume aspect of an economy), giving equal weight to the four factors mentioned on a per capita basis. This indicator was computed for each of the 31 COMECON and OECD economies in the years 1970 and 1985. The analysis shows that the consumption of materials in the countries with a lower per capita GDP rose faster relative to the countries with a higher per capita GDP and indicates convergence of aggregate materials consumption between countries but not per se absolute delinking.

Jänicke et al. (1989) also found that the correlations between per capita GDP and the TI for the whole sample in 1985 was much less significant and showed a much smaller slope than in 1970; this they interpreted as a sign of the process of delinking through structural change. This comes close to suggesting the existence of an endogenous tendency to delink with rising GDP per capita.

To empirically test the delinking hypothesis on throughput, De Bruyn and Opschoor (1997) extended the analysis of Jänicke et al. by taking a longer period of study (1966–90), using a more coherent set of indicators and applying time series analysis on a subset of 20 OECD and COMECON countries. Countries again appear to converge in their aggregate materials consumption: over time, the increase in aggregate materials consumption in the poorer countries rose faster than the increase in GDP, while the consumption in the richer countries declined in relative and absolute levels. But a most interesting outcome of the longitudinal analysis is that this development has come to an end. It appears that the economies considered are entering a period of relinking, rather than continuing on the delinking path. This becomes clear when we compare the end of the 1980s (1989) with the beginning of the 1980s (1983) using moving three-year averages. If the throughput intensities of 1989 are compared with those of 1986, it can be seen that several of these countries (Spain, Italy, Japan, Western Germany, the United Kingdom, Belgium–Luxembourg) showed an upswing in their throughput intensities. Furthermore, the Netherlands and Turkey are countries facing environmental deterioration. That is, their throughput rose more than their increase in GDP. We conclude that the observed absolute improvements in aggregate material consumption for developed economies as observed by Jänicke et al. (1989) in 1985 as compared to 1970, did not continue in the 1980s (with the exception of Norway). The observed trend to delink is indeed manifest from 1970 till the early 1980s. However, for several countries environmental pressure appears to have been relinked with the environment since the mid-1980s (de Bruijn and Opschoor 1997) (see Figure 1.2).

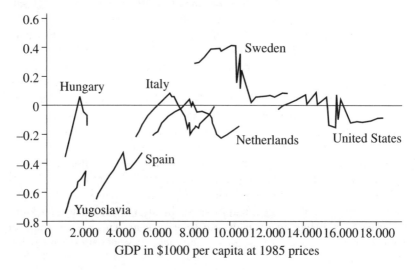

Figure 1.2   Developments in aggregated throughput index, 1966–90 (three-year moving averages of aggregated environmental index for selected countries)

Metabolism in Economies in Transition and Developing Economies

We have looked at the relationships between economic development (growth and restructuring) and environmental pressure as measured by throughput, in Central European countries from 1970–91 (Rebergen et al., 1994). As one might expect, the levels of throughput were high in comparison with Western

Europe, both in absolute terms and per unit of GDP; the specifics of the sectoral structure of the centrally planned economies and inefficiencies in the price and incentive structure account for much of these high levels. It is interesting to observe that, as in Western Europe, throughput per unit of production dropped in the 1980s, and the centrally planned economies began to decouple before 1989. This may, in part, be due to attempts by the previous regimes to increase efficiency, on one hand, to a more effective societal concern over environmental issues, and on the other, to the emerging changes in the patterns of production. It was expected that on the resources side this tendency might persist whereas on the pollution side it might yield to the need to keep prices low for competitive reasons (Rebergen et al., 1994). In a subsequent analysis energy consumption, steel production and several emissions (particulates, SO_2, NO_x, CO_2) have been analysed for Poland, Hungary, former CSFR, Czechia and former Eastern Germany. All countries investigated showed relative delinking at least since the late 1970s and absolute delinking set in after 1984. Since 1991 these economies showed economic recovery (in terms of rising GDP) but most throughput indicators continue to decline. If we look at the developments of pollution and materials intensities in these countries we can observe a fairly consistent downward-oriented pattern, independent of political regime, for most pollutants (the No_x intensity being more or less constant) and for steel production; energy intensities show less of a decline (except in Poland). The substantial decreases in emissions can therefore be ascribed mainly to the lower volumes of production since the change (some 20 per cent reduction before the recovery) and to a lesser extent to a longer-term trend of declining intensities. If growth rates pick up further, the effects of relative delinking will quickly be overtaken by the growth effect and in absolute terms there will be relinking.

Environment–growth relationships *in developing countries* have been studied mainly from the perspectives of deforestation and energy use.

Shafik and Bandyopadhyay set the scene with deforestation research (1992); they did not find a significant relationship of the annual rate of deforestation (1961–86) and income. Panayotou (1993) followed with a study explaining net deforestation by regressing it to income per capita, population density and a dummy for tropical countries. He does find inverted Us and the turning point is around $825 per capita. Cropper and Griffiths (1994) look at the percentage change in forest area between two years (1961–91) for 64 countries in Africa, Latin America and Asia and include other variables as well (for example, timber price) as time trend. They found significant turning points in Africa (PPP$4760) and Latin America (PPP$5420) only. Rock (1995) regresses the average annual rate of deforestation against measures of (PPP) income, population growth, increase in value added in agriculture, and a special dummy for countries in Asia which is highly significant and relevant. Population growth has a strong influence as well and the income variables suggest an EKC with a turning point around PPP$3500.

Bernstein (1993) has investigated the historical relationship between energy use and economic growth (GDP) for a set of 40 developing countries between 1971 and 1987. Energy growth has outstripped GDP growth, especially in situations with a history of price subsidies. In terms of energy intensities he finds that developing countries have become less efficient which leads him to argue for demand-side management, supply efficiency and technology transfer, making possible a leapfrog trajectory below the conventional development. Sengupta (1996) shows how, for countries such as Brazil, India and Indonesia the primary energy intensities (PPP) grew by some 0.6–3 per cent annually (they declined by 1.1 per cent pa in China). He expects that even if modern technology would come to such countries more rapidly, yet the processes of industrialisation, urbanisation and fuel shift away from non-commercial fuels would continue to raise the commercial energy intensity of GDP at levels in the range of 2.25–3.5 per cent pa (as compared with 1.83 per cent in the USA). Results such as these also come from Gupta and Hall (1996).

In an explorative study (Rebergen, unpublished) we analysed nine countries: two low-income countries or LICs (Burkina Faso, Bangladesh), four low-middle-income countries or LMICs (Cameroon, Philippines, Ecuador, Tunisia) and three upper-middle-income countries or UMICs (Botswana, Malaysia, Brazil), for which we derived some rather arbitrary but at least uniform throughput indicators (1970–92): (i) fertiliser use per hectare of crop land; (ii) ratio of area of harvested forest to total forest area; (iii) commercial energy consumption; and (iv) number of commercial vehicles per capita. These indices were also aggregated into one index of environmental pressure by taking an unweighted average of the individual indices (1970 = 100). In these countries we observed strong shifts in the economic structure (the sectoral composition of GDP) from 1970 to 1990 with more industry. Throughput varied with income level (with a range between 27 (LIC) and 127 (UMIC) in 1970 moving up to 158 (LIC) and 344 (UMIC) in 1991. Linear regressions of this index with PPP–income per capita gives positive and significant regression coefficients with averages moving from 0.18 (LICs) via 0.08 (LMICs) to 0.05 (UMICs); in other words the marginal impact of income on throughput declines as countries develop, or throughput per unit of GDP increases in low-income countries but seems to decrease in middle-income countries. There may thus already be some relative delinking in the latter countries, possibly as a result of leap-frogging; the ability to use newer, cleaner technology than industrialized countries would or could have done at similar levels of income. Nevertheless, due to ongoing economic growth the overall throughput levels showed increased environmental deterioration. Throughput intensities (throughput per unit of GDP) have been calculated (Table 1.1) and show a rise in LICs and a decline in MICs (as expected, much

Table 1.1   Estimated throughput intensities: selected developing countries, 1970–91

Countries with/in	1970	1980	1991
income level:			
LICs	0.104	0.139	0.157
LMICs	0.131	0.108	0.095
UMICs	0.132	0.083	0.059
population size:			
small	0.112	0.107	0.101
large	0.137	0.130	0.135
trade orientation:			
primary comm.	0.119	0.122	0.124
industrial	0.125	0.100	0.095

Source: Rebergen (unpublished).

more so in UMICs); on the whole they increased. It is very interesting to also see that countries with external trade based on primary commodities showed a slight increase over time whereas countries with an industrial orientation showed a marked decrease.

1.3   DISCUSSION AND CONCLUSIONS

This section will discuss aspects of the data and methods used in the EKC studies reviewed in Section 1.2, and take some of the results a bit further. We will also draw some conclusions on EKCs and look at broad strategies towards more sustainable economic growth.

Some Notes on Methods used in EKC Studies

The results arrived at in Section 1.2 are far from being conclusive or convergent, and that was seen as to be expected. Some of the problems underlying this may have to do with fallibilities in data and methods.

An obvious first point is that of the data used. Some studies use concentrations, others emissions, some aggregate these into integrated indexes. Data are often lacking, they may be incomparable in a cross-country or even intertemporal setting, proper weights are absent, and so on.

A second problem is that of the specifications of the equations that are being estimated in the various studies. They are rather ad hoc, and do not emerge as true reduced-form relationships from properly specified models (see Stern et al., 1994). Thus, no feedbacks from environmental quality to growth appear, generally time lags are ignored, and trade relationships are not modeled.

Thirdly, where EKCs are demonstrated, the model specifications lack correct asymptotic properties. It can easily be calculated that at some income levels these specifications will result in negative emissions where they clearly must be positive (De Bruyn and Opschoor, 1997).

There may also be confusion about the interpretation of the regression results from the panel data where a time variable is included. Typically the EKCs obtained will shift downward over time. For individual countries, however, the EKC based on panel data analysis does not describe the factual relationship between emissions and income over time for that country. The conclusion is that the turning points calculated from EKCs based on pooled data may not reveal the actual turning points for individual countries. While the EKC in cross-sectional data may reveal an inverted-U relationship between environmental pressure and economic development, there is nothing to expect that a specific country will move along such an EKC path. De Bruyn finds that if the time trend is not significantly different from zero it may well be the case that the relationship between economic growth and environmental pressure is N-shaped, even where the pooled EKC is an inverted U.

Fifthly, EK curves – in so far as they exist – say very little about system-wide consequences of environmental utilisation. They have been found – if at all – for individual pollutants only and there may have been transfers to other countries and shifts to other pollutants, and so on (see Arrow et al., 1995; see also De Bruyn and Opschoor, 1994 and Anasuategi, 1998). Also, the indicators used may not be representative of 'environmental pressure' in general (for example, there may be a bias towards pollution *vis-à-vis* natural resources).

Finally, this type of analysis appears to ignore the long-run risks to ecological processes in cases of irreversible environmental changes (Arrow et al., 1995; WRI et al., 1996).

Environmental Kuznets Curves: an Assessment

In many empirical studies results do indicate that specific forms of environmental pressure have gone down with rising average incomes. However, there is no empirical evidence for the expectation that delinking occurs endogenously or automatically.

This holds *a fortiori* when environmental change is studied at a more aggregate level (for example, throughput).

Moreover, where absolute delinking has taken place it does not always appear as a process which is stable or persistent under conditions of sustained economic growth – far from it. Also, delinking has not been studied sufficiently in a system-wide and dynamic setting.

Thus, contrary to what would have been a convenient and happy situation, Section 1.2 shows that correlations between economic growth and environmental improvement aimed at testing the hypothesis of an inverted U or parabolic relationship must be used cautiously and do not lead to unambiguous results. This is no surprise from the perspective of environmental macroeconomics (see above).

Even if EKCs as found reflect a general phenomenon, they often imply a reduction of metabolism only beyond fairly high average incomes, which, given the current levels and distribution of income and people, would entail that environmental utilisation may or will keep on growing for at least a number of decades, with subsequent risks of unsustainability. Anasuategi reviews the turning points (normally in PPP$) found. For emissions into air they appear to range between PPP\$5000–20 000 (for CO_2 even PPP\$35 000 – where Sengupta found PPP\$8700), for deforestation between PPP\$825–5500. Many emissions and processes of resource harvesting will thus continue to grow or expand in the foreseeable future (Selden and Song, 1992; Panayotou, 1993, and so on). Sengupta (1996) looked at India and China to see what would happen to CO_2 emissions. Even with his low estimate for the turning point income, it would take China to the middle of this century to reach CO_2 stabilisation and India would get there only towards the end of this century.

Sustained economic growth is not necessarily environmentally sustainable, nor will it automatically become sustainable. If and where an EKC relationship exists it is more likely to be the reflection of deliberate environmental policies and policy-induced technological innovation (see also World Bank, 1992). And given the information that is available now on turning point levels of average income (if there are turning points), these imply that with economic and population growth as expected, environmental pressure at the global level will continue to grow very far into this century.

The latter point holds especially for the developing countries and the economies in transition, but there is also reason for serious concern for the industrialised countries. At the moment the OECD countries may be entering a phase of relinking. This indicates the need to accelerate environmental policies rather than anything else.

Main Strategies to Enhance Sustainability

On what should such additional or accelerated environmental policies be focused? This chapter ends by providing a broad perspective on this, based on the analysis provided above.

Equation (1.1) can be easily expanded to $S = s \cdot y \cdot P$, where $y = Y/P$ and P is population. Then it is equivalent to an equation notorious in environmental analysis: 'I = PAT' (or Impact equals the 'product' of population, affluence and technology or metabolism). For throughput to be sustainable, some maximum has to be set to S, *ceteris paribus*.

This suggests the following approaches to unsustainability:

i.   raise ecosystems' carrying capacities for economic activity (or sustainable level of S), and/or
ii.   reduce the population size, and/or
iii. reduce income or production per capita, and/or
iv.   change the environmental impact of production technology.

Of these strategies the first and last ones appear attractive and promising: expanding the natural resource base or the absorption capacity of the environment (mostly through improved knowledge, technology and management) and the development of cleaner and leaner (or more eco-efficient) technologies in production. Reduction of P and/or Y/P are undesirable or at least socially and politically very difficult strategies.

Another option may exist, however. In fact, the y or Y in the above formula could be decomposed into ranges of different products and the S could be disaggregated into different technologies for each of these products. If one does that, the problem of reducing S to sustainable levels of impact can be approached by the additional, more sophisticated strategy of changing patterns of consumption and production in such a way that the average value of s drops.

Changes in consumption (and hence production) patterns may come about as a result of rising incomes, of improved information and education (including the emergence of new values), and of changes in relative prices. Economic growth will affect the first of these automatically and investment in produced and human capital may be instrumental to achieving it; attempts to develop ecological knowledge and consciousness may require the development of particular types of human assets and appropriate cultural institutions, and changing prices to also reflect environmental costs will require specific administrative and policy capabilities and institutions.

Changing the environmental efficiency of production may come about as a consequence of research and development in industry and scientific institutions; these will emerge in response to price changes and changes in profits, and in response to public programmes and funding stimulating innovation where the market fails to produce signals of adequate strength. Growth may generate the private and public funds necessary for financing innovation but here, again, deliberate policies and specific institutions and mechanisms appear as necessary conditions.

Possibilities for enhancing the environmental space and for raising eco-efficiency are available. Without going into details or attempting to cover this vast area, one could point at the tremendous differences in emission and waste coefficients and in energy or materials intensities in similar industries in different parts of the world; this suggests that tremendous environmental gains can be expected from technology transfers from countries with more to countries with less experience in environmental policies. Significant economic benefits can be expected through these processes of diffusion of already developed technologies, as is witnessed by the fact that even in the industrialized economies of the OECD often substantial net cost savings may result from using available energy conservation technologies. A more diverse and intensive diffusion of available technology is necessary and possible, but it still may be unlikely to be adequate in relation to the need for delinking. Additional technological innovation is required. So are institutional innovations, in the spheres of resource management and resource pricing, taxation and other fiscal incentives, mechanisms for redistributing technology and access to resources, and adjustment policies (as elaborated in, for example, Opschoor, 1996): these new institutional arrangements are to underpin, reinforce and direct technical and economic tendencies that may enhance the sustainability of the overall economic process.

NOTE

1. In fact, WCED spoke of the various societal processes of resource management and so on, to be 'in harmony' – which we feel is better replaced by 'compatible'.

REFERENCES

Anand, S. and Sen, A.K. (1996), *Sustainable Human Development: Concepts and Priorities*, Office of Development Studies, New York: UNDP. (Discussion Papers, n.1).

Anasuategi, A. (1998), 'Delinking, Relinking and the Perception of Resource Scarcity', in: J. van den Bergh and M. Hofkes (eds), *Theory and Implementation of Economic Models for Sustainable Development*, Dordrecht/London: Kluwer Academic Press, pp.165–72.

Arrow, K., Bolin, B., Costanza, R., Dasgupta, P., Folke, C., Holling, C.S., Jansson, B.-O., Levin, S., Maler, K.-G., Perrings, C. and Pimentel, D. (1995), 'Economic growth, carrying capacity and the environment', *Science*, 268, 520–21. Reprinted in *Ecological Economics*, **15** (2), 91–5.

Ayres, R.U. (1994), 'Industrial Metabolism: Theory and Policy', in: R.U. Ayres and U.E. Simonis (eds), *Industrial Metabolism: Restructuring for Sustainable Development*, New York: UNU Press, pp. 3–21.

Bernstein, M.A. (1993), *Are Developing Countries 'Delinking' Energy Demand and*

Economic Growth? Washington, DC: Economic Development Institute, World Bank (EDI, Working Papers, ns. 93–50).

Brenner Y.S. (1966), *Theories of Economic Development and Growth*, London: George Allen and Unwin.

Bruyn S.M. de and Opschoor, J.B. (1997), 'Developments in the throughput–income relationship: theoretical and empirical observations', *Ecological Economics*, **20** (3), 255–69.

Chesshire, J. (1986), 'An energy-efficient future: a strategy for the UK', *Energy Policy*, 14, 395–412.

Cropper, M. and Griffiths, C. (1994), 'The interaction of population growth and environmental quality', *American Economic Review*, 84, 250–54.

Daly, H.E. and Cobb, J.B. (1994), *For the Common Good*, Boston: Beacon Press.

Daly, H.E. (1991), *Steady State Economics: Second Edition with New Essays*, Washington, DC/Covelo: Island Press, p. 297.

Goodland, R. (1995), 'The concept of environmental sustainability', *Annual Review of Ecological Systems*, 26, 1–24.

Grossman, G.M. and Krueger, A.B. (1996), 'The inverted U: what does it mean?', *Environmental and Developmental Economics*, **1** (1), (Feb), 119–22.

Gupta, S. and Hall, S.G. (1996), 'Carbon abatement costs: an integrated approach for India', *Environmental and Developmental Economics*, **1** (1), (Feb.), 41–65.

Jänicke, M., Monch, H., Binder, M. et al. (1993), 'Ecological aspects of structural change in intereconomics', *Review of International Trade and Development*, **28**.

Jänicke, M., Monch, H., Ranneberg, Th. and Simonis, U.E. (1988), *Structural change and environmental impact:: empirical evidence on thirty-one countries in East and West*, Berlin: Science Center Berlin, FS II-88-402.

Jänicke, M., Monch, H., Ranneberg, T. and Simonis, U.E. (1989), 'Economic structure and environmental impacts: East–West comparisons', *The Environmentalist*, 9, 171–82.

Kuznets, S. (1965), *Economic Growth and Structure: Selected Essays*, London: Heinemann Educational Books Ltd.

Max-Neef, M. (1995), 'Economic growth and quality of life: a threshold hypothesis', *Ecological Economics*, **15** (2), 115–19.

Moll, H.C. (1993), *Energy counts and materials matter in models for sustainable development: dynamic lifecycle modelling as a tool for design and evaluation of long-term environmental strategies*, Groningen: Styx, 396 pp.

Nordhaus, W.D. and Tobin, J. (1972), 'Is Growth Obsolete?', in: M. Moss (ed.), *The Measurement of Economic and Social Performance*, New York: National Bureau of Economic Research, Studies in Income and Wealth, p. 38.

Opschoor, J.B. (1990), 'Ecologische duurzame economische ontwikkeling: een theoretisch idee en een weerbarstige praktijk', in: P. Nijkamp and H. Verbruggen (eds), *Het Nederlands milieu in de europese ruimte, Leiden*: Stenfert Kroese, pp.77–126.

Opschoor, J.B. (1996), 'Institutional change and development towards sustainability', in: R. Costanza, O. Segura and J. Martinez-Alier (eds), *Getting Down to Earth: Practical Applications of Ecological Economics*, Washington, DC: Island Press, pp. 327–51.

Panayotou, Th. (1993), *Empirical Tests and Policy Analysis of Environmental Degradation at Different Stages of Economic Development*, Geneva: ILO. (Technology and Employment Programme, WP 238).

Pigou, A.C. (1962), *The Economics of Welfare*, London: Macmillan (first edition 1920).

Rebergen, C. (unpublished), 'Economische structuur en milieudruk in ontwikkelings-landen, 1970–1991', Report on Practical Environmental Economics, Amsterdam: Vrije Universiteit.

Rebergen, C., van der Vegt, H. and Opschoor, J.B. (1994), 'Economische structuur en milieudruk: Centraal Europa, 1970–1991', *Milieu, 1994/4*, 145–53.

RIVM (State Institute for Public Health and Environment) (1997), 'The Future of the Global Environment: A Model-based Analysis Supporting UNEP's First Global Environment Outlook', UNEP/DEIA/TR.97-1, Nairobi: UNEP.

Rock, Michael T. (1996), 'The stork, the plow, rural social structure and tropical deforestation in poor countries', *Ecological Economics*, **18** (2), August, 113–31.

Selden, T.M. and Song, D.S. (1994), 'Environmental quality and development: is there a Kuznets curve for air pollution emissions?', *Journal of Environmental Economics and Management*, **27**, 147–62.

Sengupta, R. (1996), *Economic Development and CO$_2$-Emission: Economy–Environment Relation and Policy Approach to Choice of Emission Standard for Climate Control*, New Delhi, India: Jawaharlal Nehru University, Apr. 1996 (revised Sept. 1996).

Shafik, N. and Bandyopadhyay, S. (1992), *Economic Growth and Environmental Quality: Time-Series and Cross-Country Evidence*, Washington: World Bank, 52 pp. (Working Papers, WPS 904).

Simonis, U.E. (1989), *Industrial Restructuring for Sustainable Development: Three Points of Departure*, Berlin: Science Centre Berlin FS II 89–401.

Stern, D.I., Common, M.S. and Barbier, E.B. (1994), *Economic Growth and Environmental Degradation: a Critique of the Environmental Kuznets Curve*, University of York (Discussion Papers in Environmental Economics and Environmental Management, EEEM 9409).

Suri, V. and Chapman, D. (1996) *Economic Growth, Trade and the Environment: an Econometric Evaluation of the Environmental Kuznets Curve*, Ithaca, NY: Cornell University, Dept of Agric. Resource and Managerial Economics (WP 96-05).

Tinbergen, J. (1967), *Economic Policy: Principles and Design*, Amsterdam: North Holland, First edn.

UNDP (1997), *Human Development Report 1997*, New York/Oxford: Oxford University Press, 1997.

UNDPCSD (UN Department for Policy Coordination and Sustainable Development) (1997), *Critical trends: global change and sustainable development*, New York (UN ST/ESA/225).

UNEP (United Nations Environment Programme) (1997), *Global Environmental Outlook*, New York/Oxford: Oxford University Press.

UNGA (United Nations General Assembly) (1997), *Programme for the Further Implementation of Agenda 21*, New York: UN. Adopted by the Special Session of the General Assembly 23–27 June 1997 (Advanced text, 1 July 1997).

World Bank (1992), *Development and the Environment: World Development Report 1992*, Oxford/New York: Oxford University Press, 308 pp.

World Bank (1995), *Monitoring Environmental Progress. Environmentally Sustainable Development Publications*, Washington, DC: World Bank.

World Commission on Environment and Development (WCED) (1987), *Our Common Future*, Oxford: Oxford University Press, 383 pp.

WRI et al. (1996), (World Resources Institute; UN Environmental Programme; UN Development Programme, World Bank) *World Resources 1996–97*, New York/Oxford: Oxford University Press.

2. The impact of perverse subsidies on international trade and the environment

Cees van Beers and André de Moor

2.1 INTRODUCTION

The relationship between international trade and the natural environment has, until the end of the 1980s, received relatively little attention within both international and environmental economics. Most textbooks in both areas still do not pay much attention to this interface. For several years now there has been a great deal of research on the potential conflict between free trade and environmental regulation, on the impact of environmental regulation on international trade flows and the location choices of firms, and on the use of trade measures in environmental policy. Both international and environmental economists have contributed to this. There has been some debate on free trade versus protectionism, and the discussion in the institutional context has been, from the beginning, whether the greening of international trade agreements, notably the WTO, is useful and possible. What is accepted by most participants in the debates is that the classic theory of comparative advantage cannot be straightforwardly applied to situations in which significant environmental externalities exist.[1]

In this chapter it is argued that the discussion on the relationship between trade and environment is still incomplete. It appears that trade patterns are not only disturbed by incorrect prices as a result of market failures but also as a result of the policy failures of governments. Market failures mean that trade patterns are disturbed because prices do not incorporate environmental externalities caused by the production or consumption of commodities traded. Policy failures mean that trade patterns among countries are not optimal as government interventions work out adversely. The most notorious example of policy failures is the huge amount of so-called perverse subsidies in many production and natural resource sectors of the economy. Perverse subsidies distort market prices and it is essential to remove such policy failures first before correcting for market failures.

The next section pays attention to the relationship between trade and environment as evidenced by the existence of market failures. In Section 2.3

it is argued that the comparative advantage patterns are not only disturbed by incorrect pricing due to the absence of incorporating environmental costs in market prices, but also by the existence of huge amounts of public subsidies. Section 2.4 provides estimates about the magnitude of these subsidies. Proposals to eliminate or at least reduce the amount of subsidies are presented in Section 2.5 and in particular the role of the WTO is considered. The final section presents some conclusions.

2.2 THE ROLE OF INTERNATIONAL TRADE IN ENVIRONMENTAL DEGRADATION AND RESOURCE DEPLETION

The interface between international trade and environmental externalities has a number of facets. Trade theory shows that in a static framework specialisation of countries along the lines of their comparative advantage is efficient, that is, welfare maximising for the domestic and world economy. This is correct as long as all costs of production and consumption are included in market prices. This situation is shown for a small open economy with perfect competition in Figure 2.1.

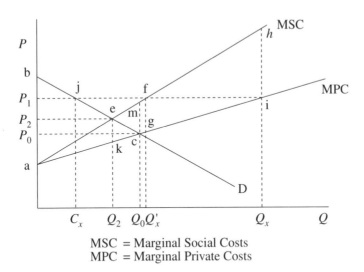

MSC = Marginal Social Costs
MPC = Marginal Private Costs

Source: Van Beers and Van den Bergh (1996, p. 153)[2]

Figure 2.1   Environmental externalities, production and trade in a small open economy

Figure 2.1 shows the situation of an exportable commodity. In case of autarky without pollution and a pollution tax, OQ_0 and OP_0 are the relevant quantities relative price of the good. Net social welfare (in the absence of externality) equals abc. If there is pollution but no pollution tax net welfare decreases and is: (area abc –/– area acm). Suppose the commodity can be exported because at the world market $P_1 > P_0$. Exports are equal to C_xQ_x. Compared with the autarky situation with pollution but no tax, production has increased from Q_0 to Q_x. The increased production for exports lead to additional pollution (fih) which is not taken into account in the price. Welfare decreases with (fih – jfe)

A pollution tax of fg will decrease exports to $C_xQ'_x$. Net social welfare is then abjf. Compared with the situation of exports without environmental policy the increase in net social welfare is fhi. This consists of less pollution (fhig) minus loss of producer surplus (fig). Subsequently net social welfare increases if fhig > fig. Therefore, compared with the autarky situation with environmental policy, net social welfare will increase with jfe. In other words opening up the closed economy will improve net welfare. Now the effect of exporting the commodity whose production is pollutive gives rise again to ambiguous conclusions regarding welfare increase or decrease. In spite of increased pollution as a result of exports, it is still possible that net social welfare increases compared with the situation of autarky. The ultimate outcome depends, among others, on the steepness of the demand and supply curves. It is not possible to draw general conclusions.

The framework sketched out is a static one. In a dynamic world international trade can affect the natural environment along a number of channels. First, international trade shows a strong correlation with economic growth. Two opposite effects can be noted. On the one hand, trade leads via economic growth to a larger use of natural resources and more pollution. Pollutive or resource-intensive intermediate sectors may deliver to export sectors. A notable example is transport. When adopting a long-run perspective, one can foresee that increased environmental damage and resource depletion will harm regional or national capacities for certain economic activities and generate related trade flows. Although in the short run trade may seem beneficial to a region, trade may thus set in motion a direction of change which ultimately may leave the region at an unsustainable path. On the other hand, a more financial (public) budget is generated which can be used for supporting environmental policy and generating technology which may curb environmental pressure per unit of GDP. In general, it is not clear which of these opposite effects at what time in the process of economic development of a country will dominate.

Second, trade flows can directly be associated with waste that can damage the natural environment but also with non-renewable resources and natural materials that are essential for an ecologically sustainable system. Examples are well known: chemical and nuclear waste, tropical hardwood, ivory, animal skins or even complete dead or living entities of threatened species. Pollution, health risks, depletion of resources and damage to ecosystems are the result.

2.3   THE ROLE OF SUBSIDIES IN ENVIRONMENTAL DEGRADATION AND RESOURCE DEPLETION

In the previous section, we argued that international trade may have positive but also negative welfare effects. The key factor in channelling these effects is whether market prices reflect environmental externalities; if they do not, the outcome will only be suboptimal. However, it may also be that observable market prices (without environmental externalities) themselves are incorrect. Government subsidies may create such distortions by sending out false price signals and, as a result, actually contribute to further environmental degradation. Generally, two main types of subsidies can be distinguished, that is support to consumption or to production. By intervening in the market prices of goods and services and setting them below the market level, governments are subsidising consumers. This underpricing is typical and quite common in developing countries, where the consumer prices of water, energy or food are kept low. Subsidies to production, on the other hand, imply a transfer of resources to producers by guaranteeing minimum prices above market level or through purchase obligations. Such producer subsidies are quite common in the developed OECD countries.[3] Consumer and producer subsidies hence both affect market prices but their full economic impact may be quite different.

In a static framework as sketched out in Figure 2.1, it is not difficult to see that consumer subsidies may cause further environmental degradation. If the government sets the domestic price below the market level OP_0 in autarky, domestic demand will be larger than the optimal market outcome Q_0. This overconsumption obviously implies further environmental degradation and resource depletion abroad. Indeed, the country experiences an increase in imports but it exports pollution. Consumer subsidies may therefore lead to or aggravate the trade deficit.

Now consider producer subsidies. In Figure 2.1, the government may set producer prices above the market level OP_0 or in case of exportables, higher than the world market price OP_1. This will encourage producers to boost production, which will lead to a further depletion of resources and environmental degradation in the domestic economy. However, contrary to underpricing, producer subsidies create a vicious cycle of more support in a dynamic framework. The production surpluses need to be transported and stored in warehouses which require further subsidies. Additional public support is necessary to export these subsidised surpluses which can only be done with the help of export subsidies since the commodities cannot be sold at the production prices or at world market prices. Finally, subsidised producer prices require protection of the domestic market since domestic producers would not be able to compete with cheaper imports. In the end, producer subsidies distort both exports and imports and lead to serious trade and environmental imbalances.

Many government subsidies are hidden and in some way linked to prices, inputs or income.[4] Such 'coupled' subsidies are particularly distortionary because by lowering the costs for consumers and users or increasing the returns to producers, they lead to rent-seeking behaviour and encourage excessive consumption or production. The consequences for the environment are negative, through more pollution, more waste and more degradation. However, since producer subsidies affect supply and induce overproduction, they impact on the early chains of economic processes and hence may have more far-reaching implications than consumer subsidies which are at the end of the economic chain. Additionally, since producer subsidies boost production over domestic consumption, it will also encourage exports and hence affect international trade. Considering that producer subsidies are dominant in OECD countries while consumer subsidies are dominant in developing countries, subsidies do have serious implications for international trade as we will see in the next section.

2.4   HOW PERVERSE SUBSIDIES AFFECT TRADE PATTERNS AND THEIR ENVIRONMENTAL IMPACT

Recent empirical evidence shows that the issue of (perverse) subsidies merits further attention only because of their sheer magnitude. Worldwide, governments are heavily engaged in providing subsidies and it is in fact such a persistent and widespread phenomenon that one can easily talk of a serious addiction. The costs associated with public support policies are huge. A recent review estimates the costs of global subsidies at $950 billion *a year* (see Table 2.1). It also demonstrates that many government subsidies do indeed provide false price signals and hence undermine sound economic structures.[5]

The largest subsidies in absolute terms can be found in OECD countries, nearly $700 billion a year, or three-quarters of all subsidies. Governments in non-OECD countries, however, dispense more support in relative terms: 4.6 per cent of GDP compared with 3.3 per cent in OECD countries. What is common, though, in both developed and developing countries, is that governments tend to subsidise economic activity in natural resource sectors and hence actively foster resource depletion and environmental degradation.

Table 2.1   The global costs of subsidies, mid 1990s (in US$ bn)

	Subsidies	
Agriculture	325	
Automobile	225	
Energy	205	
Water	60	
Manufacturing industry	55	
Forestry	35	
Mining	25	
Fisheries	20	
Total (in % GDP)	950	3.6%
Subtotal OECD (in % GDP)	690	3.3%
Subtotal non-OECD (in % GDP)	260	4.6%

Source: Van Beers and De Moor (1998)

The most heavily subsidised sector in the world is agriculture. Governments in OECD countries dispense $300 billion worth of transfers to support agriculture and in particular production by offering farmers minimum prices above the world market level (see Table 2.2).[6] The EU, Japan and the USA together account for 90 per cent of all OECD transfers. Agricultural support runs up to $334 per capita or over $1330 for a family of four. The amount of support is even more staggering per farmer; subsidies amount to nearly $15 000 for a full-time farmer in an OECD country. For individual countries, and in particular Japan, the results are simply bewildering and out of any reasonable proportions.

These massive amounts of subsidies are not only disruptive because of their size, but also because they induce farmers to overutilise their lands and

Table 2.2   Transfers from OECD agricultural policies, 1996 (in US$ bn)

	OECD	USA	EU	Japan
Total subsidies	297	69	120	77
Idem, in % of GDP	1.3	0.9	1.1	1.7
Idem, US$ per capita	334	259	322	617
Idem, US$ per full-time farmer	14 493	27 240	17 473	30 091
Idem, US$ per hectare	254	161	825	15 107

Source: OECD (1997a, 1997b), Van Beers and De Moor (1998).

to maximise production by applying more fertilisers, pesticides and inputs. This overproduction leads to land degradation and environmental pollution. Additionally, as we have argued in the previous section, producer subsidies typically create a further cycle of more support, subsidies to transport and store the surpluses and, since they cannot be sold at the prices of production, export subsidies to dump the surpluses on the world market. As a result, world market prices are depressed which further increases the OECD price subsidies, hence a full circle.

Table 2.2 only reflects the cost of support policies. But besides being very expensive, OECD agricultural support policies are also ineffective. Only 20 per cent ends up as additional farm income; the remaining leaks away, mainly as a result of using more inputs as fertiliser, pesticides and water, and through inefficiencies in production. If maintaining farm income is the primary goal, the effectiveness of OECD subsidies is extremely poor.

The trade-distorting implications of OECD agricultural subsidies are enormous. Exports are subsidised and cheaper imports need to be barred from OECD markets. As a result, developing agricultural economies suffer twice: first, from the depressed world market prices, and second, from the access barriers to OECD markets. At the same time, developing countries are also guilty as charged, but of a far more minor offence. It is estimated that developing countries spend about $25 billion a year on subsidising water, fertilisers and pesticides. Nonetheless, these subsidies exert a very negative impact on domestic agricultural production and the environment.

Energy is also heavily subsidised, both in developed and developing countries. Global energy subsidies currently run up to $205 billion each year. The common feature in energy support policy across the world is that subsidies flow to fossil fuels. Subsidies for coal, oil and gas run up to $150 billion, or 70 per cent of total energy support, and this increases to a further $180 billion, or 90 per cent, when we include subsidies for fossil fuel-based electricity generation.[7] Bluntly put, the energy policies of governments end up subsidising pollution and global warming.

OECD countries spend $85 billion on subsidising energy. That is nearly $100 per person or $400 for an average family of four. In Europe, coal is heavily supported through policies as price support and purchase obligations, while in North America, oil and gas industries are subsidised through tax breaks and capital subsidies. Former socialist countries spend some $80 billion on subsidising energy consumption by keeping user prices below the market level.[8] This subsidy of $200 per person is a firm reduction since the early 1990s when energy prices were sometimes below 10 per cent and consumer subsidies ran up to $250 billion annually.[9] In the remaining developing countries, energy subsidies run to nearly $40 billion a year, a modest $9 per person. Again, subsidies flow to fossil fuels, either directly or indirectly through electricity.

Subsidies to energy provide disincentives for energy use and conservation. Quite the contrary, the underpricing of energy provides consumers with no incentive whatsoever to save on their energy bills and hence energy consumption will be higher than necessary. Since energy (or electricity) is mostly generated from burning fossil fuels, particularly in non-OECD countries, the impact on the environment is doubly negative; first, through an excessive level of energy use, and second, through environmentally malign energy sources. Although the ultimate impact on the environment is similarly negative, subsidies to energy producers affect energy patterns in a somewhat different way. In this case, the higher price of energy induces overproduction and since most support is directed to fossil fuels, this turns out to be ecologically malign as well. Additionally, since energy is an important input in production processes, their harmful impact may spread throughout the economy by promoting energy-intensive production and hence trade patterns .

Subsidies to fisheries is an example to illustrate that not only the size of the subsidy matters. Total subsidies amount to 'only' \$20 billion per year, through a variety of measures,[10] but they do exert a highly negative influence on production, fishing stocks and trade. With the help of massive subsidies, fishing vessels have grown larger and larger; over the past 20 years, the fishing fleet has grown at a rate double that of the global catch. Additionally, fisheries subsidies also allow loss-making fishing firms to survive. The over-capacity of the fishing fleet has now led to severely depleted and overfished stocks; about 70 per cent of the world's fishing stocks is fully exploited, overexploited, depleted or recovering. Fishing stocks are not allowed to recover, and ultimately the result will be the biological extinction of species.

Introduced to maintain fishermen's income and employment, subsidies to the fisheries sector have served their purpose only in the short run. In the longer run, however, the impact of fisheries subsidies on income and employment turns out to be quite perverse. Because they have induced overfishing and severely depleted fishing stocks, the subsidies are now threatening the same employment they intended to preserve. Evidence suggests that this situation is already occurring. Fishing grounds off the coast of Newfoundland and New England had to be closed in 1992 because the fleets continued their fishing efforts and severely overfished the waters. The costs have been high: 42 000 jobs were lost and resulted in an additional \$8 billion in unemployment benefits.

A typical example of a harmful subsidy are foreign access payments, that is subsidies for the distant water fleets in developed countries to access foreign fishing grounds. These distant water fleets have enormous capacities, not only because of the number of fishing vessels but also because of their size and technological sophistication.[11] By accessing the fishing grounds of developing countries, the fish catch of distant water fleets seriously reduces

the fishing stock in developing countries' waters and threatens the employment opportunities of local fishermen. In other words, foreign access payments
may save jobs in the rich countries but at a high cost and only at the expense
of jobs in the developing countries.

Finally, consider subsidies to OECD manufacturing industries. Currently,
public support runs up to at least $55 billion but it may well be several times
larger.[12] From 1989, OECD industry subsidies have grown by at least 26 per
cent in nominal terms, a rate of 6 per cent a year. Although the ratio of
support to manufacturing GDP fluctuates between 1.2 per cent and 1.4 per
cent, this stability is more the result of the growth in GDP than of collective
policy efforts to reduce industrial support. Only 4 per cent of all OECD
industry subsidies are targeted at environmentally benign industries. Most
subsidies are directed to investment or production and hence reduce capital
costs or increases the profits of companies. Both policies alter economic
signals and will very likely lead to an increase in industrial production
capacity. They will also have direct and immediate trade- and competition-
distorting impacts. Therefore, the impact on the environment is likely to be
negative, leading to more industrial waste and pollution.

2.5   POLICY OPTIONS FOR REDUCING PERVERSE
SUBSIDIES: THE ROLE OF THE WTO

The obvious conclusion from the foregoing is that perverse subsidies need to
be eliminated or at least reformed and decoupled from production or consumption. One important barrier is that many perverse subsidies – once
provided – change the behaviour of people and firms. A typical feature is
their long history, and soon support becomes an integral part of everyday life
and gets enshrined in human behaviour and business decision-making processes. Subsidy recipients get used to support and grow dependent on them. In
particular, when subsidies are linked to economic activities, subsidy recipients get addicted. Removing subsidies would raise fierceful opposition because
recipient groups fear losing their competitiveness. In fact, at the country
level, this fear is recognized as a prisoner's dilemma; governments that may
wish to pursue subsidy reform will hesitate to move first because they fear
being confronted with (only) negative economic effects if they act alone.

One of the two main strategies suggested by De Moor and Calamai (1997)
is to initiate and stimulate an internationally coordinated policy move towards subsidy reform. The ideal forum to negotiate such an international
policy effort would be the WTO. Besides being the only truly recognized
international platform, the WTO has proved its usefulness on various trade
issues. Nevertheless, the OECD countries are in the most comfortable posi-

tion to lead such an initiative. They have more to benefit from subsidy reform; first, because OECD subsidies are the largest in the world, at least in absolute terms, and second, they are economically the most distorting.

The most successful strategy would be to aim for a phased-in reform of subsidies, gradually decreasing the level of support. This approach could well be differentiated in time and by income level, for example OECD countries could commit themselves on a complete elimination of subsidies within a period of five years, middle-income countries within ten years and low-income countries could target for a 50 per cent reduction within ten years.

What kind of incentive would OECD countries have to abolish or reduce their 'own' subsidies? None, as long as the cost implications for the economy and the environment are not clear. This is the reason why another key strategy is of importance, that is, creating transparency. Making clear how much support costs, and how it affects the economy and the environment, will reveal more clearly the often implicit choices and priorities. If the huge amount of costs for the economies of the OECD countries which are the result of subsidies will be clearly revealed, OECD governments will definitively have an incentive to reduce them. An example is the reduction of agricultural subsidies of the European Union (EU) as a result of the Agreement on Agriculture in the Uruguay Round. This negotiation result would never have been achieved if it had not been made clear that agricultural policies and subsidies in the EU were so highly expensive. The WTO may be well suited to introduce common standards for subsidy reporting and subsequently monitoring subsidy performance. Such standards could, for instance, comprise common tax benchmarks.

Domestically, creating more transparency allows for a better and more sound assessment of objectives and alternatives and enhances control of government policies. More transparency also increases the political costs of irresponsible policies and hence provides incentives for policy makers to act responsibly. To control the addiction in the long run, subsidy providers and recipients should be placed under regular and strict scrutiny. This would require institutional reform. Subsidies should be bound to a time-horizon, say for a maximum of five years; after which support should be gradually reduced. Subsidies should also be restricted to a maximum support level and policy measures with an open end should be avoided. One may consider introducing a burden of proof for subsidy policies and require that governments actually prove why support is necessary and why in that particular format.

Future international trade negotiations should pay more attention to subsidies in both developed and developing countries. In the next round on agriculture the line of reducing export subsidies as agreed upon in the Agriculture Agreement of the Uruguay Round should be continued, and extended with subsidies that are not only directly related to trade but affect trade flows and natural environment indirectly. In particular producer and input subsidies should be taken into account.

Finally, we also believe that OECD countries can do more and play an important active role in the elimination of subsidies in developing countries. It is recommendable that the OECD countries reduce their barriers against imports from developing countries which would permit the latter to eliminate or at least to reduce substantially domestic perverse subsidies. The advantage of such a deal for the OECD countries is that environmental damage done to the environment in developing countries but with a global impact (for example, deforestation causing changes in the world climate) can be reduced. In practice, we think this is an exchange to be negotiated politically that is practically achievable.[13]

2.6 CONCLUSIONS

So far, the debate on international trade and environment has been rather incomplete. Before discussing the incorporation of environmental externalities in prices, which assumes correct market prices, the debate should focus first on the existence and impact of perverse subsidies on international trade and the environment. Currently, most of the massive amount of $950 billion in government subsidies provides false price signals and hence undermines sound economic structures. Many subsidies are directed to support economic activity in natural resource sectors and the active subsidisation of production or consumption in these sectors causes further resource depletion and environmental degradation. In particular, producer subsidies are distortionary by affecting trade patterns and causing trade imbalances.

Reform of subsidies should take place within an internationally coordinated policy effort within the framework of the WTO and led by the OECD countries. The best strategy would be a phased-in reform of subsidies which leads to a gradually decrease of support. The incentive for the OECD countries to do so should be the high economic and environmental costs involved in providing subsidies. In particular the economic costs should be revealed, as most of them are hidden. Hence, our proposal is to create more transparency which makes clear the high costs in foregone alternatives (that is, what else could have been done with billions of dollars of perverse subsidies). This leads to a better and more sound assessment of objectives and alternatives and enhances control of government policies. More transparency also increases the political costs of irresponsible policies and hence provides incentives for policymakers to act responsibly. A credible, international organisation such as the WTO could play a key role in this process of desubsidisation.

In trade negotiations in the WTO framework, OECD countries can offer additional market access for developing countries in exchange for the elimination of those subsidies in developing countries that create global environmental damage. Additional market access for exports of developing countries in the domestic markets of the OECD countries provides the developing nations with means that allow them to fulfil their obligation to eliminate or reduce the most important perverse subsidies.

NOTES

1. The relationship between environment, international trade and policy is extensively discussed in Low (1992), Anderson and Blackhurst (1992, 1994) and Van Beers and Van den Bergh (1996).
2. Van Beers and Van den Bergh (2001) and Van Beers and De Moor (2001) provide a more extensive graphical treatment of the impact of perverse subsidies on international trade and external effects.
3. In De Moor and Calamai (1997), subsidies are defined as comprising all measures that keep prices for consumers below market level or keep prices for producers above market level or that reduce costs for consumers and producers by giving direct or indirect support. This subsidy concept hence comprises far more than the traditional money handouts from the government, but it also includes transfers through the tax system and different types of off-budget subsidies, such as soft loans, minimum prices and local purchase obligations.
4. For example, tax subsidies directly affect the (net) income of subsidy recipients while minimum price guarantees benefit producers and hence affect production.
5. Compare De Moor and Calamai (1997), OECD (1997a, 1998), Myers (1998) and Van Beers and De Moor (2001)
6. There are many more types of support but producer price support is most typical for OECD countries, as, for instance, in the Common Agricultural Policy of the EU.
7. At the opposite extreme, subsidies for renewable energy or energy conservation account for only 4 per cent.
8. The 1995 subsidy estimates for the socialist countries have been derived from earlier World Bank (1992) calculations by using the percentage reduction in subsidy rates and the (negative) growth rate of commercial energy use. Expressed as a percentage of GDP, subsidies have remained fairly constant. This outcome corresponds to the OECD (1997a) update for energy subsidies in Russia of $52 billion, or 8.4 per cent of GDP, exactly similar to the early 1990s.
9. In 1995, energy prices are generally at 70 per cent of the world market level.
10. For example, expenses for fleet renewal and modernisation, port facilities, withdrawal of excess supplies from the markets due to minimum prices, foreign access payment, subsidised interest rates, loan guarantees, exemptions from fuel taxes for the fleet, accelerated depreciation of fishing boats, deferral of income taxes for fishermen.
11. A typical trawl net is now one kilometre long, big enough to hold 12 jumbo jets, and able to catch 400 tons of fish in one go.
12. Not included are subsidies through procurement policies for which only a small percentage could make procurement by far the biggest subsidy to industry. Studies suggest that one-half of the $600 to $900 billion in public procurement involve non-competitive goods and services with a typical price subsidy of 30 per cent. This would bring the subsidy from public procurement at $90 to $135 billion a year.
13. These policy options have been extensively worked out in Van Beers and De Moor (2001).

REFERENCES

Anderson, K. and Blackhurst, R. (1992), *The Greening of World Trade Issues*, New York: Harvester Wheatsheaf.

Anderson, K. and Blackhurst, R. (1994), Special issue on 'Trade and the Environment', *Ecological Economics*, **9**, January.

De Moor, A. and Calamai, P. (1997), *Subsidizing unsustainable development: undermining the earth with public funds*, Institute for Research on Public Expenditure, The Hague: the Earth Council.

Low, P. (1992), 'International trade and environment', World Bank Discussion Papers, n.159.

Myers, N. (1998), *Perverse Subsidies*, Canada: International Institute for Sustainable Development.

OECD (1997a), *Reforming Energy and Transport Subsidies*, Paris: OECD.

OECD (1997b), *Agricultural Policies in OECD Countries. Monitoring and Evaluation*, Paris: OECD.

OECD (1998), *Improving the Environment Through Reducing Subsidies*, Part I: *Summary and Policy Conclusions*, Paris: OECD.

Van Beers, C. and Van den Bergh, J.C.J.M. (1996), 'An overview of methodological approaches in the analysis of trade and environment', *Journal of World Trade*, **30** (1), (Feb.), 143–67. Reprinted in: A.M. Rugman, J.J. Kirton and J.A. Soloway (eds) (1998), *Trade and Environment: Economic, Legal and Policy Perspectives*, Cheltenham: Edward Elgar.

Van Beers, C. and Van Den Bergh, J.C.J.M. (2001), 'Perseverance of Perverse Subsidies and their Impact on Trade and the Environment', *Ecological Economics*, **36**, p. 475–86.

Van Beers, C. and De Moor, A. (1998), *Scanning Subsidies and Policy Trends in Europe and Central Asia*, UNEP (Environmental Information and Assessment Technical Report, n.2)

Van Beers, C. and De Moor, A. (forthcoming, 2001), *Public Subsidies and Policy Failure*, Cheltenham: Edward Elgar.

World Bank (1992), *World Development Report 1992*, Washington, DC: World Bank.

3. Valuing statistical lives

David Pearce

INTRODUCTION: THE IMPORTANCE OF RISK VALUATION IN ENVIRONMENTAL COST–BENEFIT STUDIES

Environmental cost–benefit studies include as benefits any reductions in the risks of premature mortality and morbidity. In turn, changes in the risks of health 'end points' are given economic valuations based on the willingness to pay (WTP) of those at risk to reduce the risks. Valuations may vary with the level of risk and certainly vary with the health state that is avoided, for example, people are more averse to cancer risks than risks of accident. One feature of these cost–benefit studies is that health benefits tend to dominate overall benefit estimates. Accordingly, if the basis on which the health benefits are estimated is incorrect, then the overall cost–benefit result is very likely to be incorrect. It matters a great deal, therefore, if the underlying epidemiology is correct and if the economic valuation applied to the health effects is correct.

This chapter provides an overview of the issues as they relate to premature mortality only. It is designed as a background paper on the debate about the appropriate way to treat life risks in the context of environmental change. It does not seek to produce any new results, being designed mainly for reference and as a guide to the issues.

Table 3.1 shows the role that health benefit valuation has played in some recent European cost–benefit studies. It can be seen that the overall benefits figures are dominated by health impacts. Other studies report cost–benefit results for policies aimed directly at health effects. Here the issue is whether benefits exceed costs, an issue that is also very much affected by the approach taken to health impacts.

ECONOMIC VALUATION AND RESOURCE ALLOCATION

Economic valuation is intricately inseparable from the issue of how to allocate scarce resources. Risk reduction is not a costless activity and hence any

Table 3.1　　*Health benefits as a percentage of overall benefits in recent cost–benefit studies*

Study	Title and subject area	Health benefits as % of total benefits
Holland and Krewitt (1996)	*Benefits of an Acidification Strategy for the European Union*: reductions of SO_x, NO_x, NH_3 in the European Union	86–94%. Total benefits cover health, crops and materials.
AEA Technology (1998a)	*Cost–Benefit Analysis of Proposals Under the UNECE Multi-Effect Protocol*: reductions of SO_x, NO_x, NH_3, VOCs	80–93%. Total benefits cover health, crops, buildings, forests, ecosystems, visibility
IVM, NILU and IIASA (1997)	*Economic Evaluation of Air Quality for Sulphur Dioxide, Nitrogen Dioxide, Fine and Suspended Particulate Matter and Lead*: reductions of these pollutants	32–98%. Total benefits include health and materials damage
AEA Technology (1998b)	*Economic Evaluation of the Control of Acidification and Ground Level Ozone*: reductions of NOx and VOCs. SO_2 and NH_4 held constant.	52–85% depending on inclusion or not of chronic health benefits. Total benefits include health, crops, materials and visibility

resources used up in the reduction of one set of risks could have been used to reduce another set of risks. Taking a wider view, resources allocated to risk reduction might equally be allocated to some entirely different purpose: education, restoring national heritage, improving landscapes, and so on. Valuation attempts to provide the answer to the problem of choosing between alternative uses of resources. If risk reduction has a high value relative to other uses of resources, then risk reduction should have priority.

There have been philosophical objections to the use of economic valuation. On what might be called the 'rights approach' individuals have rights to human health and a clean environment, and such rights would have similar status to rights against discrimination (Bullard, 1994). One possible implication of the rights approach is that all environmental risks should be reduced to zero, since any positive level of risk infringes individuals' rights. Alternatively, if rights conflict and are not absolute, then some trade-off between rights has to occur. A variation of the rights-based approach extends rights to non-human species, that is, it confers 'value' on living things (and sometimes non-living things) independently of human values. This is sometimes articulated in terms of 'intrinsic' rights of species to exist.

The rights-based approach contrasts with the view based on 'trade-offs' between cost and risk reduction. Risk reduction is pursued up to some point where the costs of conservation are thought to be 'too high'. There are divergent views as to how this trade-off is to be made. In particular, there are those who favour a balancing of economically valued costs and benefits, and there are those who favour leaving the trade-off to the political system. This categorisation is not meant to be all-encompassing. More detail of the considerable variation of views within these categories can be found in Turner (1993).

One of the problems with the debate about these alternative views is that much of the discussion takes place quite independently of the real world context of environmental change. If resources were infinite there would be no problem of trade-off, and hence no problem of determining priorities. Everything deemed to be 'good' or 'right' could be done. But the real world is not like this and it is necessary to choose. The fundamental feature of choice making is cost, which is another way of saying that resources are finite. Adopting a rights-based approach implies that the choices surrendered by pursuing risk reduction as a matter of right (that is, the cost) are of a lower 'moral order' than risks to human health or risks to other species. The problem then is that risk reduction has to be pursued regardless of the foregone values sacrificed. Moreover, all risk reduction has to be pursued: it cannot be correct to reduce some risks but not others unless the rights are attenuated in some way. Risk reduction may therefore conflict with other rights, for example rights to a decent livelihood, rights to education and, especially, to freedom of choice.

Much of the motive for the rights-based approach arises from an understandable sense of frustration with the fact that trade-off approaches do involve 'acceptance' of some positive levels of risk. But it also has its foundations in a lack of appreciation of what 'cost' actually means, a perception fostered by the view that cost is 'just money', as if money is unrepresentative of human wellbeing.

Developments in risk analysis sharply underscore the unavoidability of trade-offs and the unreality of the rights-based approach. Risk–risk analysis and health–health analysis draw attention to the fact that the costs of risk reduction policies are met from reductions in household incomes – see Keeney (1990, 1994, 1997), Graham et al. (1992), Lutter and Morrall (1994), Portney and Stavins (1994), Viscusi (1994) and Viscusi and Zeckhauser (1994). It is known that households with low incomes tend to have higher exposure generally to life and health risks, so that reductions in expenditure increase risk exposure. For example, Keeney (1997) estimates that in the USA there is one fatality for each $5–11m of public expenditure on risk reduction.

Finally, rights-based approaches tend to be discussed as if whatever is deemed to be right by one or more persons constrains others who may not share the moral view. Put another way, what is right has an absolutist flavour. If there was no dispute about the moral standpoint, then, clearly, there would be a moral consensus. But in so far as hypothetical market studies have shown the existence of 'lexical' preferences (implying no trade-off) – and this is disputed – they have not characterised the whole sample. It is unclear, therefore, what role a minority believing in 'rights' should play in determining the outcome of a policy or project choice.

Overall, then, rights-based approaches fail because of their neglect of the most basic of all economic principles – opportunity cost – and because they have little to say about consensus.

THE TRADE-OFF VIEW: ECONOMICS

The economic approach to the trade-off issue operates through the aggregation of human preferences. The set of persons affected by a decision defines the set of people whose preferences count, where 'affected by' means that their wellbeing is, in one way or the other, partly dependent on the environment in question. This preference base is inherently 'democratic' – it requires that policies be responsive to preferences however they are formed. Preferences are revealed in the market-place through demand behaviour – that is, as 'willingness to pay' (WTP). Indeed, the demand curve in textbook economics is a (marginal) willingness to pay curve. If WTP is rejected as a criterion for allocating resources to risk reduction, then some explanation has to be provided as to why environmental goods and services are different to other goods and services which are allocated on a WTP basis.

But risk reduction often has no market, that is, the issue giving rise to risk is not bought and sold on the open market. Clean air would be an example. Thus the economic approach requires that preferences for risk reduction be inferred from human behaviour in other contexts.

The theory of economic valuation developed substantially in the 1980s and 1990s. This section reviews, briefly, those techniques that relate to human health risks only. Other techniques are relevant to the valuation of other environmental changes. For a detailed review see Freeman (1993).

For a change in risk that threatens life and health generally we can say that the relevant valuation is the value that the individuals at risk attached to their own health and life chances, plus what others would be willing to pay to avoid the risk to that individual, plus any costs that society at large bears and which would not otherwise occur if the individual did not suffer the effects of the risk in question. These components are:

a. $VOR_{i,i}$ where $VOR_{i,i}$ refers to the individual i's valuation of risk to herself – that is 'own risk'. The way in which these individual VORs are aggregated is dealt with shortly. Essentially, we will require the summation of such own valuations for all individuals at risk to give $\Sigma_i VOR_{i,i}$, more commonly known as the 'value of a statistical life' (see below).

b. $VOR_{i,j}$ where the i,j notation now refers to j's valuation of risks to i. Again, this will need to be summed for all j, that is for all people expressing some concern about risks to i, to give $\Sigma_j VOR_{i,j}$.

c. COI_i where COI refers to the 'cost of illness, suffered by i but which costs are borne by the rest of society. An example would be hospital costs. COI could be regarded as part of $VOR_{i,j}$.

The extent to which these three components of the value of life risks can in fact be aggregated is discussed later.

VALUING STATISTICAL LIVES

One form of health risk is the risk of premature mortality arising from some risk context, say increased air pollution. What value should be attached to such risks of mortality? The sum of individuals' own valuations of risks to their own lives is known as the value of a statistical life, VOSL. The shorthand often used for the VOSL is 'value of life', which is unfortunate. Since the idea of 'valuing life' appears odd to some and morally offensive to others, it is important to understand what a value of a statistical life (VOSL) actually is.

The way a VOSL is obtained is by aggregating up from a value (willingness to pay, WTP) of risk reduction. Imagine the probability of dying next year is 0.004 for each person and suppose we have 1000 persons in the population. Assume there is some risk reduction policy that reduces the risk to 0.003, a change of 0.001. Each person is asked to express their WTP for this change in risk and suppose the answer is £1000. The risk reduction policy is a public good: it affects everyone equally. Thus 1000 people say they are each willing to pay £1000 for the policy, that is, their aggregate willingness to pay is £1m. The change in risk will result in one statistical person being saved each year (1000 × 0.001). Thus the value of a statistical life is £1m in this example. It is important to understand that no-one is being asked their WTP to avoid themselves dying at a specified time: they are being asked to express a WTP for a change in risk. As Freeman (1993, p. 320) notes:

> the economic question being dealt with here is not about how much an individual would be willing to pay to avoid his or her certain death or how much compensation that individual would require to accept that death. In this respect, the term 'value of life' is an unfortunate phrase that does not reflect the true nature of the question at hand. Most people would be willing to pay their total wealth to avoid certain death; and there is probably no finite sum of money that could compensate an individual for the sure loss of life. Rather, the economic question is about how much the individual would be willing to pay to achieve a small reduction in the probability of death during a given period or how much compensation that individual would require to accept a small increase in that probability.

It is worth emphasising Freeman's point: the VOSL is *not* what someone is willing to pay to avoid losing their life, a confusion that is pervasive in the popular literature commenting on valuations of life risks. It is the valuation of small changes in risk. VOSL is essentially a convenient rule for aggregation.

Individuals' WTP to reduce risks can be expected to vary across different individuals. The two main reasons for this will be that:

a. people have differing attitudes to risk: some may even be 'risk lovers', that is, positively enjoying risky contexts. Most people are risk avoiders, that is they will tend to reveal a positive willingness to pay for risk reduction. But there is no particular reason why their valuations of risk should be the same;
b. incomes vary and hence willingness to pay is likely to vary in such a way that those with higher incomes have higher WTPs. This is not a necessary result since attitudes to risk may vary in such a way as to offset an income effect. Nonetheless, it raises an important equity issue about fairness between people, an issue that is not in fact confined to risk valuations but to the use of WTP measures in general.

A VOSL can also be measured by a 'willingness to accept' (WTA) compensation for increased risk. It is well known that many people do make this trade-off between risk and money, for example by accepting premia on wages to tolerate risk. It is tempting to think that the WTA approach will produce very much higher values for a VOSL than the WTP approach, simply because

WTA is not constrained by income. WTP and WTA can, indeed, be different and WTA for environmental losses may exceed WTP for environmental gains by factors of 2–5 (Gregory, 1986). Various explanations exists for this disparity, including the fact that individuals may feel they are losing an 'entitlement' if the issue is one of loss of an entitlement (WTA) rather than an increment to an existing entitlement (WTP). Another explanation, which is wholly consistent with economic theory, suggests that WTA > WTP arises mainly in contexts where there is no ready substitute for the environmental good in question (Hanemann, 1991). These issues are discussed further later on.

TECHNIQUES FOR ESTIMATING VOSL

A number of techniques have been developed to estimate VOSLs. The main ones are rooted in the general economic theory of valuation, that is they have a theoretical basis on the measurement of human wellbeing based on individuals' preferences. One widely used technique, however, has only a tenuous link to the theory.

Valuing Mortality Risks: Wage Risk Models

The wage risk, or 'hedonic wage' model estimates a willingness to accept measure of risk. Essentially, it looks at wages in risky occupations and seeks to determine the factors that determine wages. One of these factors is hypothesised to be the risk level. Other things being equal, workers will prefer jobs with less risk to jobs with high risk. This will result in a relative shortage of workers for risky jobs and hence wages in those jobs should be higher. This 'wage premium' then becomes a measure of risk valuation. It can be estimated by multiple regression techniques in which the wage is the dependent variable and the various factors influencing the wage are the independent variables. An example might be:

$$\text{Wage} = f\,(\text{Educ, Exp, Union, Risk, Occ})$$

where Educ is education, Exp is years of experience, Union is an indicator of the degree of unionisation of the labour force, Risk is the objective (or perceived) probability of fatal injury and Occ is some indicator of the desirability of the occupation. The coefficient linking Wage and Risk is then the WTA measure of risk.

One obvious problem with such approaches is that workers have to know about the differences in risks and, if they do, whether those perceptions coincide with 'objective' measures of risk such as the probability of a fatality in that industry. If there is no perception of risk, but risk exists, then the 'hedonic wage' (that is, the wage premium) may be zero, seriously understating risk values. If there is a perception of risk but it is exaggerated compared to objective risk, then risk may be overvalued. Other problems include the potential for workers in risky jobs to be 'self-selecting', that is, those tolerant of risk may be attracted into the industry in question. Lack of labour mobility will also mean that some workers will remain in jobs without full compensation for the risks involved.

What limited evidence there is suggests that workers actually overstate the risk of their jobs. But as Freeman (1993) points out, what matters for the hedonic wage model is the perception of differences in risks between jobs, not the absolute level of risk in a given job.

Most hedonic wage studies have been carried out in the USA and suggest that VOSLs range from \$2m (1994 prices) to \$3.5m.

Valuing Mortality Risks: Avertive Behaviour

Individuals spend money in trying to reduce risks, so called 'averting behaviour'. Under certain circumstances these expenditures approximate the economists' concept of WTP to reduce risk. The kinds of averting expenditures in question might be on smoke alarms, safety harnesses, tamper-proof drug storage containers, and so on. These kinds of expenditures can be regarded as part of what is called a 'health production function' in which the state of good health is 'produced' by various factors, including expenditures on averting ill-health. Note that some apparent averting expenditures are not valid measures of risk reduction. Thus, it is quite widely assumed that life insurance expenditures are measures of WTP to avoid risk. But insurance expenditures do not have the effect of reducing risks. Indeed, they may actually increase risks by encouraging less careful behaviour – the issue of 'moral hazard'. As Freeman (1993) notes, life insurance essentially values the earning capacity of the insured individual to the dependants who are the ones who will gain from any insurance policy. This is not at all the same thing as the individual's willingness to pay to reduce risks to his or her own life, which is what is required.

The health production function can be written:

$$H = f \text{(Poll, Med, Avert, Other)}$$

where Poll is the level of pollution, Med is the level of medical treatment, and Avert is the level of averting activity. Other refers to all the other factors affecting health status: age, income, smoking behaviour, and so on. Reducing pollution will reduce the time spent being unwell, say from 4 days to 3 days.

If by spending £X through avertive behaviour the same reduction in ill-health can be achieved, then £X should be the value of the reduced pollution to the individual. More formally,

WTP (Pollution Reduction) = (Reduced Time in Ill Health) × (Extra Cost of 'Producing' Health by Mitigating Activity).

In this way, expenditures on risk reduction can be interpreted as WTP for risk reduction. In practice, finding examples of avertive expenditures that are 'purely' health producing has proved difficult. Studies include seat belt use and smoke detectors and suggest VOSLs of about $0.7–$2.2 m.

Valuing Mortality Risk: Contingent Valuation

The contingent valuation method (CVM) requires that individuals express their preferences in response to a questionnaire. It is therefore very much akin to market research in which the researcher seeks to find out how a respondent would behave, in terms of WTP, for a modified or new good. Questionnaires take two forms: (a) open-ended or continuous approaches simply ask what someone is WTP (or WTA), and no prompting of likely values is permitted; and (b) discrete or dichotomous choice in which the value is posed and the respondent is then asked whether he or she is willing to pay that sum, yes or no. Yes/no questions that use the cost of providing some project or benefit as the sum to which the yes/no answer is sought are also known as 'referendum' approaches. There is now a general preference for the dichotomous choice format. The kinds of biases that may occur in CVM include:

a. Starting point bias in the dichotomous choice format, that is, respondents tend to produce WTP answers that tend towards the first 'price' put forward by the questioner. Such a bias is easily tested by seeing if the difference between the average stated WTP is statistically different to the starting point sum;

b. Strategic bias whereby the respondent understates the true value of their preference (they 'free ride') in the expectation that others will state more and thus secure the good in question for everyone. This phenomenon was long thought to be inherent with 'public goods', such as clean air, since if the clean air is provided for any one individual it is provided for everyone (clean air is said to be 'jointly consumed'). Of course, the misstatement of preferences may be biased the other way: someone may be so keen to see the good provided that they overstate their preferences, fearing that others will free ride. Tests for strategic bias suggest that, contrary to expectation, it may not be of major significance. Such tests may involve stratifying the sample deliberately to give some people strong incentives to free ride and others less of an incentive, and then seeing if their average WTPs diverge. Others involve indicating that unless more than a certain percentage of respondents vote for the good, it will not be supplied.

c. Hypothetical bias: the respondent may produce answers that are purely hypothetical, that is, if the good or policy in question is actually provided, their WTP will be less than stated in response to the questionnaire. Careful design of questionnaires can reduce the hypothetical bias problem to very low levels in WTP questionnaires. It may be more of a problem with WTA questions. Measuring the bias usually involves comparing stated preferences with actual preferences when real sums of money are involved in the CVM. Since respondents are less familiar with compensation contexts (the relevant context for WTA), their stated WTA is likely to exceed their actual WTA.

d. Part–whole or 'mental account' bias: here the problem is that, while the questionnaire may focus on a specific environmental benefit, the respondent may act as if he or she is valuing environmental improvement in general. Tests for this kind of bias involve varying the quantity of the good in question, for example a 1 per cent reduction in risk, a 10 per cent reduction in risk and so on, and seeing whether WTP varies significantly as the benefit is increased. A number of studies suggest that WTP is the same and that what individuals are 'purchasing' is not the benefit in question but the 'warm glow of giving' or 'moral satisfaction'. One response has been to ensure that questions are not asked until the respondent has been reminded that he or she has a specific budget to be allocated. The empirical evidence of part–whole bias remains mixed;

e. Information bias: the quality of information supplied to the respondent may affect the stated WTPs. Usually, the more information is supplied about the risks in question the higher the WTP. Why this is regarded by some critics of CVM as a flaw in the method is unclear. Information should influence WTP in exactly the same way as information influences WTP in the everyday market place for ordinary goods. While there is an interesting issue of how much information should be provided, what matters most is that the same level of information be provided to all respondents.

There are other problems with the CVM, but modern CVM design is capable of minimising the extent of error in stated responses. Good surveys of CVM are to be found in Pearce et al. (1994) and Bateman and Turner (1993).

Valuing Mortality Risk: The Human Capital Approach

Before the formalisation of hedonic wage, CVM and avertive behaviour approaches, the most commonly used technique to value risk to human life was the human capital approach. The idea is simple: an individual is 'worth' to society what he or she would have produced in the remainder of their lifetime, gross of taxes since the interest is in society's valuation of the individual. An argument did exist as to whether the earnings that are relevant should be net or gross of the individual's own consumption. If the individual's consumption is excluded then the value concept is simply that of how the rest of society values the individual, and that is inconsistent with the WTP approach. If the individual's consumption is included, then at least some gesture is made towards including a value from the individual's own standpoint. But there is in fact nothing to suggest that an individual's WTP need be equal to the remaining lifetime income of that individual. The link to the WTP approach is clearly tenuous at least. The WTP approach is based on how individuals value risks to their own lives, whereas the human capital approach makes no obvious reference to that concept. Indeed, the human capital approach says little about individuals' attitudes to risk. Its one virtue is that it is thought to be very easy to calculate (Rowlatt et al., 1998).

Even if the human capital approach is accepted as a rule of thumb, however, there are problems in its estimation. First, if the individuals at risk had retired from work, the human capital valuation would suggest that their VOSL is zero or even negative (if consumption is deducted). This perhaps underlines the failure of the concept in terms of its theoretical underpinnings. If human capital was a WTP concept, those out of work should have positive WTPs. Second, someone may be of median age but still not be producing marketed 'output'. A houseperson, for example, produces non-market output and this would have to be valued. Third, future earnings cannot simply be added up year by year to get a total since the individual will discount the future. Hence a discount rate is needed.

While it would be better if the human capital approach was avoided altogether, it is still widely used, no doubt because of the relative ease of computation. If used, the computation in question would be:

$$\text{'VOSL'} = \sum_{i=1,T-t} (p_{t+i} \cdot Y_{t+i})/(1 + r)^i$$

where $\Sigma_{i=1,T-t}$ denotes the sum over time from time t, the current age of the individual at risk, T is the age at which the individual ceases to work, p_{t+1} is the probability of the individual surviving from age t to age $t + i$, Y is income, and r is the discount rate.

The human capital approach does not produce a value of statistical life in the sense of Σ_i VORi,i above. But can it be used to estimate the value that others put on the life at risk? For close relatives, friends, and so on, the answer must be 'no': such people do not value risks in terms of the income forgone by the individual at risk. But what of society generally? There is a sense in which society loses the output of the individual less the consumption of that individual. But had the individual survived, the rest of society might have to produce transfer payments in the form of welfare payments, and illness costs arising from the ill-health that the individual would have suffered had they survived. Arguably, then, what the rest of society loses is i's income minus i's consumption minus i's claims on the rest of society over the expected lifetime of i without the risky event. This is perhaps the most that can be said for the human capital approach.

Willingness to Pay versus Willingness to Accept?

The valuation of statistical lives rests on the WTP or WTA principle. It is easy to see that WTP is constrained by income and/or wealth. WTA appears not to be so constrained since it is an amount in compensation for accepting a risk. Both the contingent valuation and wage-risk models have the capability to elicit WTA estimates and practice has found that WTA figures are not infinite, that is, people do not expect extremely large payments in compensation for losses of environmental quality. But WTA does tend to exceed WTP, as noted earlier, and these differences cannot generally be explained by issues of questionnaire design. There are genuine differences between WTP and WTA. This raises the issue of which measure is correct?

The answer depends on the context, and especially on property rights, although other factors help to explain the size of the discrepancy between WTP and WTA. The following matrix explains the property rights issue. Generally, WTP is the right concept when the individual whose valuation is being sought does not have a right to the improvement being valued. WTA is the correct concept when the individual does have a right to the status quo and is being asked to forgo a benefit or accept a loss.

The relevance of property rights arises in two contexts. The first is where there are clearly defined legal rights, and the second relates to the individual's perception of rights. Thus, we might expect individuals to value a unit loss much more highly than a unit gain if he or she believes they have some right to the existing amount of environmental quality or asset. There is indeed evidence that individuals have 'loss aversion', that is they regard the status quo as some kind of reference point from which gains and losses are evaluated. This view is stressed by advocates of 'prospect theory' – see Kahneman and Tversky (1979).

Valuation of a GAIN WILLINGNESS TO PAY ⇒ Property rights DO NOT rest with individual	Valuation of a LOSS WILLINGNESS TO PAY TO AVOID THE LOSS ⇒ Property rights DO NOT rest with the individual
Valuation of a GAIN WILLINGNESS TO ACCEPT COMPENSATION TO FORGO THE GAIN ⇒ Property rights DO rest with the individual	Valuation of a LOSS WILLINGNESS TO ACCEPT COMPENSATION ⇒ Property rights DO rest with the individual

A second factor explaining the wide divergence sometimes found between WTP and WTA is the degree of substitutability of the thing being valued with other goods. Suppose, for example, that what is being valued is a unique environmental or material asset – the Grand Canyon or the Taj Mahal, say. Then, as there are no ready substitutes one might expect WTA to be very much higher than WTP. And this turns out to be the case: the fewer the substitutes the larger the discrepancy between WTA and WTP, as theory would predict (Hanemann, 1991). Hanemann's explanation is not comprehensive because the same WTA/WTP discrepancy exists for commonplace goods, in which case the insights from prospect theory appear to be relevant.

The relevance to life risks is of course significant if individuals feel that risks to life or health constitute an invasion of their rights not to have to tolerate those risks. There is some evidence to suggest that those rights will be especially pronounced when the risks are not voluntary, in contrast with, say, occupational risks. If so, we might expect wage-risk models, which are WTA estimates for voluntary risk, to reveal risk valuations that are above, but not substantially above, WTP valuations. CVM models, on the other hand, might reveal substantial WTA/WTP discrepancies if the risk in question is involuntary. The problem with the evidence is that most of the VOSL studies are either wage-risk studies or CVM studies of transport risk. Transport risks may or may not be seen as voluntary compared to, say, radiation risks from a nuclear power plant, although most risk studies appear to treat transport-related risks as involuntary. Early analysis of the voluntary/involuntary risk valuation issue was fairly inconclusive.

Starr (1972) attempted a comparison of risk levels and the associated benefits and concluded that involuntary risk might be valued by a factor of ten more than voluntary risk. Reworked by Otway and Cohen (1975), Starr's ratio appears far too high and a factor of two appears more appropriate. But further analysis by Fischoff et al. (1979) reinstates the large tenfold differential between involuntary and voluntary risk values. Substantial question marks hang over these studies, however, not because of the risk data but because of the use of measures of benefit based on actual expenditures on the activity in question or the contribution the activity makes to an individual's income. There is some affinity here with the required benefit measure – WTP – but it is far from precise.

Overall, then, the conceptual contexts in which WTP and WTA should be used are fairly clear and relate to the presumption about property rights. In practice, determining the assignment of property rights is far less straightforward.

THE EVIDENCE ON VOSL

Several reviews exist of VOSLs. Pearce et al. (1992) review the various estimates of VOSL and find the mean estimates across studies shown in Table 3.2 (updated to 1997 values). The estimates also show the ratio of WTA to WTP because of the presumption that WTA studies tend to find higher values than WTP studies. The wage risk studies are fairly consistent between the UK and USA with a suggestion that a higher (average) value exists for WTA in the USA than in the UK. On the other hand, WTP studies appear to produce higher values in the UK. These data also suggests that the WTA > WTP inequality holds for the USA but not for the UK, but there is no ready explanation for these disparate results. Note, however, that the estimates shown are unweighted averages, that is, it assumed that all the studies reviewed are equally valid.

Other reviews for the USA suggest ranges of recommended VOSLs. Fisher et al. (1989) recommend a range of $2–10m; Cropper and Freeman (1991) recommend $2–6m; Viscusi (1992) recommends $3–7m and Miller (1989) recommends $1–4m. An extensive review by Industrial Economics Incorporated (1993) fits a lognormal distribution to available estimates considered to be 'reliable' (26 in all) and takes the geometric mean (that is, the mode) to obtain $4m in 1993 values, or $4.5m in 1997 values. Overall, then, VOSL estimates of around US$1.6–4.8m would appear to be 'safe'.

Use of VOSL estimates of the kind noted in Table 3.2 has come under criticism for several reasons:

Table 3.2 Values of statistical life

UK£m (1997)	USA	UK
WTA (wage risk)	2.9–4.6	2.4–2.9
WTP (CVM, CRM)	1.2–2.2	3.3–5.3
WTP (market)	0.9–1.0	0.5–2.8
WTA/WTP (WR/CVM)	1.3–3.8	0.4–0.9
WTA/WTP (WR/mkt)	2.9–5.1	0.9–5.8

Source: Pearce et al. (1992) updated to 1997 prices.

a.   There is unease about the fact that health benefits based on VOSL are so dominant in cost–benefit studies;

b.   the VOSL estimates come largely from accident contexts where the mean age of the person killed is very much lower than in pollution contexts. There is therefore a feeling that older people, perhaps with an already impaired health state, will not have the same valuation of risk as someone who is very much younger; and

c.   it is, as noted above, very easy to confuse what a VOSL is actually measuring. Wrongly translated as a 'value of life', the concept is easy prey for critics who do not invest in attempts to understand the analytical foundations of VOSL. Since this confusion is widespread, analysts often prefer not to use the VOSL concept at all.

Of these reasons, only the second has any intellectual basis, although the first does reflect a 'statistical sensitivity' issue in the sense that, if the VOSL estimates are wrong, then entire decisions may be changed.

    For these good and bad reasons, then, there have been attempts to estimate not the value of the risk of fatality but the value of the life period gained by reducing the risk. This has come to be known as the 'value of a life year' or VOLY.

Values of Life Years (VOLYs)

The underlying rationale for valuing 'life years' is that many contexts in which health risks occur relate to pollution. Clearly, pollution is more likely to affect people who are most vulnerable. In a poor country this may be the very young and the very old. In a rich country, where infant mortality risks are very low, it is more likely to affect the elderly and especially those who are already at risk from their prevailing health state. Suppose, for argument's sake, that statistically the reduced life expectancy of someone exposed to air pollution is six months. Then, the argument goes, what matters is the value the individual places on those six months of extended life. If the period is a few weeks, or even days, then the relevant value is that 'life period' rather than the actual risk. This contrasts with the VOSL where a person at risk, however old they are, is faced with a risk and they express their WTP to reduce that risk. In principle, the two values – VOSL and VOLY – should bear some relationship since the person at risk must have some idea of remaining life expectancy. Indeed, it would be extremely surprising if they did not. In expressing a WTP to reduce risk, then, they should be accounting for the remaining life period available to them.

One obvious way of approaching the problem is to see if WTP to reduce risks is functionally related to age, an issue we return to below. The surprising thing about the VOSL literature is that very little of it controls for age, so that only a few studies exist to offer a guide on how risk valuations vary with age.

Alternative approaches attempt to estimate the VOLY and, so far, two procedures have been used. The first simply takes estimates of the VOSL and converts them to values of life years; that is, no additional information is sought. The second attempts to construct VOLYs from first principles by engaging in valuation studies that directly attempt to elicit the WTP for extended periods of life.

VOLYs derived from VOSLs
One approach to estimating the VOLY is to regard it as the annuity which when discounted over the remaining life span of the individual at risk would equal the estimate of VOSL. Thus, if the VOSL of, say, £1.5m relates to traffic accidents where the mean age of those involved in fatal accidents is such that the average remaining life expectancy would have been 40 years, then

$$VOLY = VOSL/A$$

where $A = [1 - (1 + r)^{-n}]/r$ and n is years of expected life remaining and r is the utility discount rate.[1] Examples are shown in Table 3.3 for $n = 40$ years.

These VOLY numbers can then be used to produce a revised VOSL allowing for age. At age 60, for example, suppose life expectancy is 15 years. The VOSL(60) is then given by

$$VOSL(60) = \sum VOLY/(1 + r)^{T-60}$$

where T is life expectancy. In the case indicated, this would be, at 1 per cent discount rate and a 'standard' VOSL of £1m:

Table 3.3   Values of life years

£m 1997 prices	Utility discount rate = 0.3%. A = 37.6	Utility discount rate = 1.0%. A = 32.8	Utility discount rate = 1.5%. A = 29.9
1.0	26 595	30 460	33 445
1.5	39 894	45 690	50 167
2.0	53 190	60 920	66 890
3.0	79 787	91 138	100 000

$$\text{VOSL}(60) = (30\ 460) \cdot (13.87) = £422\ 480.$$

The result is that the age-related VOSL declines with age and this appears to accord with the intuition of some commentators (see the discussion below). The generalised formula for age-related VOSL is:

$$\text{VOSL}(a) = [\text{VOSL}(n)/A] \cdot \sum 1/(1 + r)^{T-a}$$

where a is the age of the individual or group at risk, T is life expectancy for that group, VOSL (a) is the age-adjusted VOSL and VOSL (n) is the 'normal' VOSL.

One advantage claimed for this approach to valuation is that it can be combined with other information on the health state of the individual at risk. This might be done via 'QALYs' – quality of life year ratings. QALYs involve weighting life expectation by quality factors that reflect individuals' own perceptions of the quality of life associated with that life expectancy. Extending a life by one year but with an associated level of pain and suffering thought to be unbearable would attract a low QALY indicator. A VOLY multiplied by this QALY would give a revised quality-adjusted VOLY (Davies and Teasdale, 1994).

While the VOLY approach may appear sound it suffers from a number of deficiencies. First, it offers no evidence that VOSL declines with age in the manner shown. If this were to be the case, we would expect to find evidence that the WTP to reduce risks varies inversely with age. As Rowlatt et al. (1998) note, there *is* some evidence for a declining WTP as people become older, but that evidence is not at all consistent with the age profile of VOSL as dictated by the VOLY approach. Ignoring any influence from health states, the VOLY approach implies a monotonically declining VOSL with age, whereas the WTP for risk literature tends to produce inverted-U shapes. In essence, the age-related VOSLs derived on this approach are arbitrary: they are imposed from outside rather than being derived from any individual-based risk assessment. Maddison (1998) suggests that there are sound reasons for supposing that VOSL is proportional to the number of discounted life years remaining to an individual and that it is inversely proportional to the survival probability in the current time period. In other words, Maddison suggests that there are rationales for a declining VOSL with age, but that this will be attenuated in old people by the reduced survival probability. For the UK, he suggests that the VOSL for a 74-year-old with six months life expectancy would be 17 per cent of the healthy 36-year-old.

Second, while the evidence on age and WTP for risk reduction is not compelling, what there is suggests a decline in WTP. Jones-Lee (1989) and Jones-Lee et al. (1993) report WTP for accident reductions in the UK and these are shown in Figure 3.1.

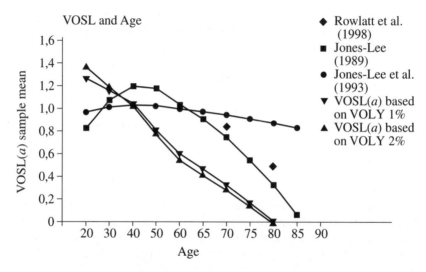

Figure 3.1   Age effects on VOSL estimates

For illustration, they are compared there to the implied VOSLs that would come from using the VOLY approach. Notice that the VOLY-based VOSLs do not exhibit the inverted U shape found in the Jones-Lee studies and they seriously understate later age VOSLs when compared to the standard VOSL approach. Also, the VOSL ratios using the VOLY approach are invariant with the value of VOSL(n), but will change with the discount rate assumed. However, Figure 3.1 shows that the VOLY-based VOSL is largely unaffected by the choice of 1 per cent or 2 per cent utility discount rates. Supporting evidence for modest declines in WTP with age can be found in Maier et al. (1989), Miller and Guria (1991), Kidholm (1995), Persson et al. (1995) and

Desaigues and Rabl (1995). Rowlatt et al. (1998) cite a Swedish paper –
Persson and Cedervall (1991) – which found rising values of WTP with age,
a result that Rowlatt et al. put down to problems in eliciting answers to
questions about small risk changes, but which could be consistent with theory
(see below). Johannesson and Johansson (1996) also find modestly increasing WTP with age.

Third, it was noted that the VOLY-based VOSL could be combined with
QALY information. Again, it appears that the VOLY approach imposes an
apparently 'logical form' on the valuations by assuming those already ill will
value remaining life periods less. But to quote a recent study for the US
Environment Protection Agency:

> it is possible that the reduced life expectancy and reduced enjoyment of life
> associated with many chronic illnesses may result in lower WTP to reduce risks of
> death. On the other hand, facing serious illness and reduced life expectancy may
> result in higher value [being] placed on protecting the remaining time. (Chestnut
> and Patterson, 1994)

Overall, Maddison's approach holds out some promise for finding age-related
VOSLs via indirect routes. These should then be tested against VOSLs derived from direct approaches in which age is specifically accounted for.

VOLYs derived from WTP experiments
An alternative procedure based on the VOLY concept is to see the WTP to
extend a lifetime conditional on having reached a certain age. Johannesson
and Johansson (1996) report a contingent valuation study in Sweden where
adults are asked their WTP for a new medical programme or technology
that would extend expected lifetimes conditional on having reached the age
of 75. Respondents are told that on reaching 75 they can expect to live for
another 10 years. They are then asked their WTP to increase lifetimes by 11
years beyond 75, that is, the 'value' of one extra year. The results suggest
average WTP across the age groups of slightly less than 10 000 SEK using
standard estimation procedures and 4000 SEK using a more conservative
approach. In dollar terms this is $600–1500.[2] Recall that this is for one year
of expected life increase. WTP actually *increases* with age, although not
dramatically – on the standard basis, 8000 SEK for the 18–34 age group,
10 000 for the 35–51 age group and 11 700 for the 51–69 age group. Using
the formula:

$$\text{VOSL}(a) = \text{VOLY} \cdot \sum 1/(1 + r)^{T-a}$$

Johannesson and Johansson suggest these values are consistent with 'normal'
VOSLs of $30 000 to $110 000, substantially less than the VOSLs derived

previously. Since $T - a$ is obviously less the older the age group, then the relevant VOSLs will decline with age. They also derive discount rates of 0.3 per cent to 3.4 per cent and these are invariant with age. Finally, they argue that these lower valuations are consistent with findings in Sweden and the USA on social attitudes to allocating resources to life saving. Thus, Cropper et al. (1994) found that survey respondents strongly favoured life saving programmes which save the lives of young people rather than old people. Earlier work by Johannesson and Johansson (1995a, 1995b) found that Swedish attitudes were similar, and that expectations about the future quality of life at old age play a significant role (regardless of what the actual quality of life is). The implications of the low WTP values for health care are hinted at in Johannesson and Johansson (1996): they observe that the VOSL values are 'negligible' compared to the costs of health treatment for the aged.

The Johannesson and Johannsson study is the only one available at present which attempts to value a life year directly. Is the WTP approach used consistent with the VOSL approach? It is arguable that the 'goods' being valued are quite different: VOSL studies value risk and the VOSL is simply an aggregation of those individual valuations of risk. The WTP for a life year is not explicitly a value of risk, but a value of extending a life year once the respondent is assumed to reach a particular age. The Johannesson and Johansson paper could be argued to be more relevant for pollution control policy if the benefits of that policy are thought to accrue mainly to the elderly.

VOSL and age again

As opposed to accidents, environmental risks are especially likely to affect the health of those already predisposed to illness, for example the elderly. Hence, it is important to know if the VOSL is likely to vary with age. At one extreme we could legitimately argue that we have no reason to suppose this WTP will vary negatively with age. Indeed, older people may be all the more risk-averse simply because the value of time itself is likely to increase the less there is of it remaining to the person at risk. Plausible reasons to suppose that WTP will fall as age increases have been advanced in the theoretical literature (for example Freeman, 1993, Chapter 10; Cropper and Simon, 1994). Freeman (1993) reviews life cycle models and shows that, in general, one might expect WTP to decline with age. This is because lifetime utility is dependent on lifetime consumption in such models and older people simply have fewer consumption years left. However, there are several reasons why such life cycle WTP models understate 'true' WTP:

a.   they tend to omit others' valuations of the life at risk (for example relatives, friends) (see below);

b. life cycle models assume that expected lifetime utility depends on expected lifetime consumption only, whereas individuals surely value survival as well. Note that this value of survival need not vary inversely with age at all, and could actually increase;

c. there is evidence to suggest that WTP for 'contemporaneous risk' is less than WTP for 'latent risk', that is WTP for avoiding accidents is less than WTP for avoiding risks of cancer (Jones-Lee et al., 1985). Yet the empirical VOSL literature is almost entirely based on accident risks. For pollution issues, then, transferring VOSLs from accident risk contexts to pollution contexts is likely to understate the 'true' degree of risk aversion.

OTHERS' VALUATION OF RISKS TO AN INDIVIDUAL

The second component of the basic valuation equation was the value placed on risks to i by others who are close to i, relatives and friends. The literature that seeks to estimate such valuations is very much smaller, but suggestive of some results. Viscusi et al. (1988) surveyed consumers to elicit risk valuations for injury risks from the use of insecticides in the USA. Consumers were asked their WTP to reduce risks from 15/10 000 to 10/10 000 for two pairs of risk: inhalation and skin poisoning and inhalation and child poisoning. The WTP figures of $1.04 and $1.84 respectively, therefore, imply values of risk of $2080 and $3680 (1.04/0.0005 and 1.84/0.0005). Individuals were then asked their WTP for an advertising campaign to reduce risks by the same amount generally, that is, to other people. The results implied valuations of the first risk pair of $10 000 for North Carolina State – where the survey was conducted – and $3070 for risks outside the state. For the second risk pair, the values were $18 100 and $4260. The state/non-state comparisons suggest that valuations decline as the individuals at risk become more 'anonymous' to the valuer, as one might expect.

An early study by Needleman (1976) sought the valuation of close relatives for reductions in risks. The study looked at kidney donors. Donors tended at that time to be close relatives to secure greater chances of acceptance of the transplanted organ. The kidney donor suffered a slight increase in risk while the recipient had dramatically improved chances of survival. By looking at data on actual kidney donations and at refusal rates – that is, situations in which the relatives refused to make the donation – Needleman estimated a 'coefficient of concern'. An average coefficient of 0.46 implies that close relatives' valuations may be 46 per cent of the value of risk of the individual at risk, that is, one might write $VOR_{i,j} = 0.46VOR_{i,i}$ where j is now close relatives. Recall that $VOR_{i,i}$ is summed across all individuals at risk and expressing a positive WTP to obtain a VOSL. It follows that $VOR_{i,j}$ should be

summed across all close relatives of those at risk. The effect could be substantial. For example, if each individual at risk has four close relatives, the
effect would be to multiply VOSL by $4 \times 0.46 = 1.64$ to obtain the summed
valuations of close relatives. Christe and Soguel (1995) conduct a contingent
valuation analysis of willingness to pay to avoid the consequences of a road
accident. WTP was estimated in two contexts: where the respondent was the
hypothetical victim and where the respondent is a relative of the hypothetical
victim. In each case, the pain and suffering of others is relevant. In the former
case, willingness to pay ($VOR_{i,i}$ in our notation) may already account for the
pain and suffering of relatives and others, that is, WTP is influenced by the
concern the victim has for the effects of an accident to him/herself on others.
In the second case, where the victim is a relative, WTP ($VOR_{i,j}$ in our
notation) may reflect both the relative's own bereavement and also some
judgement of the pain and suffering of the victim. Schwab Christe and
Soguel try to distinguish these effects. The results are:

a. $VOR_{i,i}$ for a death is 1.7m Swiss francs, or around US\$1.2m;
b. $VOR_{i,i}$ for an accident involving severe and permanent disability is slightly
      higher than $VOR_{i,i}$ for death at some 1.75m Swiss francs;
c. $VOR_{i,j}$ for relatives (*j*) is *higher* than $VOR_{i,i}$ at around 2m Swiss francs,
      and higher still for permanent and severe disablement. In general $VOR_{i,j}$
      would appear to be equal to 1.25 $VOR_{i,i}$, about three times the effect
      found by Needleman's study.

Cropper and Sussman (1988) suggest that US citizens have a willingness to pay
for children's statistical lives equal to 70–110 per cent of their own values
($VOR_{i,i}$). This is consistent with a New Zealand study by Miller and Guria
(1992) with a $VOR_{i,j}$ of 119 per cent for family members. Blomquist et al.
(1996) estimate a $VOR_{i,i}$ of \$2m and a $VOR_{i,j}$ for children by parents of \$3–5
million, that is 1.5–2.5 times the $VOR_{i,i}$. Blomquist et al. (1996) also review
other studies of $VOR_{i,j}$, finding a fairly consistent range of values between 23
and 50 per cent of $VOR_{i,i}$ when the person at risk is not a family member.

   The studies suggest that $VOR_{i,j}$ may be of the order of 100 per cent for own
family members and perhaps 20 per cent for non-family members. The implications of adding 20 per cent premia for *each person* affected by the *i*th life at
risk are fairly significant. Not only would a typical valuation of, say, \$2m be
quadrupled because of close family valuations, but a further \$0.4m (20 per
cent of $VOR_{i,i}$) might need to be added for each person thought to exhibit a
degree of concern for the individual at risk. VOSLs, then, could be seriously
understated by focusing on $VOR_{i,i}$ alone.

   However, the issue of aggregating life risks across individuals is complex.
For a discussion see Johansson (1995). Jones-Lee (1992) cautions against

assuming that $\text{VOR}_{i,i}$ and $\text{VOR}_{i,j}$ can be added but suggests a social value of a statistical life of 1.1 to 1.4 times the $\text{VOR}_{i,i}$. This is based on analysis of altruistic motives. For *pure altruism* – in which the person exhibiting the concern respects the preferences of the person at risk – the correct VOSL is the 'own' valuation. The original proof is given in Bergstrom (1982). Jones-Lee (1991) examines the case of *pure paternalism* – where j exhibits a concern for i's risks but does so on the basis of overriding i's preferences – and concludes that the same result holds, that is, $\text{VOR}_{i,i}$ is the correct valuation. Where there is a focus by j on i's 'safety', that is, risk reduction, and the utility function for j takes the form:

$$U_j = U \ (x_j, \ s_j; \ s_i)$$

where x is the private good and s is safety, then it is legitimate to add a 'premium' to the own VOSL. Thus, for any premium to be justified, j's preferences have to be paternalistic and relate only to i's safety, not to i's consumption of the private good.

VALUING FUTURE LIVES

Given that 'sustainable development' is a widely embraced goal of economic and environmental policy, and given that 'sustainability' raises the importance of impacts on future generations, one issue of some importance in risk valuation is that of how to value 'future lives'. Essentially, should a life at risk in, say, 50 years time be valued in the same way as a life today? This is an 'intergenerational equity', issue. Jones-Lee and Loomes (1995) have shown that, on balance, future lives should be valued at the current VOSL and should *not* be discounted. Or, put another way, the effective discount rate applied to future lives should be zero provided the valuations being applied are the current VOSLs. In benefit–cost analysis a similar result would be obtained by valuing future lives at a future VOSL, that is, one allowing for the expected growth of incomes which will therefore make future generations more willing to pay for risk reductions, and then discounting that value to get back to a current value. So, for a life risk 50 years hence we would have two alternative rules for valuation at the current period:

$$\text{VOSL}_{t=50} = \text{VOSL}_0,$$

the 'equal values no discounting' rule or

$$\text{VOSL}_{t=50} = \text{VOSL}_0 \cdot e^{50g} \cdot e^{-50r}$$

the 'discounted future values' rule, where g = expected rate of income growth and r = the discount rate. So long as $r = g$ the two rules are the same. The rules become more complex once we allow for the degree of aversion to inequality that might be displayed by the current generation; once a distinction is made between the discount factor for future risks and the discount factor for future income; and once survival probabilities vary between generations. In general:

a.   the greater the degree of aversion to inequality, the closer one gets to the equal values and no discounting case;
b.   the greater the survival probabilities of future generations relative to current generations the more justified is discounting future risk reduction benefits; and
c.   only if future wellbeing (as opposed to income) is discounted, can discount rates greater than zero be justified in the context where the current VOSL is used to value future risks.

More generally, either future risks are valued at future WTP levels and then discounted in the same way as income, or future risks are valued at current VOSLs and no discounting is allowed, provided there is impartiality between current and future generations.

VALUING STATISTICAL LIVES WHEN INCOMES ARE UNEQUAL

WTP and, less obviously, WTA estimates of VOSL are constrained by income. WTP and WTA estimates are also averages, that is, there is a frequency distribution from which the mean is taken, so that some people have much higher valuations of risk than the mean and some have much lower valuations than the mean. One of the reasons for these different valuations will be income differences within the nation. This procedure for deriving a VOSL has given rise to extensive misunderstanding. Imagine two countries, one rich and one poor, such that the rich country imposes a risk on the poor country through pollution. Global warming, which results from the emission of greenhouse gases, is often regarded as an example of such 'imposed' pollution costs. (Although the rich world (the OECD countries) actually emits just under 40 per cent of total greenhouse gases, with 60 per cent coming from the developing world, oil rich nations, and the ex-Soviet Union (World Resources Institute, 1994)). Estimates of VOSLs determined by WTP estimates in the rich and poor countries will produce higher values for the rich country than the poor one, WTP being (partly) determined by income levels. Suppose the rich country's pollution gives rise to an estimated 100 premature mortalities in the poor country. Assume the rich country faces the choice of spending resources on international pollution control to the benefit of the poor countries, or spending the same level of resources on a domestic issue which also saves 100 lives, that is, the marginal cost of saving lives is the same in the two countries. A cost–benefit test will result in the resources being spent domestically because the 100 'domestic' lives will be 'worth' more than the 100 overseas lives due to the higher risk valuations. Yet if 'all lives are equal' in some sense, such an outcome seems very unfair, especially if the rich country can be said to impose the pollution on the poor country. Some have argued that, if a VOSL is to be used at all, it should be the same VOSL for everyone and that VOSL should be the higher of the two figures, that is, the VOSL for the rich country.

Is the benefit–cost test then invalid in some moral sense? There are several issues to be distinguished. First, the VOSL within a country is an average, as noted above. In principle, then, the same procedure should be used where VOSLs differ across countries. The resulting VOSL will be an average of the two VOSLs, but it will not be the highest VOSL that is used. If the highest figure was chosen, then logically it must also be chosen within a country, that is, the average should not be used. Such an outcome is not logically tenable since the individual with the highest aversion to risk would then determine everyone's valuations. The idea of averaging valuations to reflect concern about the inequality of WTP is a longstanding one in cost–benefit analysis. Pearce (1986, original edition 1971) discusses a rule in which WTP is weighted by a ratio of average income to actual income, that is, an adjusted WTP for any country i becomes:

$$\text{WTP}_i^* = \text{WTP}_i \cdot \underline{} / Y_i$$

and WTP_j is

$$\text{WTP}_j^* = \text{WTP}_j \cdot \underline{} / Y_j$$

where $\underline{}$ is the average of Y_i and Y_j. The ratio of the two WTPs is then

$$\text{WTP}_i^* / \text{WTP}_j^* = \frac{\text{WTP}_i \cdot Y_i}{\text{WTP}_j \cdot Y_i}$$

This procedure will produce the same 'common VOSL value' if the value of risk as a proportion of income is the same in both i and j. Only if WTP_j as a proportion of Y_j is higher than WTP_i/Y_i will the resulting VOSL be higher in j than in i, and if the proportion is higher in i than in j, then the weighted VOSL will be higher in i than in j.

Second, regardless of the equity weighting procedure discussed above, the cost–benefit test need not produce the unfair outcome discussed in the example above. This is because the example assumes a common marginal cost of reducing risks in both countries. In practice, risk reduction is likely to be less costly in the poorer country than in the rich country. Even with 'unequal lives' then, nothing follows about the outcome of a benefit–cost test.

HEALTH VALUATION STUDIES IN BRAZIL

Seroa da Motta (1995) and Seroa da Motta and Mendes (1996) present estimates of the economic costs of premature mortality from water and air pollution in Brazil. The water pollution study (Seroa da Motta, 1995) uses a Probit model to estimate the probability of premature death due to pollution. A 1 per cent increase in clean water provision was found to result in a 2.5 per cent reduction in deaths to children under 14 years of age. A similar increase in the provision of sewage collection would result in a 1.6 per cent reduction in deaths and sewage treatment would result in a 2.1 per cent reduction. If all three services are improved by 1 per cent, the benefit is a 6.1 per cent reduction in under 14 deaths. The cost of saving one life was estimated to be $115 000 to $215 000 or $164 000 if all three services are increased. In the absence of detailed VOSL studies in Brazil (other than those based on fore-gone output which, as noted, tends to underestimate 'life' values) the cost–benefit balance is unclear. Brazil's GNP per capita is some 16 per cent of the USA per capita GNP. In the USA, VOSLs of $4m are commonplace in policy studies so that a straight income ratio adjustment would suggest a VOSL of some $640 000, making a benefit–cost ratio for investment in improved water and sanitation of nearly 4. Seroa da Motta and Mendes (1996) also extend their analysis to air pollution.

CONCLUSIONS

Few topics have proved so controversial as the 'value of statistical life'. In large part the controversy derives from unfortunate terminology, since what appears to be at stake is the 'value of life' itself. This confusion has not been helped by even the most distinguished commentators and analysts using this phrase. But what is being estimated is the value of risk reduction. VOSLs are, essentially, convenient ways of aggregating these estimates.

In a finite world there really should be no dispute that resources have to be allocated rationally across different life risks. The real focus of the debate should be on the size of the VOSL. As we saw, this is the subject of a debate which centres on two approaches to valuing risks. The first asks for the WTP to avoid risks, and the second asks for the WTP to extend an expected lifetime by some finite period, say one year. The literature on 'value of life years' turns out to be a hybrid of these approaches, deriving VOLYs from a given VOSL. As discussed, there appears to be limited theoretical justification for this hybrid approach. It is also not consistent with what we know about VOSLs as they vary with age. Nonetheless, what we know about the age–WTP relationship is not much. In turn, the literature that attempts directly to estimate VOLY is minute. Such as it is, it suggests VOSLs are very much less than those derived from standardised VOR calculations.

Other issues concern the role that others' valuation of risks should play and the role that discounting might play in valuing future risks. In general it would appear that there is a case for adding a modest premium to own VOSLs for others' paternalistic concerns, and there is no strong case for discounting future risks.

NOTES

1. The utility discount rate is the rate at which future wellbeing is discounted, not the rate at which income or consumption is discounted. The UK Treasury (1997) adopts a rate of pure utility discounting of 1. 5 per cent but little evidence exists to support this rate. Pearce and Ulph (1995) suggest a rate of 0.3 per cent.
2. The range is reported as $400–$1500 in the original article, but this looks like a misprint.

BIBLIOGRAPHY

Action Asthma (1990), *The Occurrence and Cost of Asthma*, Worthing: Action Asthma, Cambridge Medical Publications.

AEA Technology (1998a), 'Cost–benefit analysis of proposals under the UNECE multi-pollutant multi-effect protocol', Report to UK Department of Environment, Transport and Regions, London and to UNECE Task Force on Economic Aspects of Abatement Strategies, Geneva.

AEA Technology (1998b), 'Economic evaluation of the control of acidification and ground level ozone', Provisional report to DGXI of the European Commission, Brussels.

Bateman, I. and Turner, R.K. (1993), 'The Contingent Valuation Method', in: R.K. Turner (ed.), *Sustainable Environmental Economics and Management*, London: Belhaven Press.

Bergstrom, T. (1982), 'When is a man's life worth more than his human capital?', in: M. Jones-Lee (ed.), *The Value of Life and Safety*, Amsterdam: North Holland, pp. 3–26.

Bishop, R. (1978), 'Endangered species and uncertainty: the economics of a safe minimum standard', *American Journal of Agricultural Economics*, 60, 10–18.

Blomquist, G., Miller, T. and Levy, D. (1996), 'Values of risk reduction implied by motorist use of protection equipment', *Journal of Transport Economics and Policy*, (Jan.), 55–66.

Bowers, J. (1993), 'A conspectus on valuing the environment', *Journal of Environmental Planning and Management*, **36** (1), 91–100.

Brunekreef, B. (1995), *Quantifying the Health Effects for the Netherlands of Exposure to PM_{10}*, Bilthoven: National Institute of Public Health and Environmental Protection. (Report 623710002) (in Dutch).

Bullard, R.D. (1994), 'Unequal environmental protection: incorporating environmental justice in decision making', in: A. Finkel and D. Golding (eds), *Worst Things First: the Debate over Risk-based National Environmental Priorities*, Washington, DC: Resources for the Future Inc., pp.237–66.

Carson, R., Mitchell, R., Hanemann, M., Kopp, R., Presser, S. and Ruud, P. (1995), 'Contingent valuation and lost passive use damages from the Exxon Valdez', San Diego: University of California, Department of Economics, mimeo (Discussion Paper 95-02).

Chestnut, L. and Patterson, A. (1994), *Human Health Benefits Assessment of the Acid Rain Provisions of the 1990 Clean Air Act Amendments*, August, for US EPA.

Chestnut, L., Colome, L., Keller, L., Lambert, W., Ostro, B., Rowe, R. and Wojciechowski, S. (1988), *Heart Disease Patients' Averting Behavior, Costs of Illness, and Willingness to Pay to Avoid Angina Episodes*, Washington, DC: US Environmental Protection Agency Report to Office of Policy Analysis.

Cropper, M. and Freeman, A. (1991), 'Environmental health effects', in: J. Braden and C. Kolstad, (eds), *Measuring the Demand for Environmental Quality*, New York: North Holland.

Cropper, M. and Simon, N.B. (1994), *Are we Valuing Risks to Life Correctly?*, Washington, DC: World Bank, mimeo.

Cropper, M. and Sussman, F. (1988), 'Families and the economics of risk to life', *American Economic Review*, 255–60.

Cropper, M. and Sussman, F. (1990), 'Valuing future risks to life', *Journal of Environmental Economics and Management*, 19 (2), 160–74.

Cropper, M., Aydede, S. and Portney, P. (1994), 'Preferences for life saving programs: How the public discounts time and age', *Journal of Risk and Uncertainty*, 8, 243–65.

Davies, N. and Teasdale, P. (1994), *The Costs to the British Economy of Work-Related Accidents and Work-Related Ill-Health*, London: Health and Safety Executive.

Desaigues, B. and Rabl, A. (1995), 'Reference Values for Human Life: an Econometric Analysis of a Contingent Valuation in France', in: N. Schwab Christie and N. Soguel (eds), *Contingent Valuation, Transport Safety and the Value of Life*, Boston and Dordrecht: Kluwer, 85–112.

Desvousges, W. et al. (1993), 'Review of health effects resulting from exposure to air pollution', Research Triangle Institute, Task Force on Externality Costing, Nov. (Working Paper. 1, revised).

Dockery, D.W., Schwartz, J. and Spengler, J. (1992), 'Air pollution and daily mortality: association with particulates and acid aerosols', *Environmental Research*, 59, 362–73.

Dockery, D.W., Pope III, C.A., X. Xiping et al. (1993), 'An association between air pollution and mortality in six U.S. cities', *The New England Journal of Medicine*, **329** (4), 1753–808.

Fischoff, B., Slovic, P. and Lichtenstein, S. (1979), 'Weighing the risks', *Environment*, **21** (4), 17–20 and 32–38.

Fisher, A., Chestnut, L. and Violette, D. (1989), 'The value of reducing risks of death: a note on new evidence', *Journal of Policy Analysis and Management*, **8** (1), 88–100.

Flanders, D., Haddix, A., Olson, D., Romieu, I., White, M. and Williamson, G.D. (1995), *Review of Urban Air Pollution Health Impact Methodology*, Atlanta: Center for Disease Control.

Freeman III, A.M. (1986), 'On Assessing the State of the Art of the Contingent Valuation Method of Valuing Environmental Changes', in: R.G. Cummings, D. Brookshire and W. Schulze (eds), *Valuing Environmental Goods: an Assessment of the Contingent Valuation Method*, Totowa, NJ: Rowman and Allenheld, pp.148–61.

Freeman III, A.M. (1993), *The Measurement of Environmental and Resource Values*, Washington, DC: Resources for the Future.

Graham, J., Chang, B.H. and Evans, J. (1992), 'Poorer is Riskier', *Risk Analysis*, **12** (3), 333–7.

Gregory, R. (1986), 'Interpreting measures of economic loss: evidence from contingent valuation and experimental studies', *Journal of Environmental Economics and Management*, **13** (4), 325–37.

Gren, A.-M., Folke, C., Turner, K. and Bateman, I. (1994), 'Primary and secondary values of wetland ecosystems', *Environmental and Resource Economics*, **4** (1), (Feb.) 55–74.

Hanemann, M. (1991), 'Willingness to pay and willingness to accept: how much can they differ?', *American Economic Review*, 81, 635–47.

Holland, M. and Krewitt, W. (1996), *Benefits of an Acidification Strategy for the European Union*, Brussels: European Commission, DGXI.

Industrial Economics Incorporated (1993), *Review of Existing Value of Life Estimates*, Report prepared for the US Environmental Protection Agency, Washington, DC.

IVM, NILU and IIASA (1997), *Economic Evaluation of Air Quality for Sulphur Dioxide, Nitrogen Dioxide, Fine and Suspended Particulate Matter and Lead*, Report to DGXI, Brussels: European Commission.

Johannesson, M. and Johansson, P.-O. (1995a), *Is the Value of a Life Year Gained Independent of Age?*, Stockholm: Stockholm School of Economics, mimeo.

Johannesson, M. and Johansson, P.-O. (1995b), 'Quality of life and the WTP for an increased life expectancy at an advanced age', *Working Papers in Economics and Finance*, n. 85, Stockholm School of Economics.

Johannesson, M. and Johansson, P.-O. (1996), 'To be or not to be, that is the question: an empirical study of the WTP for an increased life expectancy at an advanced age', *Journal of Risk and Uncertainty*, 13, 163–74.

Johansson, P.-O. (1995), *Evaluating Health Risks: an Economic Approach*, Cambridge: Cambridge University Press.

Jones-Lee, M. (1989), *The Economics of Safety and Physical Risk*, Oxford: Blackwell.

Jones-Lee, M. (1991), 'Altruism and the value of other people's safety', *Journal of Risk and Uncertainty*, **4** (2), 213–19.

Jones-Lee, M. (1992), 'Paternalistic altruism and the value of statistical life', *The Economic Journal*, **102** (410), 80–90.

Jones-Lee, M. and Loomes, G. (1995), 'Scale and context effects in the valuation of transport safety', *Journal of Risk and Uncertainty*, **11**, 213–19.

Jones-Lee, M., Loomes, G. and Philips, P. (1995), 'Valuing the prevention of non-fatal road injuries: contingent valuation vs standard gambles', *Oxford Economic Papers*, 47.

Jones-Lee, M., Loomes, G., O'Reilly, D. and Philips, P. (1993), 'The value of pre-
    venting non-fatal road injuries: findings of a willingness to pay national sample
    survey', Crowthorn: Transport Research Laboratory Working Paper WP/SRC/2.
Jones-Lee, M., Hammerton, M. and Philips, P. (1985), 'The value of safety: results of
    a national sample survey', *The Economic Journal*, 95, 49–72.
Kahneman, D. and Tversky, A. (1979), 'Prospect theory: an analysis of decisions
    under risk', *Econometrica*, 43, 263–91.
Keeney, R. (1990), 'Mortality risks induced by economic expenditures', *Risk Analy-
    sis*, **10** (1), 147–59.
Keeney, R. (1994), 'Mortality risks induced by the costs of regulation', *Journal of
    Risk and Uncertainty*, 8, 95–110.
Keeney, R. (1997), 'Estimating fatalities induced by the economic costs of regula-
    tion', *Journal of Risk and Uncertainty*, 14, 5–23.
Kidholm, K. (1995), 'Assessing the Value of Traffic Safety Using the Contingent
    Valuation Technique: the Danish Survey', in: N. Schwab Christe and N. Soguel
    (eds), Contingent Valuation, Transport Safety and the Value of Life, Boston and
    Dordrecht: Kluwer, pp. 45–61.
Kopp, R. (1993), 'Environmental economics: not dead but thriving', *Resources*, 111,
    (Spring), 7–12.
Krupnick, A. (1986), *A Preliminary Benefits Analysis of the Control of Photochemi-
    cal Oxidants*, Washington, DC: US Environmental Protection Agency.
Krupnick, A. and Cropper, M. (1992), 'The effect of information on health risk
    valuations', *Journal of Risk and Uncertainty*, 5, 29–48.
Krupnick, A. and Cropper, M. (1989), *Valuing Chronic Morbidity Damages: Medical
    Costs, Labour Market Effects and Individual Valuations*, Report to Office of Policy
    Analysis, Washington, DC: US Environmental Protection Agency.
Krupnick, A., Harrison, K., Nickell, E. and Toman, M. (1993), *The Benefits of
    Ambient Air Quality Improvements in Central and Eastern Europe: a Preliminary
    Assessment*, Washington, DC: Resources for the Future, Discussion Paper ENR93-
    19.
Loehman, E.T., Berg, S., Arroyo, A., Hedinger, R., Schwartz, J., Shaw, M., Fahien,
    R., Dhe, V., Fishe, R., Rio, D., Rossley, W. and Green, A. (1979), 'Distributional
    analysis of regional benefits and costs of air quality control', *Journal of Environ-
    mental Economics and Management*, 6, 222–43.
Lutter, R. and Morrall, J. (1994), 'Health–health analysis: a new way to evaluate
    health and safety regulation', *Journal of Risk and Uncertainty*, 8, 43–66.
Maddison, D. (1998), *Valuing Changes in Life Expectancy in England and Wales
    Caused by Ambient Concentrations of Particulate Matter*, London: Centre for
    Social and Economic Research on the Global Environment (CSERGE) , University
    College, mimeo.
Maddison D., Johansson, O., Littman, T., Verhoef, E. and Pearce, D.W. (1996),
    Blueprint 5: the Social Costs of Transport, London: Earthscan.
Maier, G., Gerking, S. and Weiss, P. (1989), *The Economics of Traffic Accidents on
    Austrian Roads: Risk Lovers or Policy Deficit?*, Vienna: Wirtschaftuniversitat,
    mimeo. Cited in Rowlatt et al., 1998.
McMichael, A., Anderson, R., Elliott, P., Wilkinson, P., Ponce de Leon, A. and Soria,
    F. Simon (the 'London Review Group') (1995), *Review of Methods Proposed, and
    Used, for Estimating the Population Health Risks of Exposure to Urban Air Pollu-
    tion*, London: London School of Hygiene and Tropical Medicine.

Miller, T. (1989), 'Willingness to pay comes of age: will the system survive?', *Northwestern University Law Review*, 83, 876–907.

Miller, T. and Guria, J. (1991), *The Value of Statistical Life in New Zealand*, New Zealand: Ministry of Transport, Wellington NZ.

Needleman, L. (1976), 'Valuing other people's lives', *The Manchester School*, 44, 309–42.

O'Doherty, R. (1994), *Contingent Valuation as a Participatory Process*, Bristol: Department of Economics, University of West England, mimeo.

Ostro, B. (1994), *Estimating Health Effects of Air Pollution: a Method with an Application to Jakarta*, Washington, DC: World Bank, Policy Research Department, Working Paper, 1301.

Ostro, B. (1995a), 'Addressing uncertainties in the quantitative estimation of air pollution health effects', Paper presented to EC/IEA/OECD Workshop on the External Costs of Energy, Brussels, Jan.

Ostro, B. (1995b), *Air Pollution and Mortality: Results from Santiago, Chile*, Washington, DC: World Bank, Policy Research Department, Working Paper, 1453.

Otway, H. and Cohen, J. (1975), *Revealed Preferences: Comments on the Starr Benefit–Risk Relationships*, Vienna: International Institute for Applied Systems Analysis, Laxenburg, Research Memorandum 75-5.

Pearce, D.W. (1986), *Cost Benefit Analysis*, 2nd edn, Basingstoke: Macmillan.

Pearce, D.W. and Brisson, I. (1993), 'BATNEEC: the economics of technology-based environmental standards', *Oxford Review of Economic Policy*, **9** (4), (Winter) 24–40.

Pearce, D.W. and Turner, R.K. (1992), 'The ethical foundations of sustainable economic development', *Advances in Human Ecology*, 1, 177–95.

Pearce, D.W. and Ulph, D. (1999), 'A Social Discount Rate for the United Kingdom', in D.W. Pearce (ed.), *Economics and Environment: Essays in Ecological Economics and Sustainable Development*, Cheltenham: Edward Elgar.

Pearce, D.W., Markandya, A. and Barbier, E. (1989), *Blueprint for a Green Economy*, London: Earthscan.

Pearce, D.W., Bann, C. and Georgiou, S. (1992), *The Social Cost of Fuel Cycles*, London: HMSO.

Pearce, D.W., Whittington, D. and Georgiou, S. (1994), *Project and Policy Appraisal: Integrating Economics and Environment*, Paris: Organisation for Economic Cooperation and Development.

Persson, U. and Cedervall, M. (1991), 'The value of risk reduction: results of a Swedish sample survey', Swedish Institute of Health Economics, IHE Working Paper 1991:6.

Persson, U., Norinder, A. Ligner and Svensson, M. (1995), 'Valuing the Benefits of Reducing the Risk of Non-Fatal Road Injuries: the Swedish Experience', in: N. Schwab Christie and N. Soguel (eds), *Contingent Valuation, Transport Safety and the Value of Life*, Boston and Dordrecht: Kluwer, pp. 63–83.

Pimentel, D., Wilson, C., McCullum, C., Huang, R., Dwen, P., Flack, J., Tran, Q., Saltman, T. and Cliff, B. (1996), *Environmental and Economic Benefits of Biodiversity*, Ithaca, NY: College of Agriculture and Life Sciences, Cornell University, mimeo.

Pope III, C.A. and Dockery, D. (1992), 'Acute health effects of PM_{10} pollution on symptomatic and asymptomatic children', *American Review of Respiratory Disease*, 145, 1123–8.

Pope III, C.A., Schwartz, J. and Ransom, M. (1992), 'Daily mortality and PM_{10} pollution in Utah Valley', *Archives of Environmental Health*, **47** (3), 211–17.

Pope III, C.A., Thun, M.J., Namboordi, M., Dockery, D.W., Evans, J.D., Speizer, F. and Heath Jr, C.W. (1995), 'Particulate air pollution as a predictor of mortality in a prospective study of US adults', *American Journal of Respiratory and Critical Care Medicine*, **151**, 669–74.

Portney, P. and Stavins, R. (1994), 'Regulatory review of environmental policy: the potential role of health–health analysis', *Journal of Risk and Uncertainty*, 8, 111–22.

Rowe, R. and Chestnut, L. (1986), 'Oxidants and asthmatics in Los Angeles: a benefits analysis', Report to Office of Policy Analysis, US EPA, EPA-230-09-86-018, Washington, DC.

Rowe, R. and Nethercut, T. (1987), *Economic Assessment of the Impact of Cataracts*, Colorado: RCH Hagler Bailly, mimeo.

Rowe, R., Chestnut, L. and Shaw, W. (1984), 'Oxidants and Asthmatics in Los Angeles: a Benefits Analysis', in: S. Duk Lee (ed.), *Evaluation of the Ozone/ Oxidants Standard*, Pittsburgh: Air Pollution Control Association.

Rowe, R., Chestnut, L., Peterson, D. and Miller, C. (1986), *The Benefits of Air Pollution Control in California*, Energy and Resource Consultants, Boulder, for California Air Resources Board, vols 1 and 2.

Rowe, R., Chestnut, L., Lang, C., Bernow, S. and White, D. (1995), 'The New York environmental externalities cost study: summary of approach and results', Brussels: Jan. 30–31, 1995. Paper presented to European Commission, International Energy Agency and Organisation for Economic Cooperation and Development Workshop on External Costs of Energy.

Rowlatt, P., Spackman, M., Jones, S., Jones-Lee, M. and Loomes, G. (1998), *Valuation of Deaths from Air Pollution*, NERA and CASPAR, Report to UK Department of the Environment, Transport and Regions, February.

Sagoff, M. (1993), 'Environmental economics: an epitaph', *Resources*, 111, (Spring), 2–7.

Schwab, Christe, N. and Soguel, N. (1995), *The Pain of Victims and the Bereavement of their Relatives: a Contingent Valuation Experiment*, Switzerland: IDHEAP, University of Lausanne, mimeo.

Schwartz, J. (1991a), 'Particulate air pollution and daily mortality in Detroit', *Environmental Research*, **56**, 204–13.

Schwartz, J. (1991b), 'Particulate air pollution and daily mortality: a synthesis', *Public Health Reviews*, **19** (39–60).

Schwartz, J. (1993a), 'Air pollution and daily mortality in Birmingham, Alabama', *American Journal of Epidemiology*, **137**, 1136–47.

Schwartz, J. (1993b), 'Particulate air pollution and chronic respiratory disease', *Environmental Research*, **62**, 7–13.

Schwartz, J. (1994), 'Air pollution and daily mortality: a review and meta analysis', *Environmental Research*, **64**, 36–52.

Schwartz, J. and Dockery, D. (1992b), 'Increased mortality in Philadelphia associated with daily air pollution concentrations', *American Review of Respiratory Disease*, 145, 600–604.

Schwartz, J. and Dockery, D. (1992a), 'Particulate air pollution and daily mortality in Steubenville, Ohio', *American Journal of Epidemiology*, **135**, 12–19.

Schwartz, J. and Marcus, A. (1990), 'Mortality and air pollution in London: a time series analysis', *American Journal of Epidemiology*, **131** (1), 185–94.

Schwartz, J., Spix, C., Wichman, H. and Malin, E. (1991), 'Air pollution and acute respiratory illness in five German communities', *Environmental Research*, **56**, 1–14.

Schwartz, J., Slater, D., Larson, T., Pierson, W. and Koenig, J. (1993), 'Particulate air pollution and hospital emergency room visits for Asthma in Seattle', *American Review of Respiratory Disease*, **147**, 826–31.

Seaton, A., MacNee, W., Donaldson, K. and Godden, D. (1995), 'Particulate air pollution and acute health effects', *The Lancet*, **345**, Jan. 21, 176–8.

Seroa da Motta, R. (1995), 'El caso de Brasil', in: J. Quiroz, (ed.), *Análisis económico de la contaminación de aguas en América Latina*, ICEG/ILADES.

Seroa da Motta, R. and Fernandes Mendes, A.P. (1996), 'Health Costs Associated with Air Pollution in Brazil', in: P. May and R. Seroa da Motta (eds), *Pricing the Earth*, New York: Columbia University Press, Chapter 5.

Small, K. and Kazimi, C. (1995), 'On the cost of air pollution from motor vehicles', *Journal of Transport Economics and Policy*, Jan., 7–32.

Starr, C. (1972), 'Benefit Cost Studies in Sociotechnical Systems', in: *Committee on Public Engineering Policy, Perspective on benefit–cost decision-making*, Washington, DC: National Academy of Sciences.

Tolley, G.S., Babcock, L., Berger, M., Bilotti, A., Blomquist, G., Fabian, R., Fishelson, G., Kahn, C., Kelly, A., Kenkel, D., Kumm, R., Miller, T., Ohsfeldt, R., Rosen; S., Webb, W., Wils, W. and Zelder, M. (1986), *Valuation of Reductions in Human Health Symptoms and Risks*, Washington, DC: University of Chicago, Report to US EPA.

Turner, R.K. (1993), 'Sustainability: principles and practice', in: R.K. Turner (ed.), *Sustainable Environmental Economics and Management*, London: Belhaven, pp. 3–36.

UK Treasury (1997), *Appraisal and Evaluation in Central Government: the Green Book*, London: HM Treasury.

Utell, S. and Samet, J. (1993), 'Particulate air pollution and health: new evidence of an old problem', *American Review of Respiratory Disease*, **147**, 1334–5.

Vatn, A. and Bromley, D. (1994), 'Choices without prices without apologies', *Journal of Environmental Economics and Management*, 26, 129–48.

Viscusi, W.K. (1992), *Fatal Trade-offs: Public and Private Responsibilities for Risk*, Oxford and New York: Oxford University Press.

Viscusi, W.K. (1994), 'Risk–risk analysis', *Journal of Risk and Uncertainty*, 8, 5–17.

Viscusi, W.K. and Zeckhauser, R. (1994), 'The fatality and injury costs of expenditures', *Journal of Risk and Uncertainty*, 8, 19–41.

Viscusi, W.K., Magat, W. and Forrest, A. (1988), 'Altruistic and private valuations of risk reduction', *Journal of Policy Analysis and Management*, **7** (2), 227–45.

Viscusi, W.K., Magat, W. and Huber, J. (1991), 'Pricing environmental health risks: survey assessments of risk–risk and risk–dollar trade offs for chronic bronchitis', *Journal of Environmental Economics and Management*, **21** (1), 32–51.

World Resources Institute (1994), *World Resources 1994–1995*, Oxford and New York: Oxford University Press.

Xu, X., Gao, J., Dockery, D. and Chen, Y. (1994), 'Air pollution and daily mortality in residential areas of Beijing, China', *Archives of Environmental Health*, **49** (4), (Jul./Aug.), 216–22.

4. The valuation of health impacts in developing countries

Anil Markandya

4.1 INTRODUCTION

Probably the most important benefit of development is improvement in the quality of life. This improvement is measured to a large extent through increased life expectancy, reduced morbidity and reduced incidences of illness. While it is true that *general development*, which results in better nutrition and improvements in housing, water supply and sanitation, will improve the quality of life, it is not true that all investments in these areas are equally desirable. Nor are these the only investments that impact on the quality of life. Others include measures to reduce air pollution, investments in public and private health provision and education for women.

In all these areas of policy, valuing the health impacts in money terms can provide an important aid to the decision-maker. How much should we spend on controlling emissions from vehicles, and how much can we justify in investments in improving the drinking water supply? If there is a budget constraint and we have to choose between these options, which is the more valuable?

This chapter is devoted to a discussion of the values to be attached to health impacts in developing countries. It is structured as follows. Section 4.2 provides the conceptual basis for the valuation. Section 4.3 discusses how we can overcome a shortage of data and information about these values. In many developing countries, there is a shortage of data and it is not practicable to collect what is required in the time available. The chapter discusses how data from other sources can be transferred to the site and country in question. Section 4.4 focuses on the valuation of mortality effects – effects that reduce the risk of death. Section 4.5 deals with the valuation of morbidity effects. Section 4.6 concludes the chapter.

4.2 CONCEPTUAL BASIS FOR VALUATION OF HEALTH IMPACTS

Willingness to Pay and Willingness to Accept

Over the last 25 years or so, a number of techniques have been developed for estimating external environmental effects. A survey of these may be found in Markandya and Richardson (1993), with examples of their application in non-OECD countries in Winpenny (1996). In this section we describe the concepts underlying the valuation and then review the debate surrounding the use of such a system of valuation.

The underlying principle in monetary valuation is to obtain the *willingness to pay* (WTP) of the affected individual to avoid the negative impact, or the *willingness to accept* (WTA) payment as compensation if a negative impact takes place. The rationale is that values should be based on individual preferences, which are translated into money terms through individual WTP and WTA.

Once the impacts have been identified in physical terms, they can be valued using market prices, where the things impacted (crops, materials and so on) have a market price, although even in this simple case there are problems and issues that arise, which are discussed further below. For a wide range of impacts, however, such as increased risk of death or loss of recreational values, there are no direct market prices that can be used. There are three techniques that are widely used for the valuation of such. One is to elicit the WTP or WTA by direct questionnaire. This is termed the *contingent valuation method* and has been developed into a sophisticated procedure for valuing a number of environmental impacts. Another is to look at the WTP as expressed in related markets. Frequently environmental effects are reflected in property values. Thus an increase in noise or a reduction in visibility will 'show up' in reductions in the value of properties affected by the changes. This approach is called the *hedonic price method* and is widely used for noise and aesthetic effects.

Where individuals undertake expenditures to benefit from a facility such as a park or a fishing area one can determine their WTP through their expenditures on the recreational activity, including costs of travel to the park, any fees paid and so on. Economists have developed quite sophisticated procedures for estimating the values of changes in environmental facilities using such data. This method is known as the *travel cost method* and is particularly useful for valuing recreational impacts.

Categories of Value

The WTP/WTA numbers can be expressed for a number of categories of value. The most important distinction is between values arising from the use of the environment by the individual and values that arise even when there is no identifiable use made of that environment. These are called *use values* and *non-use values* respectively. Non-use values are also sometimes referred to as *existence values*.

Within the category of use values there are many different categories. *Direct-use values* arise when an individual makes use of the environment (for example, s/he breathes the air) and derives a loss of welfare if that environment is polluted. *Indirect-use values* arise when an individual's welfare is affected by what happens to another individual. For example, if you feel a loss of welfare as a result of the death or illness of a friend or relation, resulting from increased levels of air pollution, then this loss of welfare translates into a cost through your WTP. It can and has been measured in limited cases and is referred to as an *altruistic value* (see later in this section for details). Both direct and indirect use values have a time dimension; an environmental change today can result in such values now and in the future.

Another category of use value that is potentially important is that of *option value*. This arises when an action taken now can result in a change in the supply or availability of some environmental good in the future. For example, flooding a region to impound water for a hydro project would result in that area not being available for hiking. A person might have a WTP for the option to use that hiking area, even if s/he was not sure that it would be used. This WTP is the sum of the expected gain in welfare from the use of the area, plus a certain gain in welfare from the knowledge that s/he *could* use it even if it is not actually used. The latter is referred to as the option value. The literature on environmental valuation shows that in certain cases the option value will be positive, but in general it is not an important category of value. There are very few estimates of such values, and in the context of most health valuation studies the issue is not likely to be important.

The last category of value is non-use value. This is a controversial category, although values deriving from the existence of a pristine environment are real enough, even for those who never make any use of it. In some respects what constitutes 'use' and what constitutes 'non-use' is not clear. If someone sees a programme about a wilderness area but never visits it, that represents a use value, however indirect. Pure non-use value must not involve any welfare from any sensory experience related to the item being valued. In fact some environmentalists argue that such non-use or existence values are unrelated to human appreciation or otherwise of the environment, but are embedded in, or intrinsic to, the things being valued. However, that is not the position taken in this paper. The basis of valuation remains therefore an anthropocentric one that, however, does not imply an anti-environmentalist stance.

The difficulty in defining non-use values extends, not unnaturally, to measuring them. The only method available for this category is that of the questionnaire approach, or contingent valuation. This method has been tested and improved extensively in the past 20 years, and the general consensus is that the technique works effectively where 'market conditions' of exchange can be simulated effectively and where the respondent has considerable familiarity with the item being valued (Arrow et al., 1993). For most categories of non-use value this is simply not the case. Hence, for the present, non-use values are extremely difficult to value with any accuracy.

Issues Arising in the Use of Monetary Values

Thus the basic philosophy underlying the valuation is based on individual preferences, which are expressed through the willingness to pay (WTP) for something that improves individual welfare, and willingness to accept payment (WTA) for something which reduces individual welfare. The total value of environmental impacts is taken as the sum of the WTP or WTA of the individuals comprising it. Thus no special weight is given to any particular group. This approach contrasts, for example, with that of values based on expert opinion, or values based on the costs of making good any damage done to the environment by an investment programme. Such mitigation costs will only provide a valid measure of cost if society is collectively willing to pay for the mitigation, rather than suffer the damage. In such cases mitigation-based estimates can provide important values, and have in fact been used in selected areas. However, the validity of that use is dependent on the assumption that society is willing to pay for the mitigation.

Although the valuation of environmental impacts using money values is widespread and growing, there are still many people who find the idea strange at best and distasteful and unacceptable at worst. Given the central role being played by monetary valuation in this exercise, a justification of the method is warranted.

One objection often voiced in the use of WTP is that it is 'income constrained'. Since you cannot pay what you do not have, a poorer person's WTP is less than that of a richer person, other things being equal. This occurs most forcefully in connection with the valuation of a statistical life (VOSL) (which is discussed in greater detail in Section 4.3) where the WTP to avoid an increase in the risk of death is measured in terms of a VOSL. In general one would expect the VOSL for a poor person to be less than that of a rich person.

But this is no more or less objectionable than saying that a rich person can and does spend more on health protection than a poor person; or that individuals of higher social status and wealth live longer on average than person of lower status; or that better neighbourhoods will spend more on environmental protection than poorer neighbourhoods. The basic inequalities in society result in different values being put on the environment by different people. One may object to these inequalities, and make a strong case to change them but, as long as they are there, one has to accept the consequences. One could argue, for example, that increased expenditure on high technology medicine in Europe is unethical, even though the citizens of that region have a WTP that justifies such expenditures, because the same expenditure on preventative medicine in a poor developing country would save more lives. However, society does not accept such an argument, taking the view that most decisions about allocation of resources are predicated on the existing inequality of income and wealth, both between and within societies.

In conclusion, we can see that, although there are some objections to the use of WTP/WTA as a basis of valuing externalities, it is by far the most intellectually defensible basis for valuation in a liberal society. Policymakers may wish to pay attention to other aspects of externalities, such as how many people are affected, how many of them are 'poor' and so on. It is only right and proper that they should take account of such factors. The values associated with the externality, calculated within the above framework, are therefore only part of the information that will eventually determine the selected policy. But the valuation of the externality, in money terms, needs a rigorous basis and the WTP/WTA approach provides that basis.

4.3   TRANSFERABILITY OF BENEFIT ESTIMATES

Introduction

The environmental damages associated with a particular investment will depend on the precise details of that investment: location, population-impacted and so on. Clearly, it would be infeasible to estimate all environmental damages for each programme *ab initio*. Much of the work required is extremely time-consuming and expensive, making the transfer of estimates from one study to another an important part of the exercise. The difficult issue is to know when a damage estimate is transferable and what modifications, if any, need to be made before it can be used in its new context.

Benefit Transfer

Benefit transfer is 'an application of monetary values from a particular valuation study to an alternative or secondary policy decision setting, often in another geographic area than the one where the original study was performed' (Navrud, 1994). There are three main biases inherent in transferring benefits to other areas:

a. Original data sets vary from those in the place of application, and the problems inherent in non-market valuation methods are magnified if transferring to another area.
b. Monetary estimates are often stated in units other than the impacts. For example, in the case of damage by acidic deposition to freshwater fisheries, dose response functions may estimate mortality (reduced fish populations) while benefit estimates are based on behavioural changes (reduced angling days). The linkage between these two units must be established to enable damage estimation.
c. Studies often estimate benefits in average, non-marginal terms and do not use methods that are transferable in terms of site, region and population characteristics.

Benefit transfer application can be based on: (a) expert opinion, or (b) meta analysis. Expert opinion looks at the reasonableness involved in making the transfer and in determining what modifications or proxies are needed to make the transfer more accurate. In many cases expert opinion has been resorted to in making benefit transfers. In general the more 'conditional' the original data estimates (for example, damages per person, per unit of dispersed pollution, for a given age distribution) the better the benefit transfer will be. In one particular case (that of recreational benefits) an attempt was made to check on the accuracy of a benefit transfer by comparing the transferred damage estimate with that obtained by a direct study of the costs. The finding there was not encouraging in that the two figures varied by a wide margin.

Meta-Analysis

Where several studies reporting a similar final estimate of environmental damage exist, and where there are significant differences between them in terms of the background variables, a procedure known as *meta-analysis* has been developed to transfer the results from one study across to other applications. What such an analysis does is to take the estimated damages from a range of studies of, for example, coal-fired plants and see how they vary systematically, according to affected population, building areas, crops, level of income of the population, and so on. The analysis is carried out using econometric techniques, which yield estimates of the responsiveness of damages to the various factors that render them more transferable across situations. This can then be used to derive a simple formula relating environmental costs to per capita income, which could then be employed to calculate damages in countries where no relevant studies were available.

Estimates of damages based on meta-analysis have been provided in a formal sense in two studies carried out in the US on recreation demand (Smith and Kaoru, 1990, Walsh et al., 1989), and on air pollution (Smith and Huang, 1993). The results in the recreation studies indicate that, as one would expect, the nature of the site is significant for the WTP attached to a visit, as are the costs of substitutes and the opportunity cost of time. Choice of functional form in the estimating equations also appears to play a part. In the air pollution study referred to above, it was found that damages per unit of concentration vary inversely with the average price of property in the study (the higher the price the lower the unit value of damage). If correct, it would enable an adjustment to the estimated value to be made on the basis of the average prices of properties in the area being investigated. However, the authors are cautious about the validity of the estimates obtained.

A formal meta-analysis is difficult to carry out. However, sometimes 'expert' adjustments can provide an informal meta analysis. For example, adjusting estimates of damages for size of population to obtain a per capita estimate and transferring that to the new study implicitly assumes that damages are proportional to population. Such adjustments are frequently made.

Adjusting for WTP on the Basis of Per Capita Income

An important rule of thumb that has been used in arriving at values of WTP for countries where there are no studies is to take the WTP estimates from the EC, US, or other OECD countries and adjust them for the differences in real per capita income. This was suggested by Markandya (1994), and has been applied by Krupnick et al. (1996) and others, including the World Bank studies on the valuation of air quality.

In making the adjustment the underlying assumption is that there is an 'elasticity', of WTP with respect to real income. The elasticity measures the percentage by which the WTP for a particular benefit declines for each percentage fall in the real income of the person concerned. One assumption that has been commonly used is that the elasticity is one. Another value, taken from Mitchell and Carson's (1986) work in the US is for an elasticity of 0.35. In the case of Brazil, for example, the per capita income, adjusted for purchasing power was $5400 in 1994 (calculated in 1994 prices). In the same year, the real per capita income of the US was $25 880. If we take an elasticity of one, the implication is that an impact which has a value of $1 in the US would have a value of 21 cents in Brazil. If the elasticity is 0.35, the same impact will have a value of 58 cents in Brazil. In some of the key values reported below, both sets of estimates have been taken, and indeed similar estimates have been made for a range of countries. Although crude, this method is considered to provide a rough guide to health damage values that can be used for many investment decisions.

Conclusions on Benefit Transfer

Transferability depends on being able to use a large body of data from different studies and estimating the systematic factors that would result in variations in the estimates. In most cases the range of studies available are few. More can be done to carry out meta-analysis of the type indicated, but it will take time. The best practice in the meantime is to use estimates from sources as close as possible to the one in which they are being applied and adjust them for differences in underlying variables where that is possible. Often the most important obstacle to systematic benefit transfer, however, is a lack of documentation in the existing valuation studies.

From the environmental damage–energy source linkages identified above, one can identify an increasing order of difficulty (in terms of modifications that have to be made) with which estimates can be transferred from the original study to the situation in which they are to be used;

a. The most easily transferred data is the dose-response function itself, relating environmental impacts adjusted for population. Thus numbers in the form: 0.8×10^{-6} excess deaths per $\mu g/m^3$ would be transferable across studies as long as adjustments to the other variables in the dose-response function were made (for example, relative humidity, population at risk and so on). The *additional* local information that is required to use such data is simply local market conditions, costs and prices.

b. The next ones in order of difficulty are monetary estimates of damages per unit of pollutant *by concentration*. Results are reported, for example, in ECU/$\mu g\ m^{-3}$, or in $/km/person of lost visibility. Estimates may vary according to population affected, in which case an analysis of such variations would be desirable. Other socio-economic variables that would be of relevance are income levels of the affected population, age, background environmental variables such as rainfall and so on, and socio-economic variables such as medical services and how they are paid for. If enough studies are available a meta-analysis can be performed (see below), in which the mean estimated value is regressed against these variables. Then the relevant adjustment to the estimates is made, given the local values of the explanatory variables. No additional local variables should be required. In other cases the income elasticity may be used, as was done in the previous section.

c.   Similar to (b) above are estimates of monetary damages in terms of emissions or units of energy produced. In such cases one needs all the information listed above, plus details of how the emissions or energy units relate to the concentrations or whatever impacts are responsible for the damages. For example, damages may be quoted as x/kWh for coal. The relevance of this estimate to a different situation will depend on how the kWh is related to emissions and how the emissions are converted into concentrations in the area where the impacts were measured, *plus* the variables with which the relationship between concentrations and damages vary. Thus most work will have to be done in these cases, and for many purposes it is unlikely that such estimates can be used at all.

It is important to note that national boundaries themselves are not of any relevance in transferring estimates, except that there may be cultural differences that will influence factors such as the frequency with which a person visits a doctor, or how he perceives a loss of visibility. In this sense there is no reason why a Brazilian project should not draw on the US and other studies, or transfer estimates from one country to another within Europe, as long as the above consideration is taken into account.

4.4   VALUATION OF HEALTH IMPACTS – MORTALITY

The final subsection here deals with the most important of the direct impacts of air pollutants – those on human health. These are divided into mortality effects and morbidity effects.

The mortality approach in the valuation literature has been mainly based on the estimation of the willingness to pay for a change in the risk of death. This is converted into the 'value of a statistical life' (VSL) by dividing the WTP by the change in risk. So, for example, if the estimated WTP is $100 for a reduction in the risk of death of 1/10 000, the value of a statistical life is estimated at 100*10 000, which equals $1m. This way of conceptualising the willingness to pay for a change in the risk of death has many assumptions, primary among them being the 'linearity' between risk and payment. For example, a risk of death of 1/1000 would then be valued at $1m/1000, or $1000 using the VSL approach. Within a small range of the risk of death at which the VSL is established this may not be a bad assumption, but it is clearly indefensible for risk levels very different from the one used in obtaining the original estimate.

Estimates of the WTP for a reduction in risk or the WTA of an increase in risk have been made by three methods. First, there are studies that look at the increased compensation individuals need, other things being equal, to work in occupations where the risk of death at work is higher. This provides an estimate of the WTA. Second, there are studies based on the CVM method, where individuals are questioned about their WTP and WTA for measures that reduce the risk of death from certain activities (for example, driving); or their WTA for measures that, conceivably, increase it (for example, increased road traffic in a given area). Third, researchers have looked at actual voluntary expenditures on items that reduce death risk from certain activities, such as cigarette smoking, or purchasing air bags for cars.

In the environmental economics literature, mortality impacts are valued by multiplying the change in risk of death by a 'Value of Statistical Life' (VSL). This methodology has been extensively surveyed (for a recent review see ExternE, 1999). Although there are good reasons for thinking that alternative methods of valuation may be preferable (for example based on the value of life years lost), the VOSL method of valuation has been widely used and has some general acceptance. For the EU countries ExternE (1995) estimated a central VOSL at ECU 2.6m ($3.1m), which is broadly consistent with figures used for the US. This was in 1990 prices. Converting to 1995 prices gives a VOSL of ECU 3.14m ($3.9m). PACE (1992) used a VOSL for the US of $4.0m and Krupnick et al. (1996) used a value of $3.6m. For non-OECD countries, such a value is almost certainly too high; it broadly measures individual willingness-to-pay to reduce the risk of death by a small amount.

The above values of VSL can be transferred to other countries through the use of an 'income elasticity' as outlined above. In order to assist researchers in estimating the health benefits of employment, Table 4.1 provides the VSL for different countries based on an income elasticity of 1.0 and Table 4.2 the VSL for an elasticity of 0.35. Both sets of figures use a VOSL for the US of $4.0m. The PPP GDP per capita for the US is $25,880 based on data from the World Bank Development Report.[1]

Issues Arising in the Estimation of the Value of a Statistical Life

The main issues that arise with the application of the value of a statistical life in these studies are the following:

a. The validity of the methods used in estimating the value of a statistical life.
b. The distinction between voluntary and involuntary risk.

Table 4.1   *Value of statistical life for various countries, income elasticity*
                1.0

Country	PPP GNP US$ 1994	VSL US $'000 1995	Country	PPP GNP US$ 1994	VSL US $'000 1995
Argentina	8.720	1.348	Malawi	650	100
Armenia	2.160	334	Malaysia	8.440	1.304
Australia	18.120	2.801	Mali	520	80
Azerbaijan	1.510	233	Mauritania	1.570	243
Bangladesh	1.330	206	Mauritius	12.720	1.966
Belarus	4.320	668	Mexico	7.040	1.088
Benin	1.630	252	Morocco	3.470	536
Bolivia	2.400	371	Mozambique	860	133
Botswana	5.210	805	Namibia	4.320	668
Brazil	5.400	835	Nepal	1.230	190
Bulgaria	4.380	677	New Zealand	15.870	2.453
Burkina Faso	800	124	Nicaragua	1.800	278
Burundi	700	108	Niger	770	119
Cameroon	1.950	301	Nigeria	1.190	184
Canada	19.960	3.085	Norway	20.210	3.124
Central Afr. Rep.	1.160	179	Oman	8.590	1.328
Chad	720	111	Pakistan	2.130	329
Chile	8.890	1.374	Panama	5.730	886
China	2.510	388	Papua New Guinea	2.680	414
Colombia	5.330	824	Paraguay	3.550	549
Czech Republic	8.900	1.376	Peru	3.610	558
Dominican Rep.	3.760	581	Philippines	2.740	423
Ecuador	4.190	648	Poland	5.480	847
Egypt	3.720	575	Romania	4.090	632
El Salvador	2.410	372	Russian Fed.	4.610	713
Estonia	4.510	697	Rwanda	330	51
Ethiopia	430	66	Saudi Arabia	9.480	1.465
Gambia	1.100	170	Senegal	1.580	244
Ghana	2.050	317	Sierra Leone	700	108
Guatemala	3.440	532	Singapore	21.900	3.385
Guinea-Bissau	820	127	Slovenia	6.230	963
Haiti	930	144	South Africa	5.130	793
Honduras	1.940	300	Sri Lanka	3.160	488
Hungary	6.080	940	Switzerland	25.150	3.887
India	1.280	198	Tajikistan	970	150
Indonesia	3.600	556	Tanzania	620	96
Israel	15.300	2.365	Thailand	6.970	1.077
Jamaica	3.400	526	Togo	1.130	175

Table 4.1   continued

Country	PPP GNP US$ 1994	VSL US $'000 1995	Country	PPP GNP US$ 1994	VSL US $'000 1995
Japan	21.140	3.267	Trinidad & Tobago	8.670	1.340
Jordan	4.100	634	Tunisia	5.020	776
Kazakstan	2.810	434	Turkey	4.710	728
Kenya	1.310	202	Uganda	1.410	218
Korea	10.330	1.597	Ukraine	2.620	405
Kuwait	24.730	3.822	Uruguay	7.710	1.192
Kyrgyz Republic	1.730	267	USA	25.880	4.000
Latvia	3.220	498	Uzbekistan	2.370	366
Lesotho	1.730	267	Venezuela	7.770	1.201
Lithuania	3.290	509	Zambia	860	133
Madagascar	640	99	Zimbabwe	2.040	315

Notes:
Countries are arranged alphabetically.
Elasticity is assumed to be 1.00.
VOSL is assumed to be US $4.0m (1995).

Source: World Bank (1996).

c.   The transfer of risk estimates from different probability ranges.
d.   The question of the treatment of acute versus chronic mortality, and more generally the treatment of age dependent mortality.

Validity of different methods of estimating VSL
All three methods of valuing a statistical life have been subject to criticism. The wage-risk method relies on the assumption that there is enough labour mobility to permit individuals to choose their occupations to reflect all their preferences, one of which is the preference for a level of risk. In economies suffering from longstanding structural imbalances in the labour markets this is at best a questionable assumption. Second, it is difficult to distinguish between risks of mortality and morbidity. Third, the WTA will depend on perceived probabilities of death. Almost all studies, however, use a measure of the long-run frequency of death as a measure of risk. This makes the results quoted unsatisfactory. Fourth, the probabilities for which the risks are measured are generally higher than those faced in most of the environmental impacts. This point is returned to below, but a related factor is that the high risk occupations involve individuals whose WTA for an increase in the risk of death is not typical of the population at large (for example, steeplejacks).[2]

Table 4.2   *Value of statistical life for various countries, income elasticity*
              0.35

Country	PPP GNP US$ 1994	VSL US $'000 1995	Country	PPP GNP US$ 1994	VSL US $'000 1995
Argentina	8.720	2.733	Malawi	650	1.102
Armenia	2.160	1.677	Malaysia	8.440	2.702
Australia	18.120	3.531	Mali	520	1.019
Azerbaijan	1.510	1.480	Mauritania	1.570	1.500
Bangladesh	1.330	1.415	Mauritius	12.720	3.120
Belarus	4.320	2.138	Mexico	7.040	2.536
Benin	1.630	1.520	Morocco	3.470	1.980
Bolivia	2.400	1.740	Mozambique	860	1.215
Botswana	5.210	2.283	Namibia	4.320	2.138
Brazil	5.400	2.311	Nepal	1.230	1.377
Bulgaria	4.380	2.148	New Zealand	15.870	3.371
Burkina Faso	800	1.185	Nicaragua	1.800	1.574
Burundi	700	1.131	Niger	770	1.169
Cameroon	1.950	1.618	Nigeria	1.190	1.361
Canada	19.960	3.652	Norway	20.210	3.668
Central Afr. Rep.	1.160	1.349	Oman	8.590	2.719
Chad	720	1.142	Pakistan	2.130	1.669
Chile	8.890	2.752	Panama	5.730	2.360
China	2.510	1.768	Papua New Guinea	2.680	1.809
Colombia	5.330	2.301	Paraguay	3.550	1.996
Czech Republic	8.900	2.753	Peru	3.610	2.007
Dominican Rep.	3.760	2.036	Philippines	2.740	1.823
Ecuador	4.190	2.115	Poland	5.480	2.323
Egypt	3.720	2.029	Romania	4.090	2.097
El Salvador	2.410	1.743	Russian Fed.	4.610	2.187
Estonia	4.510	2.170	Rwanda	330	869
Ethiopia	430	953	Saudi Arabia	9.480	2.815
Gambia	1.100	1.324	Senegal	1.580	1.503
Ghana	2.050	1.647	Sierra Leone	700	1.131
Guatemala	3.440	1.974	Singapore	21.900	3.773
Guinea-Bissau	820	1.195	Slovenia	6.230	2.430
Haiti	930	1.249	South Africa	5.130	2.270
Honduras	1.940	1.615	Sri Lanka	3.160	1.916
Hungary	6.080	2.409	Switzerland	25.150	3.960
India	1.280	1.397	Tajikistan	970	1.267
Indonesia	3.600	2.006	Tanzania	620	1.084
Israel	15.300	3.328	Thailand	6.970	2.527
Jamaica	3.400	1.966	Togo	1.130	1.337

Table 4.2   continued

Country	PPP GNP US$ 1994	VSL US $'000 1995	Country	PPP GNP US$ 1994	VSL US $'000 1995
Japan	21.140	3.727	Trinidad & Tobago	8.670	2.728
Jordan	4.100	2.099	Tunisia	5.020	2.253
Kazakstan	2.810	1.839	Turkey	4.710	2.203
Kenya	1.310	1.408	Uganda	1.410	1.445
Korea	10.330	2.900	Ukraine	2.620	1.794
Kuwait	24.730	3.937	Uruguay	7.710	2.618
Kyrgyz Republic	1.730	1.552	USA	25.880	4.000
Latvia	3.220	1.929	Uzbekistan	2.370	1.733
Lesotho	1.730	1.552	Venezuela	7.770	2.625
Lithuania	3.290	1.943	Zambia	860	1.215
Madagascar	640	1.096	Zimbabwe	2.040	1.644

Notes:
Countries are arranged alphabetically.
Elasticity is assumed to be 0.35.
VOSL is assumed to be US$4.0m (1995).

Source: World Bank (1996)

The net impact of all these factors is difficult to gauge but it is *likely* that the estimated WTA will be lower than the true WTA.

Voluntary and involuntary risk
There is strong evidence to suggest that individuals treat voluntary risk differently from involuntary risk, with the WTA for a voluntary risk being much lower than that for an involuntary risk. Starr (1976) has estimated, on a judgmental basis, the difference between the willingness to accept a voluntary increase in risk and an involuntary increase. He finds the latter to be around ten times as high as the former for probabilities of death in the range 10^{-6}–10^{-7}. Interestingly, for lower probabilities that are typical of the impacts of particle pollution, estimates of the differences are not available. In another study of the difference (Litai, 1980), it has been argued that the difference could be as much as 100 times.

The CVM methods are subject to the criticism that the choices are hypothetical and that individuals are not familiar with the concepts of risk involved. Certainly, there have been serious difficulties in conveying the impact of different probability changes through questionnaire methods. Finally, the consumer expenditure approach is subject to the difficulties that perceived probabilities are very different from objective probabilities, and that the effects of the expenditures are to reduce the risk of death as well as of illness following an accident. It is difficult to separate the two impacts in the studies.

Probability ranges for the estimation of VSL
Finally, there is the issue of the probability range over which the estimation is carried out and over which it is applied. Typically one is dealing with much lower probabilities of death in most environmental cases (of the order of 10^{-6} and lower), whereas the studies on which the estimated value of a statistical life is based are dealing with probabilities of between 10^{-1} and 10^{-5}. Furthermore, as the survey by Fisher et al. (1989) has pointed out, the results from studies at the higher end of the probability range are less reliable. As mentioned earlier, theoretical models would tend to predict that the WTA for lower risks should be lower but, if anything, the empirical literature shows the opposite. Partly this is due to the fact that the groups are not homogeneous. The issue remains unresolved and there is little that can be done about this problem at this stage. In the medium term, research on the theoretical and empirical aspects of the problem is needed.

For all these reasons the studies are likely to be biased, with the wage- risk studies producing values that are too low and the CVM studies values that are too high. Taking an average, as has been done here, is averaging unknown errors. One cannot say what the final impact will be. One can, however, draw some comfort from the fact that the values are, in broad terms, consistent and in a plausible range.

The treatment of age-dependent mortality, ill health and latency effects
In the case of air pollution from electricity generation the key questions that arise are: (a) should we adjust the VSL values for the fact that many of those affected are old? (b) should some adjustment be made for their state of health? and (c) should some adjustment be made for a lapse of time between the exposure and the impact? The analysis of all these issues is relatively recent in the literature and therefore there are not many studies that can be quoted. This section provides, however, a state-of-the-art review of a developing area of research.

Age dependence for VSL
The issue of age has arisen because some of the studies and much of the clinical evidence suggests that particle pollution has health effects disproportionately on the elderly. For example, Schwartz and Dockery (1992) report a relative risk for under 65s as 1.049 per $100\mu g/M^3$ of PM_{10} and for over 65s as 1.166. Other studies that look at age as a distinct variable also find this effect.

The literature on age and VSL points to a relationship that is non-linear. The VSL increases with age in the early years and then declines, with a peak value at 40–50 years of age. This is supported by both theoretical and empirical studies. In turn, several empirical studies have produced evidence of a significant inverse relationship between the VOSL and age, at least beyond middle years, perhaps the most marked example being the pronounced inverted-U life cycle for the roads VOSL which emerged from the data generated by a nationally representative sample survey employing the contingent valuation (CV) approach carried out in 1982 and reported in Jones-Lee (1989). The results from that study are summarised in Table 4.3 below.

Table 4.3   *Estimates of VSL for different ages as a percentage of VSL at age 40*

Age	20	25	30	35	40	45	50	55	60	65	70	75
VSL as % at age 40	68	79	88	95	100	103	104	102	99	94	86	77

Source: Jones-Lee et al. (1985).

All these issues about the relationship between age and VSL lead inescapably to the conclusion that VSL *should be adjusted for age*. The above table could be used to adjust VSL for age, *if data on health impacts were available on an age basis*. Unfortunately, this is rarely the case in the empirical literature.

Impact of health impairment
Apart from the effects of age, one might expect VSL to vary with the state of health. There are two dimensions to this. One is the effect of pure health impairment and the other is the effect of shortening of life span. If a person's quality of life is poor this may effect his or her WTP for a reduction in the risk of death. There is little evidence, however, that points to this, although health service professionals do use a 'Quality Adjusted Life Years' (or QUALY) approach in which resources are allocated on the basis of paying no more than a certain amount for a QUALY. We return to this method below. At this point we simply note that the VSL approach does not adjust for pure health impairment. Nor does it adjust for reductions in life expectancy. For particle pollution this is particularly important, because there is a lot of clinical experience to suggest that the life expectancy of those who die from such exposure is already very short, perhaps only a few months.

Most observers agree that it is inappropriate to take a value for VSL based on a population with normal life expectancy and apply it to a population with a much shortened life expectancy. One way to approach this is to value life years directly. The issue is of particular importance when the impacts of air pollution are classified as 'acute mortality'. For such cases the mechanism is the number of air pollution days contributing to a higher number of deaths on the same day or on immediately following days. In this case, the 'at-risk' population consists mainly of elderly people (>65 years of age) with existing (serious) cardio-respiratory problems. The expectation is that persons affected are already quite ill and have only a short life expectancy.

The other kind of mortality impact is classified as chronic mortality. Here the mechanism is long-term exposure to air pollution, which leads to disease, which in turn contributes to premature death. In this case it is formally irrelevant whether death follows a higher pollution day. Cohort studies generally show increased mortality from cardio-respiratory disease, and from lung cancer.

The acute effects of various pollutants across a range of health endpoints are reasonably well established. These include respiratory infections, asthma attacks and restrictive activity days. Research has tried to establish reliable exposure-response functions for such effects. It is more difficult to establish relationships for chronic effects such as bronchitis or other longer term respiratory infections.

Impacts of latency on VSL
If exposure to particle pollution today causes the risk of death to increase T years from now, the WTP to avoid that risk is not the same as that associated with an increase in the risk of death now. The accepted way to deal with such latency is to discount future risks, so that if the WTP for an immediate reduction in risk is X, then the WTP for a reduction in a risk with a latency of T years is $X \cdot (1 + r)^{-T}$. The key question, of course, is what value should r take?

In ExternE (1995) this issue has been discussed at great length. It is noted there that there is a case for relatively high rates (around 11 per cent), as well as one for low rates, in the region of 3 per cent. Given the lack of agreement among economists as to which rate is the appropriate rate, it is recommended that calculations be done with both rates and the resulting range of values reported.

Value of life years lost
An alternative approach to analysing changes in the risk of death is to look at them in terms of the WTP for life years and to report a value for a life year lost (VLYL). The advantage of such a method is that it allows greater flexibility in valuation, and, furthermore, one that clinicians are more comfortable in

estimating. It also brings the WTP approach closer to the QUALY (quality of life years) approach which is widely used in health planning work. This has been studied and developed by Moore and Viscusi (1988), and Johannesson and Johansson (1996)

If we are to use VLYL what numbers should we use? As a first approximation it is reasonable to take a constant VLYL over the remaining lifetime of the person and to assume that the VSL for that person is the expected discounted present value sum of future life years. Thus, if VSL is $4m for a person of 40 years of age, and if the probability of a person of age 40 surviving to age t is $p_{40,\,t}$, then the VLYL is the solution to equal to:

$$\text{VSL} = \text{VLYL} \sum_{t=40}^{t=100} (1+r)^{-t} p_{40,t}$$

Such a calculation has been carried out below based on survival probabilities for European males and are shown in Table 4.4. The values emerging are around $200 000 with a discount rate of 3 per cent and around $415 000 for a discount rate of 11 per cent.

Table 4.4   VLYL values for European males in good health

Discount rate	VLYL with $4mn VSL for age 35	VLYL with $4mn VSL for age 45
0%	$107 134	$147 770
3%	$179 746	$214 648
11%	$402 620	$430 710

The transfer of these values to industrialising countries such as Brazil can be based on the same coefficients as were applied to VSL. Thus Tables 4.3 and 4.4 can be used to scale VLYL figures in the same way. It is desirable for the VLYL values to be calculated for the survival probabilities appropriate to the country concerned. If these are very different from the ones in Europe, the VLYL values will differ for that reason as well.

These values can be used for both acute and chronic mortality impacts. In each case an estimate has to be made of the number of life years lost per unit exposure. This information has to be provided by the epidemiologists.

4.5   THE VALUATION OF MORBIDITY EFFECTS

Epidemiological data has identified a relationship between certain health 'endpoints' and particle pollution. The following are the endpoints for which some valuation is, therefore, sought:

- Bronchodilator use in asthmatics
- Cough in asthmatics
- Lower respiratory symptoms in asthmatics (wheeze)
- Prevalence of child bronchitis
- Prevalence of child chronic cough
- Restricted activity days
- Chronic bronchitis in adults
- Hospital admissions for congestive heart failure
- Chronic admissions for ischaemic heart disease
- Respiratory hospital admissions
- Cerebrovascular hospital admissions

The full cost for an illness is composed of the following parts: (a) the value of the time lost because of the illness, (b) the value of the lost utility because of the pain and suffering, and (c) the costs of any expenditures on averting and/ or mitigating the effects of the illness. The last category includes both expenditures on prophylactics, as well as on the treatment of the illness once it has occurred. To value these components researchers have estimated the costs of illness, and used CVM methods as well as models of avertive behaviour.

The costs of illness (COI) are the easiest to measure, based either on the actual expenditures associated with different illnesses, or on the expected frequency of the use of different services for different illnesses. Part of these costs may be incurred by the individual directly and others through private insurance or through general taxation. In many countries a significant portion of the costs of respiratory illness (at least of the serious kind) are paid for through general taxation. The use of COI measures in estimating the costs of air pollution has been carried out in Brazil by Seroa da Motta and Fernandes Mendes (1996). These figures are useful for policy purposes but, as the discussion in this section shows, the full morbidity costs should be taken to be higher than the COI costs.

The costs of lost time are typically valued at the post-tax wage rate (for the work time lost), and at the opportunity cost of leisure (for the leisure time lost). Typically the latter is between one-half and one-third of the post-tax wage. Complications arise when the worker can work but is not performing at his full capacity. In that case an estimate of the productivity loss has to be made.

It is important to note that COI is only a component of the total cost and, furthermore, it is not necessarily a part of the WTP to avoid an illness. For example, if a person's medical costs are paid for through general taxation, the stated WTP to avoid a particular health 'endpoint' will not include such costs. Hence the relationship between COI and WTP are complex, and one cannot add the two items together to arrive at the total cost. In part this relationship has been studied by making a direct comparison of the two estimates and looking at their ratio. Rowe et al. (1995) have done this for US data and find that the ratio of WTP to COI is in the range 1.3 to 2.4. On the basis of their analysis they recommend a value of 2 for adverse health effects other than cancer and a value of 1.5 for non-fatal cancers. To arrive at the total cost of an illness, however, one should take WTP *plus* the part of COI that is not reflected in WTP. This will be the component that is paid for through taxation and, possibly, through insurance. Even in the USA, some 68 per cent of health costs are paid for by third parties.

Although the relationship between COI and WTP is complex, it offers one method of arriving at a realistic cost figure for morbidity endpoints, for many of which we do not have any WTP studies. In this section we report on morbidity estimates from two sets of figures: (a) US and European WTP studies for certain endpoints, (b) UK COI estimates 'grossed up' for the difference between WTP and COI.

The WTP for health endpoints can be measured either through the CVM approach, or through models of avertive behaviour. The latter involves the estimation of a 'health production function', from which one estimates the inputs used by the individual in different health states, and taking the difference in value between these obtains the cost of moving from one health state to another. The difficulty is in estimating that function, where many 'inputs' provide more than one service (for example, bottled water, air conditioners), and where the changes in consumption as a function of the state of illness are difficult to estimate. There are few estimates of health endpoints based on such models, and none for the industrialising countries.

In the ExternE work, we took values of endpoints from US studies, adjusted them for inflation and converted them into ECU. In Table 4.5 we report these figures. The figures reported here are from ExternE (1995), updated from some recent US work. It would be interesting to compare the costs implied by these figures with those obtained by, for example, Seroa da Motta, and Fernandes Mendes (1996).

In making these and other transfers, the key issue is their validity in local conditions. Transferability is most questionable when medical service costs influence the WTP. Since the provision of health services is different in different countries, and costs vary a lot, simply converting the US costs into

Table 4.5   Morbidity health endpoints and their valuation (values are in
            $1996)

Endpoint	(ExternE and this study)	Comments on transferability
Bronchodilator use in asthmatics	40	Use the PPPGDP adjustment factors given in the main text.
Cough in asthmatics	8	
Lower respiratory symptoms in asthmatics (wheeze)	8	
Prevalence of child bronchitis	237	
Prevalence of child chronic cough	237	
Restricted activity days	80	
Chronic bronchitis in adults	256 000	
Hospital admissions for congestive heart failure	5 760	These values are of the UK, based on UK health costs, grossed up for the ratio of WTP to COL A similar exercise can be carried out in each country, based on COI data.
Chronic admissions for ischaemic heart disease	5 760	
Respiratory hospital admissions	3 520	
Cerebrovascular hospital admissions	5 760	

Source: ExternE (1995), updated for present study.

Korean or any other costs at the PPP adjustment factors as given in Tables 4.3 and 4.4 must be considered as a doubtful practice. For this reason the above transfer is recommended only for those US studies for which the WTP is not medical cost sensitive (restricted activity days, cough days, symptom days and prevalence of chronic cough). For endpoints involving hospital treatment we have suggested taking local health cost data and scaling up on the basis of the ratio of COI to WTP.

Where an estimate of the value can be made on the basis of PPPGDP the correction factors have to use the EU PPPGDP as the baseline value and not that of the US. Thus the estimate of values to country i are: $WTP_{EU} \cdot (PPPGDP_i/PPPGDP_{EU})^{0.35}$ for the case of an income elasticity of 0.35, and $WTP_{EU} \cdot (PPPGDP_i/PPPGDP_{EU})$ for the case of an income elasticity of 1.

The PPPGDP$_{EU}$ is \$17 900. Thus, for example, a case of a cough in asthamatics is valued in Korea as {8 · (10330/17900)$^{0.35}$} for an income elasticity of 0.35 and {8 · (10330/17900)$^{1.0}$} for an income elasticity of 1.0. This gives the values of \$6.6 and \$4.6 respectively.

4.6   CONCLUSIONS ON THE VALUATION OF HEALTH IMPACTS

Summary of Results

This chapter has reviewed the different studies of the costs of mortality and morbidity arising from air pollution and has made some broad recommendations of values.

For mortality the 'Value of a Statistical Life' (VSL) has been taken at \$4m from the risk literature, with high bounds of uncertainty (perhaps a factor of 10). For industrialising countries such as Brazil, Tables 4.3 and 4.4 provide approximate values, based on a real income adjustment.

An alternative to the VSL is the VLYL, or value of a life year lost. Based on the VSL of 2m, the VLYL would (depending on the discount rate) amount to between \$160 000 and \$330 000. Transfer of these to industrialising countries can be made on the same basis as for VSL – that is, using Tables 4.3 and 4.4 and replacing the \$4m with the appropriate value of VLYL.

There is no agreed discount rate for latent effects and for effects that will be spread out over a number of years. There is a case of a rate of around 1–3 per cent and for a rate of around 8–11 per cent. There is also a case for a time variant discount rate, but this needs further research for the precise parameters to be established.

For morbidity impacts the key endpoints arising from air pollution have been identified. The estimation of the money values of these is based on a number of sources. For non-hospital-related endpoints, studies from the US and one from Norway have been considered and values derived. For hospital related endpoints UK Department of Health figures have been adjusted for the difference between the 'Costs of Illness' (COI) and the WTP. In the case of an industrialising country transfers of health endpoints that do not involve extensive medical costs can be made by using the PPPGDP adjustment, as indicated in the text. For other health points we recommend the direct estimation of the costs of the illness and then a scaling up by the ratio of WTP to COI.

How Should These Results be Used

The purpose of this approach is to aid decision-makers in making better decisions – that is, ones that use scarce resources more efficiently. While such valuations of resources in areas other than health raise few objections, when it comes to health issues, especially mortality, the critics are more vociferous. This was made clear, for example, in the last IPCC report (1996), where the valuation of damages required an estimate of loss of life from the impacts of global warming. The authors responsible for that section of the report took values somewhat similar to those suggested in Table 4.1 – that is, based on an income elasticity of one. National governments, however, objected to this, arguing that it was not appropriate to value the deaths of the citizens of a poorer country differently from those of another (richer) country. In other words they rejected the application of the above methodology for the purposes of valuing climate change effects.

This example serves to make an important point. The purpose of valuing health impacts, as was noted at the beginning of this chapter, is to provide a better basis for decision-making. In the case of climate change, no one would wish to arrive at a policy in which the critical factor was the different values attached to the deaths of the rich and the poor. That would, rightly, be seen as immoral. Hence the appropriate thing to have done would have been to value all deaths at the world GDP average. Indeed, when the VSL method is applied at the national level – for example for transport planning – no one even thinks of taking different values for the deaths of the rich and the poor citizens. A single national value is applied. It is important, however, that the correct national value be applied. If it is too high we will devote too much to safety, and if it is too low we will not devote enough.

The values provided in this paper are guides to the valuation of health impacts in national programmes of investment. They are not intended to serve as comparisons between nations. Nor are they to be used in policies involving global pollutants. A good example of how they might be used is to compare the costs of programmes of health improvement with the lives saved and obtain the 'cost per life saved'. This has been done for Brazil recently by Seroa da Motta (1995). Looking at the costs of drinking water treatment, sewage collection and sewage treatment, he finds a cost per life saved in Brazil of around $18 000. From the figures obtained as an average for Brazil in Tables 4.3 and 4.4 this is very small; the estimate on the basis of an elasticity of one for the value of a statistical life is $835 000. Hence such programmes of water quality improvement are amply justified. Of course, if funds are not available to finance all projects in which the cost of a life saved is less than $835 000, then the government has to choose between them. In that event, the programmes with the lowest cost per life saved should be implemented first.

NOTES

1. In order to facilitate the comparison of economic activity between countries, the UN's International Comparison Programme (ICP) developed internationally comparable measures of GNP, known as purchasing power parity (PPP) estimates of GNP; these are derived using purchasing power parities as opposed to exchange rates as conversion factors. The PPP conversion factor is defined as the number of units of a country's currency required to buy the same amounts of goods in the domestic market as one dollar would buy in the United States (World Bank, 1996). Data on the average domestic prices of a representative basket of goods and services are collected by the ICP, and PPPs are derived in relation to the average international prices that are implicitly derived from the prices of all participating countries (World Bank, 1996). No data are available for a number of countries that are in political turmoil.
2. This is probably one reason that the estimated value of life declines as the mean risk level in a group increases. From a theoretical perspective one would expect the opposite if the populations were homogeneous.

BIBLIOGRAPHY

Arrow et al. (1993), 'Report of the NOAA on contingent valuation', *Federal Register*, **58** (10).

Braden, J.B. and Kolstad, C.D. (eds) (1991), *Measuring the Demand for Environmental Quality*, New York: North- Holland, Elsevier Science Publishers.

Chestnut, L.G. and Rowe, R.D. (1988), 'Ambient particulate matter and ozone benefit analysis for Denver', Draft report prepared for US Environmental Protection Agency, Denver, Colorado, Jan.

Cropper, M., Aydede, S.K. and Portney, P.R. (1994), 'Preferences for life saving programs: how the public discounts time and age', *Journal of Risk and Uncertainty*, 8, 243–65.

ExternE (1995), *Externalities of Fuel Cycles: Economic Valuation – an Impact Pathway Approach*, Brussels: European Commission, vols 1–6.

ExternE (1999), Externalities of Energy: Methodology, 1998 update, Luxembourg: European Commission.

Fisher, A., Chestnut, L.G. and Violette, D.M. (1989), 'The value of reducing risks of death: a note on new evidence', *Journal of Policy Analysis and Management*, **8** (1), 88–100.

Freeman, A.M. (1991), 'Welfare measurement and the benefit-cost analysis of projects affecting risks', *Southern Economic Journal*, **58** (1), July, 65–76.

IPCC (1996), *Climate Change 1995. Economic and Social Dimensions of Climate Change: Scientific-Technical Analysis*, Contribution of Working Group III to the Second Assessment Report of the Intergovernmental Panel on Climate Change, Cambridge: Cambridge University Press.

Johannesson, M. and Johansson, P.-O. (1996), 'To be or not to be, that is the question: an empirical study of the WTP for an increased life expectancy at an advanced age', *Journal of Risk and Uncertainty*, **13**, 163–74.

Jones-Lee, M.W. (1989), *The Economics of Safety and Physical Risk*, Oxford: Basil Blackwell.

Jones-Lee, M., Hammerton, M. and Philips, P. (1985), 'The value of transport safety: results of a national sample survey', *The Economic Journal*, 95, (March), 49–72.

Krupnick, A.J., Harrison, K., Nickell, E. and Toman, M. (1996), 'The value of health benefits from ambient air quality improvements in Central and Eastern Europe', *Environmental and Resource Economics*, **7** (4), 307–32.

Litai, D. (1980), 'A risk comparison methodology for the assessment of acceptable risk', Massachussets Institute of Technology, PhD Thesis.

Markandya, A. (1994), 'Measuring the External Costs of Fuel Cycles', in: O. Hohmeyer and R.L. Ottinger (eds), *External Environmental Costs of Electric Power*, Berlin: Springer Verlag.

Markandya, A. and Richardson, J. (1993), *The Earthscan Reader in Environmental Economics*, London: Earthscan.

Mitchell, R.C. and Carson, R.T. (1986), *Valuing Drinking Water Risk Reduction Using the Contingent: Valuation Method: a Methodological Study of Risks from THM and Girardia*, Washington, DC. Report for the US Environmental Protection Agency.

Moore, M.J. and Viscusi, W. Kip (1988), 'The quantity adjusted value of life', *Economic Inquiry*, 26, 368–88.

Navrud, S. (1994), 'Economic Valuation of External Costs of Fuel Cycles; Testing the Benefit Transfer Approach', in A.T. De Almeida (ed.), *Models for Integrated Electricity Resource Planning*, Amsterdam: Kluwer Academic Publisher.

PACE (1992), *Environmental Costs of Electricity*, New York: PACE, University Centre for Environmental Legal Studies, Oceana Publications.

RER Inc and TRC Environmental Consultants (1994), *The Air Quality Valuation Model*, Regional Economic Research Inc. and TRC Environmental Consultants.

Rowe, R.D., Lang, C., Bernow, S. and White, D. (1995), 'The New York Environmental Externalities Cost Study: Summary of Approach and Results', in: *The External Costs of Energy: Proceedings*, Brussels: CEC.

Schwartz, J. and Dockery, D. (1992), 'Increased mortality in Philadelphia associated with daily air pollution concentrations', *American Review of Respiratory Disease*, 145, 600–604.

Seroa da Motta, R. (1995), 'El Caso de Brasil', in: J. Quiroz (ed.), *Análisis Económico de la contaminación de Aguas en América Latina*, ICEG/ILADES.

Seroa da Motta, R. and Fernandes Mendes, A.P. (1995), 'Health Costs Associated with Air Pollution in Brazil', in: J. Quiroz (ed.), *Análisis Económico de la contaminación de Aguas en América Latina*, ICEG/ILADES.

Seroa da Motta, R. and Fernandes Mendes, A.P. (1995), 'Health Costs Associated with Air Pollution in Brazil', in: P. May and R. Seroa da Motta (eds), *Pricing the Earth*, New York: Columbia University Press, Chapter 5.

Smith, V.K. and Huang, J.C. (1993), 'Hedonic models and air pollution: 25 years and counting', *Environmental and Resource Economics*, **3** (4), 381–94.

Smith, V.K. and Kaoru, Y. (1990), 'Signals or noise? Explaining the variation in recreation benefit estimates', *American Journal of Agricultural Economics*, **68**, 280–90.

Starr, C. (1976), 'General Philosophy of Risk Benefit Analysis', in: H. Ashley, R. Rudman and C. Whipple (eds), *Energy and the Environment: a Risk–Benefit Approach*, Oxford: Pergamon.

Viscusi, W.K. (1992), 'Pricing environmental risks', Policy Study, n.112, St. Louis, Mo., Washington University Center for the Study of American Business.

Viscusi, W. Kip and Moore, M.J. (1989), 'Rates of time preference and valuations of the duration of life', *Journal of Public Economics*, **38**, 297–317.

Walsh, R.G., Johnson, D. and McKean, J. (1989), 'Review of outdoor recreation economic demand studies with non-market: benefit estimates, 1968–1988'. mimeo.

Winpenny (1996), *Values for the Environment: a guide to economic appraisal*, Paris: OECD.

World Bank (1996), *World Development: Report*, New York: Oxford University Press.

5. Economic instruments for waste management in Brazil

Ronaldo Seroa da Motta and Daiane Ely Sayago

INTRODUCTION

This chapter presents some possibilities of introducing economic instruments to improve waste management in Brazil

The service of urban waste collection covers approximately 70 per cent of Brazilian households and its expansion has been at the pace of urban population growth. Moreover, less than a quarter of this collected waste is properly disposed of and treated. Municipalities are facing serious budget constraints to cope with the increasing demand on these services.

Estimates of recycling levels in Brazil are shown in Table 5.1. Considering only paper and aluminium cans, the Brazilian levels are as high as those observed in most OECD countries.

Table 5.1   Recycling levels in Brazil, 1997

	Aluminium cans	Glass	Paper		Plastic			Steel
			Office	Carton	Film	Rigid	PET	
Recycling level as % of primary production	61	28	37	60	15	15	21	18

Source: CEMPRE (1997).

To clarify this chapter's aims, we present the following rationale. Waste management problems can be generalised in physical terms, as:

$$W = Y - R$$

Where:

W = total solid waste to be collected and treated.
Y = total materials produced which can end up as waste.
R = materials which were recycled.

This chapter will not address the problems of financing the collecting and treating of W, although it recognises them as an important issue. This study, instead, is devoted to analysing and presenting proposals to reduce the level of Y and increase the level of R. In doing so, the level of W will also decrease, thereby reducing budget constraints of waste management services.

In the last decades, the increase of urbanisation and industrialisation intensities in the Brazilian economy have also increased the level of package waste in total waste generated in urban areas. Therefore, we will focus our analysis on package waste.

The following section analyses the options of economic instruments whereas the third section estimates the economic benefits of recycling. Based on that, the next section indicates some results for the proposed economic instruments. Finally, we present some brief conclusions.

THE CHOICE OF ECONOMIC INSTRUMENTS

The use of economic instruments (EIs) in waste management is usually related to pricing mechanisms,[1] such as subsidies for recycling activities, taxes on package contents, tipping fees and so on.

In this study we will only take into account indirect devices, such as subsidies and package taxes. In Brazil, the introduction of fees and payments for waste generated and disposed of faces legal and fiscal constraints stricter than those for subsidies and product taxation. Moreover, we are aware of the institutional fragility in the country in coping with illegal dumping which usually arises with direct waste pricing.

However, any pricing instrument has, first, to make explicit its pricing criteria. That is, what are the pricing criteria to be applied to the chosen instrument? Pricing procedures can be applied to accomplish three distinct criteria:

Achievement of the optimal use level: pricing full negative external costs in production and consumption activities to adjust output to optimal levels.
Improvement of cost-effectiveness: pricing natural resource users in order to allow them far more flexibility to achieve environmental goals with lower costs.

Generation of revenue: pricing natural resource uses to generate revenue.

The choice of one of these three criteria is important and is not always recognised through the design, implementation and performance analysis of an economic instrument. Moreover, the reconciliation of them into a single criteria is not easy. Based on this, three criteria can be suggested to formulate pricing rules for EIs: externality prices, behaviour prices and financing prices.

Externality pricing adopts the Pigouvian tax concept of internalising full degradation costs into the producer's marginal cost functions in order to equalise marginal social costs to marginal benefit costs, as a first order condition to market efficiency. In doing so, it is possible, for example, that market clears at the social optimum level of pollution. Here, damage cost functions are paramount to the pricing set. Such a task of environmental damage estimation is always complex and controversial, particularly with multiple damage sources and variant assimilative capacity.[2]

Behaviour pricing moves away from social optimisation to individual optimisation since it assumes that there is a previously established environmental target, not necessarily the economic optimum, which has to be met. Once this target is defined, prices will create the incentive for private agents to behave in a way that the aggregation of their individual use levels will meet the desirable target. Note that in this case targets are ambient standards and agents are free of individual standards. Agents will behave according to their own optimization strategies, equalising their marginal user costs, arising from user prices, to their marginal costs of reducing the use level. In this approach, for example, a polluter will equalise pollution prices to its marginal control costs to determine its optimum pollution level at this price level. Such flexibility allows for cost-effectiveness since all pollution with control costs lower than the pollution price, set by the EI, will be willing to abate. In this case, regulators need to know agents' marginal control or opportunity costs which cannot be easy if information asymmetry exists between regulators and polluters.

Financing pricing is related to setting optimal prices to attain certain budget needs rather than to meeting optimal degradation levels or private optimal control levels. In other words, optimal prices are set to achieve a certain level of revenue and, therefore, they are basically related to the agents' demand curves of the natural resources being priced, that is, the public prices rule[3] criteria which state that prices should be set by marginal provision costs inversely proportionate to each user's demand price-elasticity. In doing so, users with less elastic demand pay more than those with more elastic demand in order to avoid revenue losses. In this case note that regulators have a budget goal to make provision of some services to which an EI will be applied to finance this budget. Knowing the users' provision for marginal

Table 5.2   Environmental management mechanisms incorporating economic incentives

<------- CONTROL-ORIENTED ------->		<----- MARKET-ORIENTED ----->		<----- LITIGATION-ORIENTED ----->	
Regulations & sanctions	Charges, taxes & fees	Market creation	Final demand intervention	Liability legislation	

General Examples

Standards: Government restricts nature and amount of pollution or resource use for individual polluters or resource users. Compliance is monitored and sanctions made (fines, closure, jail terms) for non-compliance.

Effluent or user charges: Government charges fee to individual polluters or resource users based on amount of pollution or resource use and nature of receiving medium. Fee is high enough to create incentive to reduce impacts.

Tradable permits: Government establishes a system of tradable pollution or resource use permits, auctions or distributes permits, and monitors compliance. Polluters or resource users trade permits at unregulated market prices.

Eco-labels: Government supports a labelling program that requires disclosure of environmental information of the final end-use product. Eco-labels are attached to 'environmentally friendly' products.

Strict liability legislation: The polluter or resource user by law is required to pay any damages to those affected. Damaged parties collect settlements through litigation and court system

Specific Examples

Pollution standards	Non-compliance pollution charges	Market-based expropriation for construction, including 'environmental values'	Consumer product labelling relating to problem materials (e.g., phosphates in detergents)	Damages compensation.
Licensing of economic activities	Greening of conventional taxes	Property rights attached to resources potentially impacted by urban development (forests, lands, artisanal fish)	Education regarding recycling and re-use	Liability on neglecting firm's managers and environmental authorities
Land-use restrictions	Royalties and financial compensation for natural resources exploitation	Deposit–refund systems for solid and hazardous wastes	Disclosure legislation requiring manufacturers to publish solid, liquid and toxic waste generation	Long-term performance bonds posted for potential or uncertain hazards from infrastructure construction
Construction impact regulations for roads, pipelines, ports, or communications grids	Performance bonds posted for construction standards	Tradable permits for water abstraction rights, and water and air pollution emissions	Blacklist of polluters	'Zero Net Impact' requirements for road alignments, pipelines or utility rights of way, and water crossings
Environmental guidelines for urban road alignments	Taxes affecting inter-modal transport choices			
Fines for spills from port or land-based storage facilities	Taxes to encourage re-use or recycling of problem materials (e.g., tyre taxes, battery taxes)			
Bans applied to materials deemed unacceptable for solid waste collection service	Source-based effluent charges to reduce downstream water treating requirements			
Water use quotas	Tipping fees of solid wastes			
	User charges for water			

111

Source: Seroa da Motta, Huber and Ruitenbeek (1999).

costs and demand price-elasticities, a price set can be determined. As can be seen, such an information requirement is less complex, although pricing may be politically weak since demand characteristics will be the key pricing factor without any environmental justification.

Note that in any of the criteria presented above prices can be set with restrictions based on distributive criteria on their objective functions, such as the ability to pay and the minimum free use level. That is, prices will be set with a distributive weighting.

Table 5.2 shows the range of policy instruments which can be used in environmental policies and their degree of flexibility and market orientation. As can be seen, fines, sanctions and litigation are the most common instruments currently used everywhere and they are known as command and control (CAC) instruments. Those usually recognised as EIs are charges, taxes and fees and market creation mechanisms.

Literature on EIs is vast and it is not intended to review it. However, before some examples are presented in the following section, the reader must bear in mind that EIs are widely regarded as being an economically efficient and environmentally effective alternative to strict CAC approaches. As pointed by Seroa da Motta et al. (1999), in theory, by providing incentives to control pollution or other environmental damages, EIs have lower compliance costs and can provide much needed revenue for local government coffers. Administration costs associated with EIs, however, may be higher. Monitoring requirements and other enforcement activities remain as for CAC, and additional administration efforts may be required to cope with the design and institutional changes arising from the application of EIs. The recognition of this extra institutional burden is one of the main determinants of the successful implementation of EIs.

In this study we will only analyse externality pricing devices which can be used to reduce package contents and increase its recycling.

THE SOCIAL BENEFIT OF RECYCLING IN BRAZIL

As already proposed by Pearce and Brisson (1994), the social net benefit of recycling (SNBR) can be calculated as such:

$$SNBR = WCE + ED + (RWS - ICR)$$

where:
WCE = actual expenditure on urban waste collection and treatment.
ED = environmental damage due to the lack of proper collection and treatment of urban waste;

RWS = raw (primary) material savings due to recycling; and
ICR = industrial costs incurred to undertake recycling

The value of SNBR can be seen as the externality value of recycling and, therefore, it can be used as a reference for subsidies or taxation levels based on externality pricing.

WCE was estimated from the average costs incurred by major municipalities in Brazil. To skip from the complexity of direct estimation of environmental damages, we account in *ED* for the cost of providing the adequate waste collection and treatment services which would avoid these environmental damages.

The estimation of (RWS – ICR) was based on two assumptions:

1. The current price of materials sold for recycling is a good proxy of their opportunity costs in term of material savings since the recycling market can be considered functioning efficiently.
2. The recycling market is not perfect, it is either oligopsonic or oligopolist and, therefore, market prices are not the efficient ones. The component (RWS – ICR) is measured as the total material savings, deducted from processing costs, which it is possible to gain with recycling minus the cost of a selective collection which makes that possible by offering good waste quality for recycling.

Table 5.3   Estimates of SNBR (1997 R$/t)

	Aluminium	Glass	Paper	Plastic	Steel
Assumption 1					
WCE	23.98	23.98	23.98	23.98	23.98
ED	19.02	19.02	19.02	19.02	19.02
RWS-ICR	459.33	39.29	73.52	113.23	36.27
Total	502.33	82.29	116.52	156.23	79.27
Weighted Total	5.58	13.72	50.49	32.98	14.10
Average Value = 117.00					
Assumption 2					
WCE	23.98	23.98	23.98	23.98	23.98
ED	19.02	19.02	19.02	19.02	19.02
RWS-ICR .	431.72	–119.45	190.71	1262.02	81.74
Total	474.72	(76.45)	233.71	1305.02	124.74
Weighted Total	5.27	(12.74)	101.27	275.49	22.18
Average Value = 391.00					

In assumption 2 we based our estimates on Calderoni (1997) for material savings and IPT/CEMPRE (1994) for selective collection costs.

Estimations in both assumptions were made for tons of waste and are presented in Table 5.3. The weighted total is given by the share of each material in the total package waste generated in urban areas in Brazil. The average value is the sum of each material value.

Results in Table 5.3 indicate that market imperfections may reduce private agents' perception of the recycling value from R\$391.00 to R\$117.00/ton. Since we cannot precisely identify these imperfections, externality reductions from recycling may vary along this range in urban areas of Brazil.

FORMULATING THE EI

In Brazil, material residuals (those generated from both production and consumption phases) which are introduced again in industrial processing do not carry industrial value added tax. However, tax was paid on this material as a final product. Therefore, we have designed a subsidy which is offered as a tax credit for the value added tax contents (tax actually paid) of the package which is recycled.

Note that this tax content when accruing as tax credit reduces the final value added tax (VAT) payments of those who introduce them in their industrial processing, thereby reducing their tax burden.

The subsidy credit tax level (C) is then a proportion (β) of the VAT level levied on the package (I), such as:

$$C = \beta \times I \qquad (5.1)$$

According to externality pricing criteria, the maximum amount of subsidy ($S_{\max}$) should be equal to social benefit of recycling, as follows:

$$S_{\max} = \text{SNBR} \times Q_s^* \qquad (5.2)$$

where Q_s^* is the quantity of material residuals for recycling.

Assuming this environmental restriction, C can be determined from:

$$C \times P_s \times Q_s^* \leq \text{SNBR} \times Q_s^* \qquad (5.3)$$

Using expression (5.1), we have:

$$\beta \leq \text{SNBR} / P_s \times I \qquad (5.4)$$

where P_s is the price of material residuals for recycling.

Note that the lower the SNBR is the lower will be β and thereby the total amount of subsidy.

Considering the current fiscal crisis in Brazil, we have applied a fiscal constraint on the estimation of β. This constraint was to make subsidy amount equal to VAT revenue from recycled products, such as,

$$C_F \times P_s \times Q_s^* \le I_r \times P_r \times Q_s^* \qquad (5.5)$$

where C_F is the fiscal constrained C while I_r and P_r are the tax level and price of the recycled product. Note that in the previous expressions, price and tax levels are related to material residuals while in expression (5.5) they are those prevailing for the recycled product made of the processing of residuals.

Then $C_F = \beta_F \times I_r$, where β_F is the relevant proportion of I_r to be credited to those producing recycled products, such as:

$$\beta \le P_r / P_s \qquad (5.6)$$

Note that fiscal restrictions in expression (5.6) are related to price differences between recycled and residuals and not to SNBR as in the environmental case of expression (5.4).

As already pointed out elsewhere, only recycling subsidies do not max-imise efficiency gains on waste management,[4] particularly in the case of packages. Subsidy-tax schemes are more efficient. In addition to a subsidy, then, a tax on package production should be levied as well. Such a 'de-posit–return' production scheme can also compensate for losses on tax revenue.

This tax level should be set in order to make private package costs (P_m^*) equal to its social costs. Following the same rationale for estimating β, one can set this tax level (E) as:

$$E \le \text{SNBR} / P_m^* \qquad (5.7)$$

A bill has been proposed in the National Congress to set up a deposit–return scheme of 5 per cent on the price of products with packages made of PET. A new bill covering other types of packaging materials is now under discussion. If deposit–return levels (G) are estimated following our proce-dures, they would be, for each material, equivalent to:

$$G = \text{SNBR} / P_p \qquad (5.8)$$

where P_p is the product price.

Table 5.4   Estimates of subsidy and tax levels (%)

Material/Tax level	C	C_F	E	G
Aluminium – Case 1[1]	85	146	6	0
Aluminium – Case 2[2]	85	18	6	–
Glass[3]	996	116	86	14
Glass[4]	996	300	50	3
Plastic[5]	346	159	22	1
Paper[6]	532	125	34	–

Notes:
1. Cans;
2. Bars;
3. Beer one-way;
4. Mayonnaise;
5. Soft drink PET;
6. Paper box.

Using our estimates of SNBR and current market values for P_r, P_s, P_P and P_m^*, we present in Table 5.4 some estimation exercises for C, C_F, E and G for Brazil considering some package materials.

As can be seen in Table 5.4 C values, as expected, are much higher than C_F ones since they are not constrained by fiscal restrictions. E values are being applied on package prices and therefore cannot be compared to subsidy values, although they are theoretically equivalent to C values. For G values, one can see that they are very much away from the 5 per cent level proposed by the bill.

FINAL COMMENTS

Our study was an attempt to analyse options of EIs applicable to reduce waste and stimulate recycling, particularly pricing devices based on externality correction. As our estimation exercise has shown, this requires a great deal of effort and data collection.

Regarding options for recycling subsidies, the current tax structure in Brazil offers options based on VAT credit, whereas for package taxes there will be a need to pass a law creating this new tax. The deposit–return scheme is already under discussion in the National Congress.

We have also tried to formulate these options regarding the current fiscal crisis and estimating subsidies based on budget constraints. In this case, the environmental benefit achieved with such a subsidy level can be estimated only if one knows the demand function of primary and residual materials, which was not within the scope of this study.

Our estimates have shown that environmental costs are key parameters to set subsidy, tax or deposit–return levels. However, they are very sensitive to market assumptions and data availability. Bearing this in mind, one can accept ad hoc proposals of these levels to avoid controversial estimation procedures and values.

Finally, the importance of recycling must be emphasised for the labour market of non-qualified workers in urban areas of Brazil. This other social cost was not taken directly into account in our estimate, but it would certainly increase our estimate of the social net benefit of recycling.[5]

NOTES

1. See, for example, Curzio et al. (1994).
2. In Seroa da Motta (1998a) a comprehensive review of methodological issues and case studies on environmental valuation is presented.
3. Ramsey rule, see Seroa da Motta (1998b), where it is applied to water pricing.
4. See, for example, Palmer and Walls (1997).
5. See Seroa da Motta and Saygago (1998) for an overview on these issues.

REFERENCES

Calderoni, S. (1997), Os *bilhões perdidos no lixo*, São Paulo: USP, Tese de Doutorado.
CEMPRE (1997), *Fichas técnicas, 1997*, São Paulo: CEMPRE.
Curzio, A.Q., Prosperetti, L. and Zoboli, R. (eds) (1994), *The Management of Municipal Solid Waste in Europe*, Amsterdam: Elsevier.
IPT/CEMPRE (1994), *Pesquisa Ciclosoft*, São Paulo: IPT.
Palmer, K. and Walls, M. (1997), 'Optimal policies for solid waste disposal: taxes, subsidies and standards', *Journal of Public Economics*, 65, 193–205.
Pearce, D. and Brisson, I. (1994), 'Using Economic Incentives for the Control of Municipal Solid Waste', in: A.Q. Curzio, et al. (eds), *The Management: of Municipal Solid Waste in Europe*, Amsterdam: Elsevier.
Seroa da Motta, R. (1998a), *Manual de Valoração Econômica de Recursos Ambientais*, Brasília: MMA/IBAMA.
Seroa da Motta, R. (1998b), *Utilização de Critérios Econômicos para a Valorização da Água no Brasil*, Projeto Planagua, SEMA-GTZ.
Seroa da Motta, R. and Sayago, D.E. (1998), *Propostas de Instrumentos Econômicos Ambientais para a Redução do Lixo Urbano e o Reaproveitamento de Sucatas no Brasil*, Rio de Janeiro: IPEA (Texto para Discussão, n.608).
Seroa da Motta, R., Huber, R. and Ruintenbeek, J. (1999), 'Market based instruments for environmental policymaking in Latin America and the Caribbean: lessons from eleven countries', *Environmental Development Economics*, **4** (2).

6. Deforestation, land degradation and rural poverty in Latin America: examining the evidence

Edward B. Barbier

6.1 INTRODUCTION

The main purpose of this chapter is to provide an overview of aggregate empirical evidence of the potential links between rural poverty and resource degradation in Latin America. Recent studies suggest that there are two overall aspects of poverty–environment linkages that are critical to this relationship in developing countries (see Barbier, 1997, for a review).

First, poverty may not be a direct cause of environmental degradation but instead may operate as a constraining factor on poorer rural households' ability to avoid resource degradation or to invest in mitigating strategies. Empirical evidence suggests that poorer households in rural Latin America are more constrained in their access to credit, inputs and research and extension services necessary for investments in improved resource management (Barbier, 2000; López and Valdés, 2000). Poverty, imperfect capital markets and insecure land tenure may reinforce the tendency towards short-term time horizons in production decisions, which may bias land-use decisions against long-term resource management strategies. Consequently, a rational strategy for poor rural households with limited access to capital and alternative economic opportunities may be to extract short-term rents through resource conversion and degradation, so long as there are sufficient additional resources available in frontier areas to exploit relatively cheaply and the cost of access remains low.

Second, poverty may severely constrain poor households' ability to compete for resource access. In periods of commodity booms and land speculation, wealthier households generally take advantage of their superior political and market power to ensure initial access to better quality resources in order to capture a larger share of the resource rents. Poorer households are either confined to marginal environmental areas where resource rents are limited or only have access to higher quality resources once resources are degraded and rents are dissipated. This relationship between poverty, resource access and resource degradation is perhaps less well-documented for Latin America but may be significant, particularly in frontier areas characterised by open access resource exploitation (Barbier, 2000; Schneider, 1994; Mahar and Schneider, 1994; Sunderlin and Rodrígez, 1996).

The outline of the chapter is as follows. The next section examines overall trends in land degradation and deforestation in Latin America, as well as the geographical 'location' of the rural poor. The evidence suggests that there might be a 'cumulative causation' link between rural poverty, deforestation and land degradation: poor rural households abandoning degraded land for 'frontier' forested lands, which results in deforestation and cropping of poor soils leading to erosion, which is in turn followed by land abandonment and additional conversion further into the forest frontier, and so on. If such an aggregate relationship exists, then cross- country statistical analyses of defor- estation and land expansion should provide some evidence of this linkage. In Section 6.3, three statistical analyses of the factors affecting deforestation are examined, and the results are interpreted in light of potential rural poverty- resource degradation linkages. Finally, the conclusion to this chapter discusses briefly the implications for policy of the overview of aggregate evidence of a cumulative causation link between rural poverty, deforestation and land deg- radation in Latin America.

6.2   LAND DEGRADATION AND DEFORESTATION IN LATIN AMERICA: AN OVERVIEW

The 1990 global forest resource assessment of tropical deforestation indi- cated that the annual deforestation rate across tropical Latin America over 1981–90 was approximately 0.8 per cent, which is par with the global aver- age (see Table 6.1). However, the area of tropical forests cleared on average each year in Latin America, 7.4 million hectares (ha), is almost as much as the first area cleared in Asia and Africa put together. Although most of the deforestation is currently occurring in tropical South America (6.4 million ha), the highest rate of deforestation is being experienced in Central America and Mexico (1.5 per cent annually).

Table 6.2 compares global and Latin American trends in human-induced soil erosion over the period 1945–90. Over 15 per cent of the world's de- graded land is located in Latin American countries. Central America and Mexico have the highest proportion of degraded area to all vegetated land of any region in the world. Much of the degradation in this region appears to be moderate, severe or extreme. South America also has a significant amount of human-induced soil degradation, although much of it is light degradation.

Table 6.1 Global tropical deforestation trends

Region	Number of countries	Land area (million ha)	Forest cover		Annual deforestation 1981–90	
			1980 (million ha)	1990 (million ha)	million ha	% per annum
Africa	**40**	**2236.1**	**568.6**	**527.6**	**4.1**	**0.7**
West Sahelian Africa	6	528.0	43.7	40.8	0.3	0.7
East Sahelian Africa	9	489.7	71.4	65.5	0.6	0.9
West Africa	8	203.8	61.5	55.6	0.6	1.0
Central Africa	6	398.3	215.5	204.1	1.1	0.5
Trop. Southern Africa	10	558.1	159.3	145.9	1.3	0.9
Insular Africa	1	58.2	17.1	15.8	0.1	0.8
Asia & Pacific	**17**	**892.1**	**349.6**	**310.6**	**3.9**	**1.2**
South Asia	6	412.2	69.4	63.9	0.6	0.8
Continental S.E. Asia	5	190.2	88.4	75.2	1.3	1.6
Insular S.E. Asia	5	244.4	154.7	135.4	1.9	1.3
Pacific	1	45.3	37.1	36.0	0.1	0.3
Latin America & Caribbean	**33**	**1650.1**	**992.2**	**918.1**	**7.4**	**0.8**
C. America & Mexico	7	239.6	79.2	68.1	1.1	1.5
Caribbean	19	69.0	48.3	47.1	0.1	0.3
Trop. South America	7	1341.6	864.6	802.9	6.2	0.7
Total	**90**	**4778.3**	**1910.4**	**1756.3**	**15.4**	**0.8**

Source: FAO (1993).

Agricultural activities cause the most degradation in Central America and Mexico, with deforestation also a significant factor. In South America, deforestation is the main cause of human-induced degradation, although over-grazing and agricultural activities are also significant.

Together Tables 6.1 and 6.2 suggest that in recent years the major rural resource use trends in Latin America have resulted in both processes of deforestation and land degradation. Moreover these two processes are clearly linked, as deforestation appears to be a major source of human-induced soil degradation in the region. Underlying both recent deforestation and land degradation trends in Latin America has been rapid change in land-use patterns. This is illustrated in Table 6.3.

Virtually all Latin American countries have experienced an expansion in cropland area since 1979–81, while at the same time forest and woodland area has declined substantially (see Table 6.3).[1] Permanent pasture has also increased in most Latin American countries. Continued conversion of forest and woodland to other uses is perhaps inevitable given the pressures of population density and the high proportion of forested land in Latin America.

For example, although in Central America and Mexico approximately 50 per cent of the land area is already either cropland or pasture, just under 25 per cent of the remaining land is still forest and woodland. Population density is on average over 1200 people per square kilometre (km^2). With the exception of Costa Rica and Nicaragua, timber production appears to be relatively insignificant at present across the region. It is not surprising that population pressure in particular may be forcing further expansion of cropland and permanent pasture at the expense of forest and woodlands.

In comparison, South America still retains vast areas of forest and woodlands, with just under 50 per cent of its total land area still forested. Timber production also seems more significant in the region, although Brazil is clearly the dominant timber producer of the region. However, in South America cropland and permanent pasture are also expanding rapidly at the expense of forest and woodlands, particularly the tropical forests.

It is extremely difficult to find aggregate statistics linking rural resource poverty to land degradation and deforestation trends in Latin America. However, an analysis by Leonard et al. (1989) attempted to determine how the poorest 20 per cent of the rural population in developing countries were distributed across 'high' and 'low potential' lands. The latter are defined as resource-poor or marginal agricultural lands, where inadequate or unreliable rainfall, adverse soil conditions, fertility and topography limit agricultural productivity and increase the risk of chronic land degradation. The results are indicated in Figure 6.1. Although the rural areas of Latin America have a much lower total number of extreme poor than Asia or Africa, a higher proportion of Latin America's poorest people are concentrated on low poten-

Table 6.2 *Global trends in human-induced soil degradation, 1945–90*

Region	Total degraded area (million ha)	Degraded area as a % of vegetated land	Causes of soil degradation (%)				
			Deforestation	Over-exploitation[a]	Over-grazing	Agricultural activities	Industrialisation[b]
World	**1964.4**	**17.0**	**30**	**7**	**35**	**28**	**1**
Moderate, severe[c] extreme	1215.4	10.5					
Light[d]	749.0	6.5					
Europe	**218.9**	**23.1**	**38**	–	**23**	**29**	**9**
Moderate, severe extreme	158.3	16.7					
Light	60.6	6.4					
Africa	**494.2**	**22.1**	**14**	**13**	**49**	**24**	–
Moderate, severe extreme	320.6	14.4					
Light	173.6	7.8					
Asia	**747.0**	**19.8**	**40**	**6**	**26**	**27**	–
Moderate, severe extreme	452.5	12.0					
Light	294.5	7.8					
Oceania	**102.9**	**13.1**	**12**	–	**80**	**8**	–
Moderate, severe extreme	6.2	0.8					
Light	96.6	12.3					

North America	**95.5**	**5.3**	**4**	—	**30**	**66**	—
Moderate, severe	78.7	4.4					
extreme	16.8	0.9					
Light							
Central America and Mexico	**62.8**	**24.8**	**22**	**18**	**15**	**45**	—
Moderate, severe	60.9	24.1					
extreme	1.9	0.7					
Light							
South America	**243.4**	**14.0**	**41**	**5**	**28**	**26**	—
Moderate, severe	138.5	8.0					
extreme	104.8	6.0					
Light							

Notes:

– represents less than 1 per cent contribution.

a *Over-exploitation* refers to over-exploitation for fuelwood use

b *Industrialisation* includes industrial and waste accumulation, excessive pesticide use and acidification by airborne pollutants.

c *Extreme degradation* – degradation has occurred on poor soils and restoration is impossible. *Severe degradation* – degradation involves severe nutrient depletion and deeper, more frequent gullies and hollows; extensive restoration is required, involving physical structures, drainage works, terraces, mechanised deep ploughing, and reseeding. *Moderate degradation* – degradation that involves loss of topsoil from water and wind erosion, nutrient decline, some salinisation and soil compaction, all of which contribute to loss of potential productivity; restoration is essential to reverse productivity declines, and requires both soil conservation practices and major structural interventions, such as drainage for waterlogging or salinity, contour ridging, bunds, and so on

d *Light degradation* – degradation on good soils that show signs of degradation – some topsoil loss, nutrient decline and increased salinity – which can be restored through standard conservation practices, such as crop rotation, minimum tillage, and other on-farm practices.

Source: Oldeman et al. (1990) and WRI (1992).

Table 6.3   Latin America – land area and use, 1979–91

	Land area (000 ha)	1993 Population density (per 000 ha)	Cropland and pasture as % of land area	Forest as % of land area	Cropland	
					1989–91 (000 ha)	% change since 1979–81
Central America						
and Mexico	**262.005**	**1.219**	**50.3**	**23.9**	**37.730**	**4.5**
Belize	2.280	89	4.6	44.4	56	9.0
Costa Rica	5.106	640	55.9	32.1	529	4.5
Cuba	10.982	993	57.4	25.1	3.330	4.0
Dominican Republic	4.838	1.575	73.1	12.7	1.446	2.4
El Salvador	2.072	2.663	64.8	5.0	733	1.1
Guatemala	10.843	925	30.3	34.6	1.882	7.9
Haiti	2.756	2.501	50.9	1.4	905	1.7
Honduras	11.189	503	39.2	29.1	1.824	3.7
Jamaica	1.083	2.304	42.5	17.1	270	1.8
Mexico	190.869	472	52.0	22.2	24.713	0.7
Nicaragua	11.875	346	56.2	28.5	1.273	2.1
Panama	7.599	337	29.1	43.4	649	16.7
Trinidad & Tobago	513	2.493	25.5	42.9	120	3.4
South America	**1742.693**	**173**	**34.8**	**47.2**	**113.697**	**10**
Argentina	273.669	122	61.9	21.6	27.200	0.0
Bolivia	108.438	71	26.7	51.3	2.328	12.9
Brazil	845.651	185	28.9	58.3	59.933	23.1
Chile	74.880	184	23.9	11.8	4.400	3.9
Colombia	103.670	327	44.2	48.5	5.410	4.1
Ecuador	27.684	409	28.4	39.4	2.732	9.4
Guyana	19.685	41	8.8	6.2	495	0.1
Paraguay	39.730	117	58.6	34.7	2.199	26.7
Peru	128.000	179	24.1	53.4	3.730	6.1
Suriname	15.600	29	0.6	95.2	68	39.7
Uruguay	17.481	180	84.8	3.8	1.304	–9.5
Venezuela	88.205	234	24.5	34.2	3.898	4.3
All countries	**2004.698**	**717**	**36.8**	**44.1**	**151.427**	**7.2**

Source: WRI (1994).

tial lands. Almost three-quarters of the poorest 20 per cent of the rural population in Latin America can be found on low potential lands, as opposed to 51 per cent and 57 per cent in Africa and Asia respectively. One factor explaining the larger share of the rural poor on 'low' potential lands in Latin America is that this region has a greater amount of high-yield and mechanised commercial agriculture than either Africa or Asia.

As low potential lands are considered to be prone to chronic land degradation, then clearly the problems of rural poverty and human-induced soil degradation are linked in Latin America. Moreover, given that in Latin America

Permanent Pasture		Forest and woodland		Other land		Annual logging of closed broadleaved forest, 1981–90	
1989–91 (000 ha)	% change since 1979–81	1989–91 (000 ha)	% change since 1979–81	1989–91 (000 ha)	% change since 1979–81	Extent (000 ha)	% of closed forest
94.164	**5.2**	**62.724**	**−12.8**	**67.388**	**7.1**	**102**	**1.1**
48	9.1	1.012	0.0	1.164	−0.7	3	0.2
2.327	15.6	1.640	−9.9	611	−20.3	34	2.6
2.970	15.3	2.760	9.1	1.922	−28.1	3	0.2
2.092	0.0	615	−3.1	685	−2.0	0	0.0
610	0.0	104	−25.7	625	4.7	na	na
1.400	7.7	3.750	−17.6	3.811	17.3	3	0.1
497	−2.4	38	−34.1	1.316	1.3	1	7.7
2.560	6.2	3.260	−18.8	3.545	17.9	2	0.1
190	−8.1	185	−5.1	438	5.3	1	0.4
74.499	0.0	42.460	−11.4	49.197	12.1	4	0.0
5.400	10.7	3.380	−24.7	1.822	44.6	45	0.9
1.560	13.9	3.300	−20.4	2.090	36.9	3	0.1
11	0.0	220	−4.3	162	3.8	3	1.8
492.730	**6.8**	**822.086**	**−5.9**	**314.379**	**8.1**	**2.466**	**0.3**
142.200	−0.7	59.200	−1.4	45.069	4.3	na	na
26.600	−1.7	55.590	−1.1	23.920	3.4	12	0.0
184.200	7.5	493.030	−4.9	108.488	1.2	1.982	0.5
13.500	3.8	8.800	1.3	48.180	−1.6	na	na
40.400	5.8	50.300	−5.6	7.760	7.8	108	0.2
5.140	29.2	10.900	−21.9	8.912	22.8	152	1.3
1.230	0.8	16.369	0.0	1.591	−0.6	9	0.0
21.100	33.5	13.800	−31.6	2.631	30.3	49	1.8
27.120	0.0	68.400	−3.5	28.750	8.6	89	0.1
20	1.7	14.853	−0.2	658	2.7	11	0.1
13.520	−0.8	669	6.8	1.988	11.4	na	na
17.700	2.9	30.175	−8.8	36.432	6.6	54	0.1
586.894	**6.0**	**884.810**	**−9.5**	**381.767**	**7.6**	**2.568**	**0.7**

many marginal and resource-poor lands are also likely to have been previously forested lands, then a strong rural poverty–deforestation link may also exist. Finally, as depicted in Table 6.2, deforestation may itself may be an important cause of human-induced soil degradation across Latin America. This raises the possibility of a 'cumulative causation' link between rural poverty, deforestation and land degradation: poor rural households abandoning degraded land for 'frontier' forested lands, deforestation and cropping of poor soils lead to further degradation, which in turn lead to land abandonment and additional forest land conversion, and so on.

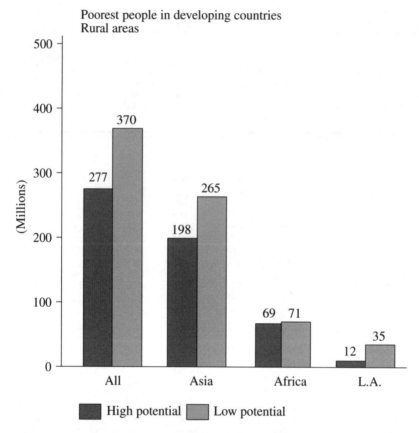

Notes:
High Potential = High potential agricultural lands; that is highly productive, favourable agricultural lands that are either irrigated or have reliable and adequate rainfall, as well as generally
high or potentially high soil fertility.
Low Potential = Low potential lands; that is, resource-poor or marginal agricultural lands.
Where inadequate or unreliable rainfall, adverse soil conditions, fertility and topography limit
agricultural productivity and increase the risk of chronic land degradation.
The 'poorest people' are defined as the poorest 20 per cent of the population in developing
countries.

Source: Leonard et al. (1989).

Figure 6.1   The rural poor and ecologically fragile areas

If there is a linkage between aggregate levels of rural poverty, land degradation and deforestation in Latin America, then cross-country statistical analyses
of the regions should provide some evidence of this linkage. The next section

looks at three recent statistical analyses of the factors underlying deforestation across Latin America, and discusses whether their findings provide evidence of a relationship between rural poverty and resource degradation.

6.3   STATISTICAL ANALYSIS OF DEFORESTATION IN LATIN AMERICA

Several recent studies have conducted statistical analysis of deforestation in Latin America, especially emphasising the role of agricultural conversion. Although most studies have focussed on individual countries, a few have attempted to elicit regional trends. In this section, two regional analyses of relevance to this chapter are examined, and an additional analysis conducted for this study is also discussed.

Data on closed forest area and annual deforestation rates are notoriously unreliable across Latin American countries. A common approach is to assume that expansion of agricultural land or permanent pasture is a proxy measure for forest land conversion. As discussed in the previous section, this is not an unreasonable assumption for Latin America.

For example, Southgate (1994) employs data from 24 Latin American countries to explore the causes of agricultural frontier expansion and thus forest clearance. The dependent variable used in the analysis is average annual agricultural land (that is, permanent pasture and cropland) growth over 1982–87. The results are indicated in Table 6.4, and suggest that the expansion of agricultural land across Latin America – and thus by proxy deforestation – are causally related to a number of key growth variables. Population growth appears to be positively correlated with agricultural frontier expansion, reflecting perhaps both the direct demand for agricultural land as populations increase as well as the indirect demand as increasing numbers of consumers raises the demand for agricultural commodities and production. Agricultural export growth also appears to be positively related to agricultural land expansion, again most likely indicating the influence of a strong export performance on the demand for land. In contrast, growth in agricultural yields across Latin American countries seems to reduce agricultural land expansion. Yield increases appear to be offsetting the demand for converting and bringing new agricultural land into production. Finally, Southgate also includes a 'land constraint' variable, reflecting the physical constraints of the land. The negative coefficient on this variable indicates that, where there is little appropriate land available for additional conversion, then the growth in arable land is significantly reduced.

Cropper and Griffiths (1994) used pooled cross-section and time-series data over the period 1961–88 for Latin America, Asia and Africa separately

Table 6.4   Analysis of agricultural frontier expansion in Latin America

Dependent variable: annual agricultural land growth, 1982–87

Explanatory variable		Estimated coefficients (t statistic)
Constant		0.463
		(2.876)
POPGRO (Annual population growth, 1980–88)		0.249
		(3.773)
EXPGRO (Annual agricultural export growth, 1984–88)		0.031
		(2.214)
YLDGRO (Annual increase in crop production per unit area of crop land, 1982–89)		−0.198
		(−6.000)
NOLAND (Land constraint dummy)		−0.641
		(−3.127)
Adjusted R^2:	0.511	F Statistic: 12.098
Sum of Squared Residuals:	0.062	Durbin-Watson: 2.065

Source: Southgate (1994).

to determine the effects of both income and population pressure on annual deforestation rates. Developing countries roughly in the tropical belt and containing forest area of over one million ha were included in the analysis. The purpose of examining the income relationships was to test for the environmental Kuznets curve or 'inverted U' hypothesis; i.e., to what extent does deforestation first rise, even out and then fall with increases in per capita income across developing regions. In addition, the authors wanted to determine the additional influence of population pressure on tropical deforestation.

In order to conduct a pooled analysis of deforestation from 1961–88, Cropper and Griffiths use the percentage change in forest area in each developing country during each year of this time period. This calculation is based on the time series for forests and woodlands provided by the FAO's *Production Yearbook*. Although as the authors note this time series is consistent, for many developing countries the annual statistics for forests and woodland are in themselves estimates derived from annualised deforestation rates derived from more periodic surveys and assessments of the status of forest resources.[2] These surveys are generally frequent and intermittent, and usually only conducted in accordance with the FAO's own ten-yearly global assessments of tropical forest resources (FAO and UNEP, 1982; FAO, 1993). In addition, for most tropical forest countries, estimates of both forest resources and annual

Table 6.5   Pooled analysis of tropical deforestation in Latin America

Dependent variable: annual rate of deforestation, 1961–88

Explanatory variable	Estimated coefficients (t statistic)
Per capita income (US$ millions)	6.03 (1.93)
Per capita income squared	–556.29 (–1.54)
Percentage change in per capita income	–0.0123 (–3.23)
Price of tropical logs (US$ thousands)	0.000192 (2.41)
Percentage change in population	0.0196 (0.39)
Rural population density	0.0363 (1.08)
Time trend	–0.0000063 (–0.05)

R^2:   0.47   Turning point: $5420
No of observations: 450

Source: Cropper and Griffiths (1994).

rates of deforestation are notoriously unreliable before the 1980 FAO tropical forest resource assessment.

Table 6.5 displays the results of Cropper and Griffiths' analysis for Latin America. The overall results suggest that an inverted-U-shaped relationship between income and deforestation does exist in Latin American countries. However, the level of income at which rates of deforestation peaks in the region is US$5420, and Cropper and Griffiths note that most countries are at income levels below this threshold. Thus the authors interpret these results to imply that the increase in the rate of deforestation in Latin America tends to level off as income rises. Income growth also appears to have a negative influence on deforestation, although the magnitude of this effect is small. In Latin America, increasing the rate of growth of per capita income by 8 per cent reduces the rate of deforestation by one-tenth of a percentage point.

A surprising result of Cropper and Griffiths' analysis is that, although both population growth and rural population density are positively correlated with tropical deforestation in Latin America, neither variable is highly significant (see Table 6.5). The authors do find a significant positive relationship between (border-equivalent) prices for tropical logs and deforestation in Latin America. This may suggest a strong correlation between logging activities and deforestation, both directly through 'unsustainable' extraction and indirectly through the process of 'opening up' previously inaccessible forest areas for agricultural settlement and conversion (Amelung and Diehl, 1991; Barbier et al., 1994; Schneider, 1994; Mahar and Schneider, 1994).

A further analysis of tropical deforestation in Latin America was conducted by Barbier (2000). The analysis was estimated for 21 tropical countries in Latin America over the 1980–85 period, examining the relationship between forest clearance and several key influences on deforestation identified by Southgate (1994), Cropper and Griffiths (1994) and individual country studies in Latin America: population pressure, agricultural yields, logging and income.[3] The approach of the analysis was similar to that for all tropical developing countries undertaken by Barbier and Burgess (1997).

Once again, a critical issue in the deforestation analysis is the choice of dependent variable. Sufficient data now exist on forest cover in Latin America so that it is not necessary to follow the approach of Southgate (1994) and use changes in arable land as a proxy for changes in forest cover. On the other hand, as discussed above, estimating annual changes in forest cover from the FAO time series used by Cropper and Griffiths (1994) is probably too inaccurate a measure of yearly deforestation rates. The most reliable data on changes in tropical forest area are currently derived from the global Forest Resource Assessment exercise conducted every ten years by the FAO and supplemented by interim assessments (FAO and UNEP, 1982; FAO, 1988, 1993; Schmidt, 1990). Unfortunately, changes in forest area in the 1990 Assessment for many tropical countries were estimated from population growth rates over the 1980–90 period which, as argued by Cropper and Griffiths (1994), makes it impossible to employ such data in an empirical analysis of deforestation if population or population density are considered to be important explanatory variables of changing forest cover. However, FAO data on forest area (in 000 ha) for 1980 and 1985 can be used to estimate a five-yearly change in forest cover for tropical countries. The change in forest cover over 1980–85 was therefore chosen as the dependent variable for forest conversion in the analysis conducted by Barbier (2000).

The results of the analysis are shown in Table 6.6. The five-year change in forest cover is represented by the logarithm of the forest area in 1985 minus the logarithm of the forest area in 1980. This leads to a semi-logarithmic specification of the regression, as the explanatory variables are based on the initial period (1980) data.[4] Three explanatory variables proved to be significant: (i) industrial roundwood production per capita, (ii) agricultural yields, and

Table 6.6   Analysis of forest clearance in tropical Latin American countries, 1980–85

Dependent variable: five-year change in closed forest area
(log forest area 1985 – log forest area 1980)[a]

Explanatory variable	Estimated coefficients (t statistic)	Estimated elasticities
Constant	−0.1340	−0.0363
X1 Rural population density 1980	(−3.267)	−0.0380
X2 Roundwood production per capita 1980	−0.0001	0.1161
X3 Agricultural yield 1980	(−3.195)	
	−0.1923	
	(−2.965)	
	0.0578	
	(2.891)	
R² (adjusted R²): 0.511 (0.425)	F Statistic:	5.926
S.E. of regression: 0.062	No of observations:	21

Notes: [a]As the dependent variable is negative, the positive coefficient for X3 indicates that forest conversion is decreasing with a unit change in this variable, whereas the negative coefficients for X1 and X2 indicate that forest conversion is increasing with a unit change in these variables.

Source: Barbier (1998).

(iii) rural population density. Income per capita proved not to be correlated with change in forest cover across tropical Latin America, and was omitted from the regression results.[5]

The analysis indicates that industrial roundwood production and rural population pressure are positively associated with forest clearance in tropical Latin America for the 1980–85 period, that is, increasing levels of industrial roundwood production per capita and population density lead to higher rates of forest loss. These factors seemed to have about equal impacts. A 1 per cent increase in rural population density across Latin America in 1980 increased the level of tropical forest area converted over the 1980–85 period by around 0.036 per cent. Similarly, a 1 per cent increase in logging per capita led to a 0.038 per cent rise in forest clearance.[6] The positive influence of rural population density on tropical deforestation suggests that population pressure is correlated with forest clearance in Latin America. As noted above, the direct correlation between log production and deforestation over 1980–85 would confirm the results of Cropper and Griffiths (1994) that recent forestry practices and policies in Latin America have directly and indirectly encouraged forest conversion, as many studies have suggested (Amelung and Diehl, 1991; Barbier et al., 1994; Repetto and Gillis, 1988).

The analysis by Barbier (2000) also indicates that agricultural yields are negatively associated with tropical forest conversion in Latin America, i.e., improvements in overall agricultural performance appear to reduce the demand for more forest clearance (see Table 6.6). The influence of agricultural yields is the strongest of all the explanatory variables. A 1 per cent increase in agricultural yields across tropical Latin America in 1980 reduces the level of forest conversion by almost 0.12 per cent over the 1980–85 period, which is double the effect of the other two variables put together. This confirms the result of Southgate (1994) that yield increases on existing arable land in Latin America appears to offset the demand for converting and bringing new agricultural land into production, thus counteracting deforestation.

Putting together the results of the above three statistical analyses of deforestation across Latin America can provide some interesting insights into the possible relationships between rural poverty and resource degradation.

First, although an indicator for rural poverty was not included in any of the analyses, it is probably reasonable to assume that over the long term the aggregate level of rural poverty in Latin America would decline with increases in per capita income. If deforestation is negatively affected by rising per capita income in the long run as indicated by the analyses of Cropper and Griffiths (1994) and Southgate (1994), then it follows that overall economic development and thus rural poverty alleviation would act to reduce forest clearance, if not rural resource degradation generally. The converse may also be true: increasing rural resource poverty across Latin America may be positively correlated with deforestation and resource degradation. However, as pointed out by Kaimowitz (1996), rising per capita income in Latin American countries may also generate higher demand for agricultural products and provide resources for large, capital-intensive projects and subsidies to agriculture, all of which may increase deforestation. Kaimowitz found that the latter two factors may be particularly relevant in Bolivia for explaining its relatively low deforestation rates, as the country is one of the poorest in Latin America and has suffered sluggish economic growth for some time. In contrast, for a relatively wealthier country such as Mexico, the positive correlation between state-level rises in per capita income and expansion of livestock numbers, and thus deforestation, is largely attributable to the effect of rising incomes on the demand for beef and other livestock prices (Barbier and Burgess, 1996).

Second, the counteracting effect of increasing agricultural yields on deforestation and the positive correlation of rural population density on forest clearance may actually be related to the overall process of frontier agricultural expansion in Latin America, particularly with regard to the migration of poor rural house-holds to frontier forested areas. Such households are generally dependent on their land holdings as their main income-earning assets. If yields are increasing on existing agricultural land, then there is less incentive for poor households to abandon these holdings, migrate to frontier areas and convert new land. How-ever, as noted in the previous section and as illustrated particularly by Figure 6.1, a substantial proportion of Latin America's rural poor are located on marginal lands. As these lands are degraded and yields decrease, then poor households will have an incentive to migrate to the frontier and clear forest lands. The positive relationship between rural population density and deforesta-tion may in fact be picking up on the trend of increased forest conversion by migrating poor rural households in many parts of Latin America.

Finally, it was suggested that the positive relationship between logging and deforestation in Latin America could be reflecting both the direct and indirect impact of timber production on forest clearance. However, as shown in Table 6.3, the total area of closed forest currently being logged in most Latin American countries is still relatively small. Even if this logging is unsustain-able or involves substantial clear cutting, the contribution of this direct deforestation impact is probably small relative to the conversion of forest land by other activities, such as agriculture. A recent review of deforestation models has concluded that logging is generally not directly related to defor-estation in Latin America (Kaimowitz and Angelsen, 1998). The direct impact of logging on deforestation may also be limited to certain regions within Latin American countries. For example, only in the Southeast of Brazil is there evidence that logging alone is the main cause of deforestation of native forests; in the Amazon and other regions, wood extraction is mainly associ-ated with clearing forests for agriculture (Seroa da Motta, 1996).

Nevertheless, several analysts have pointed out that in Latin America tim-ber production may have a more important indirect role in deforestation by 'opening up' previously inaccessible forest lands, particularly through the construction of roads (Amelung and Diehl, 1991; Chomitz and Gray, 1994; Reis and Guzmán, 1994; Schneider et al., 1990).

Reducing the costs of access to frontier forest lands may again be an important factor in encouraging migration of poor rural households who are sensitive to such costs to these frontier areas. As Seroa da Motta (1996) has shown, in the Brazilian Amazon land conversion for agriculture and wood production are actually part of the same process. Wood extraction from frontier forests finances their clearance, and licenses obtained for agricultural clearing effectively legalises timber harvesting. In addition, by agreeing in advance to purchase wood harvested from cleared forest land, sawmills ob-tain wood supplies cheaply while at the same time providing up-front capital for land conversion.

These relationships are also supported by recent statistical analyses of deforestation in individual Latin American countries. Population pressure combined with tenure insecurity and road expansion were found to be the main factors influencing forest land clearance for agriculture in Ecuador (Southgate et al., 1991). Population pressure was also found to increase agricultural land expansion in Mexico, whereas rising state-level per capita income appears to reduce forest clearance for agriculture (Barbier and Burgess, 1996). Road building was also discovered to be highly correlated with deforestation in Belize (Chomitz and Gray, 1994) and Brazil (Reis and Guzmán, 1994).

6.4   CONCLUSION

This chapter has reviewed recent evidence of linkages between rural poverty and resource degradation in Latin America. Three regional statistical analyses of the factors contributing to deforestation across the region were also examined, and the possible influence of rural poverty on these relationships were discussed.

A major problem in examining empirically poverty–environment linkages in Latin America is the difficulty in obtaining reliable data on rural poverty rates across countries and geographical areas in the region. Nevertheless, the negative impacts of aggregate per capita income on deforestation in statistical studies across Latin America may provide some evidence that over the long term land conversion and degradation is correlated with persistent rural poverty. In addition, the counteracting effect of increasing agricultural yields on deforestation and the positive correlation of rural population density on forest clearance may actually be related to the overall process of frontier agricultural expansion in Latin America, particularly with regard to the migration of poor rural households to frontier forested areas.

However, one should not be overly optimistic in drawing policy conclusions from this evidence. Although it is fair to argue that empirical studies indicate that overall economic development and thus rural poverty alleviation would act to reduce forest clearance, if not rural resource degradation generally, it is certainly not reasonable to conclude that policies that encourage greater economic growth and rising per capita income are alone sufficient to break the rural poverty–resource degradation linkage in Latin America.

First, as the analysis by Cropper and Griffiths (1994) shows, per capita income may have to rise a great deal before deforestation in Latin America starts to level off and fall with increasing income. For example, their analysis indicates that the average regional level of income at which rates of deforestation peaks is US$5420, and Cropper and Griffiths note that most countries are at income levels well below this threshold. Moreover, given the highly skewed distribution of income across much of Latin America, it is entirely possible that a country could reach this threshold income level and still have substantial numbers of rural poor. As noted in Section 6.2, the rural poor seem to be geographically concentrated on fragile and degradable land, including forest frontier regions.

Second, as stressed throughout this chapter, the rural poverty–resource degradation linkage in Latin America appears to be highly dynamic, and possibly more complex than a direct causal relationship. For example, poverty may not be a direct cause of environmental degradation but instead may operate as a constraining factor on poorer rural households' ability to avoid resource degradation or to invest in mitigating strategies. Consequently, a rational strategy for poor rural households with limited access to capital and alternative economic opportunities may be to extract short-term rents through resource conversion and degradation, so long as there are sufficient additional resources available in frontier areas to exploit relatively cheaply and the cost of access remains low. An important 'push' factor in this dynamic may be the inability of poor rural households to compete with wealthier households in existing land, credit and resource markets in established and productive rural areas. An equally important 'pull' factor is likely to be the 'opening up' of previously inaccessible forest areas by major mining, timber and agricultural mining investments.

What appears to drive the dynamic of this rural poverty–resource degradation linkage is the prevailing set of economic institutions and incentives in Latin America, which are in turn a product of the existing policy structure (Barbier, 2000). As Heath and Binswanger (1996) have observed in Colombia, 'rural poverty, inefficient resource allocation and natural resource degradation are joint phenomena, often induced by a common nexus of policy failures', which leads to 'the concentration of impoverished populations with few investment resources on marginal lands, at tropical forest frontiers and on erodible hillsides'.

As argued by Barbier (2000), current policy distortions in Latin America reinforce this 'joint phenomena' through three principal mechanisms:

- repressing the economic returns to farming on existing agricultural land relative to the price of land in markets, so that this land is effectively 'overpriced';
- making relatively cheap and abundant frontier and marginal land more accessible for poor farmers to exploit at even low rates of economic returns, leading to effectively 'underpriced' frontier and marginal land; and
- distorting the comparative economic returns from the existing and

frontier or marginal land opportunities faced by poor rural households, thus encouraging land abandonment and migration by these households to the forest frontier and onto other marginal lands.

Clearly, these three processes are not peripheral to economic development in Latin America but represent major structural imbalances in the rural economy. Poverty alleviation in Latin America will not succeed without addressing these imbalances. This in turn implies that policy reform can no longer afford to ignore rural poverty–resource degradation linkages, and focus solely on overall macroeconomic and development policies in the hope that eventually there may be some 'trickle down' effect on reducing both rural poverty and resource degradation.

Instead, policymakers in Latin America must begin to recognise that the economic incentives determining the resource management decisions of households lie at the heart of the poverty problem, and thus must be a key focus in the design of policies to alleviate rural poverty. Existing reforms aimed at economic liberalization and removing policy distortions in agriculture may reduce some of the incentives that have led to excessive land degradation and forest conversion. However, more targeted policies and investment are required to raise the comparative returns to existing agricultural lands, improve the access of poor rural households to land and credit markets, extend key infrastructure, extension and marketing services to the rural poor, and remove tax and pricing distortions that benefit mainly wealthier farmers and landowners.

NOTES

1. The few countries in Table 6.3 which show an expansion of forest area over 1981–90, include Chile, Cuba and Uruguay, all of which have expanded plantation and/or reforestation efforts.
2. That is, the usual procedure is for a country to survey (at best) its forest resources every five years, say 1975, 1980 and 1985, and to use these periodic surveys to calculate the annual average rate of deforestation for the intervening years. Estimates of the forest resource base for these intervening years are adjusted accordingly. For many developing countries, the gap between accurate surveying of their forest stock and measurements of rates of deforestation has been much longer, particularly before 1980. Thus the most recent global assessment of tropical forest resources conducted by FAO (1993) has concluded: 'So far a statistically designed pan-tropical forest survey has not been attempted ... There is considerable variation among regions with respect to completeness and quality of the information, with Asia faring better than tropical America and the latter better than tropical Africa ... It is unlikely that the state and change information on forest cover area and biomass could be made available on a statistically reliable basis at the regional or global levels within the next ten or twenty years unless a concerted effort is made to enhance the country capacity in forest inventory and monitoring.'
3. Tropical counties are taken to be those countries with the majority of their land mass lying

between the tropics. This definition does not distinguish between moist and dry forests that lie between the tropics. The 21 tropical Latin American countries used in the analysis include all the countries listed in Table 6.3, with the exceptions of Argentina, Chile and Uruguay (considered predominantly temperate) and Cuba (data limitations).

4. A second version of the regression model was also run, representing the five yearly change in forest cover by the ratio of forest area in 1985 to forest area in 1980. This leads to a linear specification of the model. Although the second linear version is not shown here, it yields similar elasticities for the explanatory variables and overall explanatory power as the semi-log version depicted in Table 6.6. As a check on these two versions of the model, another linear specification of the regression equation was run using the percentage change in forest area (that is the change in closed forest area from 1980 to 1985 divided by closed forest area in 1980) as an alternative dependent variable. This third regression yielded virtually the same results as the linear regression with the ratio of 1985 to 1980 closed forest areas as the dependent variable. Thus it appears that using the latter ratio as the dependent variable is a good approximation of the half-decade rate of deforestation. It follows that the log of this ratio will also serve as a good approximation.

5. The t-statistic for real income per capita was 1.2258; however, inclusion of the variable also reduced the significance of agricultural yields in the regression (t = 1.295) as well as the overall explanatory power of the regression. In addition, the sample size was reduced to 19 countries, as observations on income were not available in 1980 for Belize and Suriname. The data for industrial non-coniferous roundwood production are taken from FAO Yearbook of Forest Products (FAO, 1992b), and were expressed in per capita terms (m^3/total population) in the model. Real gross national product per capita in 1980 (in US$/1000) and population density in 1980 (people/1000 ha) are derived from World Bank (1992). The indicator for agricultural yield is approximated by cereal output per unit of cereal production area in 1980 (mt/ha) and is based on data from FAO (1992a).

6. Several alternatives were also tried for these two explanatory variables. For example, following Cropper and Griffiths (1994), industrial roundwood export unit values expressed in terms of domestic currencies were used as an alternative to per capita industrial roundwood production. The former proved to reduce the overall significance of the regression by one half, and in itself was not significant: (t = 0.163516). Using border-equivalent log export prices may be inappropriate in this analysis because only just under 0.2 per cent of industrial roundwood production in tropical Central and South America is exported, the widespread prevalence of price distortions and policy interventions in the forestry industry of the region has probably meant that there is little relationship between border-equivalent log prices and actual domestic prices faced by loggers. Total population and total population density were also used as alternative variables for rural population density in the analysis, but these alternatives again proved to be less significant.

REFERENCES

Amelung, T. and Diehl, M. (1991), *Deforestation of Tropical Rainforests: Economic Causes and Impact on Development*, Tubingen: Mohr. (Kieler Studien 241).

Barbier, E.B. (1997), 'The economic determinants of land degradation in developing countries', *Philosophical Transactions of the Royal Society B*, 352, 891–9.

Barbier, E.B. (2000), 'Rural Poverty and Natural Resource Degradation', in: R. López and A. Valdés (eds), *Rural Poverty in Latin America*, New York: St Martin's Press, 152–84.

Barbier, E.B. and Burgess, J.C. (1996), 'Economic analysis of deforestation in Mexico', *Environment and Development Economics*, **1** (2), 203–40.

Barbier, E.B. and Burgess, J.C. (1997), 'The economic analysis of tropical forest land use options', *Land Economics*, **73** (2), 174–95.

Barbier, E.B., Burgess, J.C., Bishop, J.T. and Aylward, B.A. (1994), 'The Economics of the Tropical Timber Trade', London: Earthscan Publications.

Chomitz, K.M. and Gray, D.A. (1995), *Roads, Lands, Markets and Deforestation*, Washington, DC: The World Bank, Policy Research Department (Policy Research Working Paper, 1444).

Cropper, M. and Griffiths, C. (1994), 'The interaction of population growth and environmental quality', *American Economic Review, Papers and Proceedings*, **2** (84), 250–54.

Food and Agricultural Organization (FAO) (1988), *An Interim Report on the State of Forest Resources in Developing Countries*, Rome: FAO.

Food and Agricultural Organization (FAO) (1992a), *1991 Production Yearbook*, v. 45, Rome: FAO.

Food and Agricultural Organization (FAO) (1992b), *1990 Yearbook of Forest Products, 1978–1990*, Rome: FAO.

Food and Agricultural Organization (FAO) (1993), *Forest Resources Assessment 1990: Tropical Countries*, Rome: FAO.

Food and Agricultural Organization (FAO) and United Nations Environment Programme (UNEP) (1982), *Tropical Forest Resources Assessment Project*, Rome: FAO.

Heath, J. and Binswanger, H. (1996), 'Natural resource degradation effects of poverty and population growth are largely policy-induced: the case of Columbia', *Environment and Development Economics*, 1, 65–83.

Kaimowitz, D. (1996), *Factors Determining Low Deforestation: Insights from the Bolivian Amazon*, Bogor, Indonesia: Center for International Forestry Research, mimeo.

Kaimowitz, D. and Angelsen, A. (1998), *Economic Models of Tropical Deforestation: a Review*, Bogor, Indonesia: Center for International Forestry Research.

Leonard, H.J., Yudelman, M., Stryker, J.D., Browder, J.O., De Boer, A.J., Campbell, T. and Jolly, A. (1989), *Environment and the Poor: Development Strategies for a Common Agenda*, New Brunswick, NJ: Transaction Books.

López, R. and Valdés, A. (eds) (2000), *Rural Poverty in Latin America*, New York: St Martin's Press, 343.

Mahar, D. and Schneider, R.R. (1994), 'Incentives for tropical deforestation: some examples from Latin America', in: K. Brown and D.W. Pearce (eds), *The Causes of Tropical Deforestation*, London: University College London Press.

Oldeman, L.R., Van Engelen, V.W.P. and Pulles, J.H.M. (1990), 'The Extent of Human-Induced Soil Degradation', Annex 5, in: L.R. Oldeman, R.T.A. Hakkeling and W.G. Sombroek (eds), *World Map of the Status of Human-Induced Soil Erosion: an Explanatory Note*, 2nd edn, Wageningen, The Netherlands: International Soil Reference and Information Centre.

Reis, E. and Guzmán, R. (1994), 'An Econometric Model of Amazonian Deforestation', in: K. Brown and D.W. Pearce (eds), *The Causes of Tropical Deforestation*, London: University College London Press.

Repetto, R. and Gillis, M. (1988), *Public Policies and the Misuse of Forest Resources*, Cambridge: Cambridge University Press.

Schmidt, R. (1990), 'Sustainable management of tropical moist forests', ASEAN Sub-Regional Seminar, Indonesia.

Schneider, R.R. (1994), *Government and the Economy on the Amazon Frontier*, Washington, DC: The World Bank, Latin America and the Caribbean Technical Department (Regional Studies Program, Report n.34)

Schneider, R., Veríssimo, A. and Viana, V. (1991), 'Logging and Tropical Forest Conservation', mimeo, Brasília: The World Bank/IMAZON.

Seroa da Motta, R. (1997), 'The economics of biodiversity in Brazil: the case of forest conversion', in: OECD, *OECD Proceedings: Investing in Biological Diversity – The Cairns Conference*, Paris: OECD, 283–304.

Southgate, D. (1994), 'Tropical Deforestation and Agricultural Development in Latin America', in: K. Brown and D.W. Pearce (eds), *The Causes Of Tropical Deforestation*, London: University College London Press.

Southgate, D., Sierra, R. and Brown, L. (1991), 'The causes of tropical deforestation in Ecuador: a statistical analysis', *World Development*, **19** (9), September, 1145–51.

Sunderlin, W.D. and Rodrígez, J.A. (1996), *Cattle, Broadleaf Forests and the Agricultural Modernization Law of Honduras*, Jakarta, Indonesia: CIFOR, Center for International Forestry Research, (Occasional Paper, n. 7).

World Bank (1992), *World Bank Tables*, Washington, DC: World Bank.

World Resources Institute (1992), *World Resources 1992–93*, New York: Oxford University Press.

World Resource Institute (1994), *World Resources 1994–95*, New York: Oxford University Press.

7. Public policies and deforestation in the Brazilian Amazon*

Carlos Eduardo Frickmann Young

7.1 THE CAUSES OF MIGRATION AND DEFORESTATION IN THE BRAZILIAN AMAZON

The literature on Brazilian development has consistently emphasised the damaging social and economic consequences of land tenure concentration. Production on tiny properties – 'minifúndios' – tends to be insufficient to afford subsistence levels of wellbeing to all members of the family. Extra income, obtained from labouring in cash-oriented farms, is often necessary to complement the household budget. On the other hand, very large estates – 'latifúndios' – are not labour-intensive. Seasonal demand for extra labour during planting and harvesting is easily covered by landless agricultural workers, hired on a daily basis (*bóias-frias*). As a consequence of both effects, the rural labour market tends to be unstable and seasonal, unable to employ all the labour surplus. Squatting and other forms of land conflict, and migration to open access land in the frontier or to urban centres, become the ultimate options for the landless agricultural work force.

Historically, the expansion of the agricultural frontier into forest areas has been used as a 'safety valve' to accommodate landless farmers. Therefore, forest areas have been reduced considerably in the Southeast, South and part of the Northeast regions, where agricultural activities have been established for a long time. The strategy of 'peopleless land for landless people', rather than agrarian reform in already occupied land, was pursued with particular intensity during the military regime (1964–85). Consequently, there was a considerable population increase in the North and Centre-West regions, which embraces almost all of the Brazilian Amazon. Because of internal migration, these regions presented population growth rates considerably higher than the national average. This 'solution' was important for two crucial problems faced by the national security strategy: it would enforce Brazilian sovereignty over the Amazon and it would decrease the political instability caused by land conflicts in many places in the country.

The migration boom corresponded to the acceleration of deforestation in the Amazonian states. In spite of the fact that there has been a reduction in the speed at which the forest has been converted into agricultural areas, the total area being deforested is still alarming. For a better comprehension of this process, it is important to understand the contribution of specific governmental policies that directly or indirectly resulted in the acceleration of deforestation.

Export Promotion Policies

Export promotion policies had a decisive influence on the process of pushing migrants to the Amazon (Almeida, 1992). One important strategy for increasing export revenues was the expansion of large-scale modern crop cultivation in the traditional family-based agriculture in the South and in the more recently occupied Centre-West *cerrado* (savannah) region. Large-scale modernisation reduced the demand for labour: the regions with higher level of mechanisation presented negative rates of rural population growth in the periods 1960–70 (Southeast) and 1970–80 (Southeast and South).

At the same time, export incentives and other support to the expansion of commercial production resulted in a considerable increase in land prices in the South and Southeast. This constituted an incentive to small farmers to sell land in the South and buy larger properties at the agricultural frontier. This led to a speculative boom in land prices, which only stopped with the explosion of the real interest rate in the late 1980s. During the 1970s and early 1980s, the agricultural rental ratio to land prices fell systematically. This is an indication that the appreciation of land prices cannot be entirely explained by increasing returns of productivity which are usually captured in the value of the rental: much of the land price appreciation was a result of speculation about future prices, combined with the macroeconomic uncertainty which led to an increasing demand for real (non-monetary) assets.

Moved by the possibility of buying much larger properties with the profits obtained from selling their original farms, southern settlers first moved to the *cerrados* in the Centre-West region, which proved to be particularly suitable to soybean cultivation, a major export crop. After some time, land prices in this region also increased following the grain production boom. More recently, areas in the south of the North region were occupied, especially in Rondônia.

This expansion of the commercial agriculture frontier northwards results in a similar movement of the social frontier, that is the subsistence or small-scale farming settlements which occupied the land previously. Given their lower opportunity costs, subsistence farmers were willing to sell their plots of land to the newcomers, and move into the Amazon.

Regional Development Programmes

From the government perspective, there was no separation of the goals of intensifying national integration, promoting regional development and the economic benefits expected from such policies. Population growth and economic expansion were seen as synonymous, and the historical vocation of the Amazonian economy was considered to be one of serving international markets. Therefore, it is not surprising that the objectives of improving exports or attracting foreign capital were always used as justifications for the policies carried out. The adopted framework of infrastructure, land concessions, fiscal and credit subsidies followed the typical approach of Brazilian industrialisation since the 1930s: public incentives were anticipated in order to attract private investment.

The most important incentives to the Amazon region were the establishment of a road building network (the Belém-Brasília road being the North–South axis and the Transamazônica road the East–West axis), colonisation projects (governmental and private), investment in regional development programmes (POLONOROESTE, Carajás) , and economic incentives to agricultural, ranching and logging activities.

The relationship between agricultural policy and deforestation is not as simple as usually presented in the literature. Policies supporting agricultural production may increase the demand for land, encouraging the expansion of the agricultural frontier through the incorporation of previously forested land. Nevertheless, the economic failure of agriculture in settlement areas, together with increasing rural poverty, may result in migration towards unoccupied forest areas.

This problem is referred to by many authors discussing the problems of colonisation, particularly in Rondônia (Mahar, 1988; Wilson and Alicbusan-Schwab, 1991; Redwood III, 1993). Coffee, cocoa and other perennial crops were considered a good protection for fragile soils against leaching and erosion. Planners believed that perennial plantations would provide a solid foundation for a mixed small farm agriculture incorporating food and cash crops, avoiding the need for further migrations. Therefore, special credit lines were set up for coffee cultivation, to compensate the lag between planting and the first harvest (3–5 years), and the high costs in terms of labour and non-labour inputs. However, before the coffee could be harvested, these credit lines were cut. At the same time, the costs of non-labour inputs increased, and tough monetary policies resulted in very high interest rates for normal credit operations. Because of the high costs involved and the fall of the international price, many coffee plantations were abandoned after some years, being converted to annual plantations or replaced by pastures.

The same dilemma is present in the debate about road building and other infrastructure programmes affecting settlements in the Amazon. Roads are an important incentive to migration to areas recently cleared, since it lowers transportation costs considerably. But, again, there is another side in the debate. The lack of infrastructure reduces the incentive to the settler to invest in farming practices that present results in the long term, such as soil conservation and erosion control. Thus, impoverished farmers may be encouraged to 'mine' the natural resource allowance of their plots – selling timber extraction rights and slash-and-burn cultivation of annual crops provide profits only in the first years of occupation. Once the resource allowance is depleted to the point where subsistence can no longer be assured, they sell their plots (if they have property rights) to buy cheaper land, or just move to 'mine' new plots of unoccupied forest land.

This point of view is highlighted mainly by the authors studying the colonisation process:

> In addition to constraints of an ecological nature, the small farmers in the Marechal Dutra project had also to cope with a lack of feeder roads or the lack of maintenance of these roads once they are constructed. Poor transport infrastructure is a problem that has been cited in nearly all case studies of settlement projects throughout the Amazon. (Wilson and Alicbusan-Schwab, 1991, p. 9)

Austerity Measures and their Implication over the Labour Market

Migration flows were also affected by the economic slowdown and successive recession periods in the last twenty years. Workers suffered from declining real wages and increasing unemployment caused by policies to reduce real wages, particularly in the 1980s. The urban poor were the most affected by redundancies, falling real income and cutbacks in social expenditure. Therefore, the traditional destination of the Southern and Northeastern rural exodus became less attractive than the Northern 'Eldorado', where people were believed to succeed very quickly. This phenomenon, aggravated by the expansion of mineral prospecting activities (*garimpo*) in areas such as the gold-rich Serra Pelada, allied to the official propaganda, disseminated the image of 'getting rich' in the Amazon at a time most Brazilians were severely affected by the economic crisis.

Another consequence of restrictive monetary policies was the gradual withdrawal of subsidised credit to agriculture, resulting in a significant growth in the number of indebted farmers. Selling land to pay financial arrears also contributed to move farmers northwards. This point is closely connected to the issue of agricultural policy, discussed in the next sub-section.

Recession depressed wages and reduced employment, thus lowering the opportunity cost of labour. This induced migration to the Amazon because, despite the hardship of life in the frontier, the settlers were more likely to succeed and accumulate wealth there than if they had decided to risk their chances in the urban labour market or stayed in the poorer rural areas in the Northeast.[1] This view is supported by empirical evidence showing that the probability of a settler being economically successful was considerably higher in the Amazon than in most of the other places migrants were likely to move in, considering the level of education and capital allowance (FAO/UNDP/MARA, 1992). However, there were many problems to be faced concerning the lack of assistance and the hardship of getting established, and health risks were especially higher.

The adjustment objective of reducing the public deficit implied higher constraints faced by the public agencies responsible for controlling encroachment in protected areas. For example, in the POLONOROESTE programme, colonisation projects were expanded at the same time the official agencies responsible for the control of Amerindian and ecological preservation areas suffered drastic cutbacks.

A considerable part of the Amazon is officially designated as either reserves or parks (over 1.1 million km^2 if indigenous reserves are included). However, it was estimated that, in the early 1990s, only one park guard was available, on average, for 6161 km^2 of parks and reserves (World Bank, 1992). The evident lack of control results in poaching or even clearing of preserved forest land, and the continuation of illegal trade of endangered fauna and flora species. The violence surrounding the encroachment of protected areas and indigenous reserves has become widely known by the tragic assassination of Chico Mendes, a leader of rubber tappers in the state of Acre. Because of his fight for the establishment of extractivist reserves in areas coveted by local landowners, there was a plot which resulted in his murder.

The lack of control over protected areas is part of a larger problem of law enforcement in the Amazon. The issue of privatisation of land ownership is particularly important, and is a major issue in the debate about the institutional causes of deforestation. As discussed previously, the formal or informal colonisation of the Amazon was a safety valve against claims for proper agrarian reforms. One instrument was the concession of tenure rights after the occupation of state-owned land (*terras devolutas*). According to the legislation, one year was usually enough to assure the land title and after a few more years the land could be sold. The possibilities of capital gains with reselling the land added fuel to the race for property rights, and deforestation was a main source of enforcing land claims: the actual productivity of the economic activity carried out after deforestation might be low, but the asset value was increased by the expectation of higher land prices (Almeida and Campari, 1994). In other words:

Rather than the agricultural suitability of land and settlers, the problem is better understood by focusing on the supply and demand for property rights. (Mueller et: al., 1994, p. 274)

7.2   EMPIRICAL EXERCISE: THE CONTRIBUTION OF ADJUSTMENT POLICIES TO DEFORESTATION, BRAZIL: 1970–85

The discussion in the previous section provides the theoretical background for an empirical exercise that tests the contribution of adjustment-related variables to the process of deforestation. The selected policies refer, directly or indirectly, to the economic incentives to land clearing in Brazil. Two are directly related to the profitability of agriculture: agricultural pricing and agricultural credit. The link between road building and deforestation is more indirect, through changes in transportation costs. Finally, two other variables were chosen because of their strong connection with the macroeconomic management: rural wages and land prices. Rural wages are related to the official stipulation of minimum wages and the overall performance of the economy (in the sense that recessionary policies depress labour markets, therefore reducing the opportunity cost of labour and favouring migration to the frontier). Land price increases in the 1970s and 1980s were connected to the boom in the agricultural export sector, which resulted in the expansion of the 'economic' frontier, notably the cultivation of soybeans in the South-western borders of the Amazon.

Selected Policies

Agricultural credit and pricing policies
The existence of special credit lines with negative real interest rates has been frequently pointed out as a major cause of deforestation (see the discussion in Section 7.1). Furthermore, considerable incentives were directed to one of the most damaging activities in environmental terms: cattle ranching. The consequences were doubly perverse: it represented an additional direct source of deforestation (forest being converted into pastures), and changed the existing pattern of land use in areas already cleared, encouraging the shift from less damaging activities, such as perennial plantations. The introduction of tighter monetary policies in the 1980s has reduced both the total amount of credit and the implicit subsidy of the real interest rate. Therefore, a positive relationship between credit and deforestation would provide an argument in favour of the hypothesis that adjustment policies tend to favour the preservation of the forest.

However, this position should be balanced by the consideration of pricing policies as a main incentive to agricultural production. One of the most important elements of adjustment policies refers to the removal of the bias against agriculture through the realignment of relative prices. In the Brazilian case, this has been done through the adoption of more 'realistic' indexation instruments to defend agricultural prices against rampant inflation. This has more than compensated the retraction of credit lines and incentives, and was a major factor in the agricultural boom in the 1980s. Therefore, a positive relationship between agricultural prices and deforestation reverses the previous conclusion, in the sense that adjustment had indeed contributed to forest land clearing.

Road building

The previous discussion shows that deforestation is expected to increase in areas where the road network is expanded, despite some controversy about the impacts on other regions. The cutbacks in public spending affected the completion of the planned road structure for the Amazon. This would have represented a positive contribution of adjustment policies to curb the process of deforestation.

Rural wages

The Brazilian government adopted explicit measures to reduce real wages during much of the 1980s. This policy was part of the stabilisation strategy of reducing aggregate demand and import requirements. The policy of reducing real wages combined with the overall recession induced by very high interest rates resulted in a contraction of the labour market. The reduction of employment opportunities and the depreciation of the minimum wage, a main reference for the unskilled labour force, represented a double incentive to the deforestation process: directly because it reduced the labour cost, particularly important in land clearing decisions, and indirectly because it restricted the possibilities of landless rural workers succeeding in the labour market, turning migration to the frontier into a more attractive option. In other words, the reduction in real wages and other stabilisation policies contributed to the increase in the level of poverty, which resulted in extra pressure for consumption of quasi-open natural resources (forests): the expansion of deforestation is the other side of the same process of increasing social exclusion and violence which exploded in urban centres in Brazil since the 1980s.

Land prices

Land prices are not directly determined by governmental action, but the role of agricultural and other government policies is essential to their formation. The adjustment objective resulted in export incentives and other agricultural promotion policies have influenced land prices positively. Since most of the boom was concentrated in the South and Southeast regions, it initially resulted in an increasing discrepancy between property prices in different regions. This process has added fuel to speculation in the land market, which is also blamed as a major cause of deforestation.

Description of the Variables

Deforestation (dependent variable)
There is a wide controversy about the proper measurement of deforestation in the Amazon (Fearnside, 1993a,b). The most precise method is based on screening satellite images. However, many difficulties undermine the use of direct estimates of deforestation. First, there are considerable discrepancies in the way the images are obtained and interpreted. Second, systematic observations exist only for the period 1987–91, with just one observation in the 1970s (1978).

Instead, a proxy based on the expansion of agricultural density (*DE*: total agricultural area divided by the total state area) according to the agricultural censuses has been used to estimate deforestation (similar proxies were used by Reis and Margulis, 1991; and Reis and Guzmán, 1994). These censuses were carried out in the years 1970, 1975, 1980 and 1985. Therefore, it was possible to estimate deforestation as the expansion of agricultural area during these years according to the same methodological principles.

One important consideration refers to the use of observations for states outside the Amazon. This procedure was adopted for two main reasons: the expansion of the frontier in the Amazon is the final stage of the land conversion process started in the other regions of the country; and the use of data for other states increases the number of observations, therefore improving the statistical quality of the analysis.

Another problem concerned the states which suffered partition or fusion during the period. To avoid this problem, the following states and territories were kept unified: Rio de Janeiro and Guanabara, Mato Grosso and Mato Grosso do Sul, Pernambuco and Fernando de Noronha, and Goiás and Tocantins. Given its very small size, the Federal District (Brasília) was also considered part of Goiás.

Agricultural credit
Agricultural credit density (*CR*) was estimated by the total credit destined to agricultural activities divided by the total area of the state. The primary source of data was the Brazilian Central Bank, and the values were deflated by the general price index (IGP-FGV).

Agricultural prices

An index for agricultural prices (*PA*) was built using data from the agricultural censuses (1970–80) and the statistical yearbook (1985), both published by IBGE. The index considered the four more important crops to small farmers: beans, rice, cassava and corn. Market prices for each crop were obtained dividing the total value of production by the total output (in physical units). A (Paasche) nominal price index was created, assuming the national average in 1980 as the basis. Finally, a real price index was estimated dividing the nominal indices by the implicit GDP deflator.

Road building

Road density (*RO*) was calculated by dividing the total extension of roads (as presented in the IBGE censuses) by the total area of the state.

Rural wages and land prices

The (nominal) indices for land prices (*PL*) and agricultural wages (*WA*) were taken from the agricultural survey, carried out every semester by the Fundação Getúlio Vargas. The values were taken from the series of prices for cultivated land and the cost of hiring temporary labour, respectively. The year value was obtained by the average value observed during the year (usually, one observation per semester).[2] The implicit GDP deflator was again used to convert the series into real values.

Estimation Procedures and Results

The contribution of the selected variables to the deforestation process, as discussed above, is summarised by equation (7.1).

$$DE = f(CR^+, PA^+, RO^+, WA^-, PL^+) \tag{7.1}$$

A panel data regression was carried out in order to test the impact of policy-related variables to deforestation, according to the data described in the previous sub-section. Equation (7.2) presents the functional form chosen for the demand for agricultural land in state i at time t, considering A_i as a constant referring to the specific conditions of state i.

$$DE_{i,t} = A_i \cdot PA_{i,t}^{\alpha_1} \cdot PL_{i,t}^{\alpha_2} \cdot WA_{i,t}^{\alpha_3} \cdot CR_{i,t}^{\alpha_4} \cdot RO_{i,t}^{\alpha_5} \tag{7.2}$$

The deforestation problem is essentially a flow problem, therefore the dependent variable is better expressed in terms of change in time. Applying logarithms, and using the notation x_t to represent $\ln(X_t/X_{t-1}) = \ln X_t - \ln X_{t-1}$, this equation can be transformed into a linear relation:

Table 7.1 Regression results

Variable	Coefficient	Std. error	t	P > |t|	[95% Conf. interval]	
pa (agric. prices)	0.1604414	0.061041	2.628	0.011	0.0380088	0.2828741
pl (land prices)	0.1681642	0.0679067	2.476	0.016	0.0319606	0.3043679
wa (rural wages)	−0.4117057	0.2002435	−2.056	0.045	−0.8133432	−0.0100682
cr (rural credit)	0.3752031	0.0658824	5.695	0.000	0.2430598	0.5073464
ro (road building)	0.4072768	0.0799577	5.094	0.000	0.246902	0.567516
dummy 75/80	0.4374081	0.077124	5.671	0.000	0.282717	0.5920992
dummy 80/85	0.3933003	0.1236985	3.180	0.002	0.1451936	0.641407
Constant	−0.2514704	0.1016744	0.2.473	0.017	−0.4554304	−0.0475373
Number of observations	61					
R-square	0.5526					
Adj. R-square	0.4935					
Root MSE	0.1573					

$$de_{i,t} = \alpha_1 \cdot pa_{i,t} + \alpha_2 \cdot pl_{i,t} + \alpha_3 \cdot wa_{i,t} + \alpha_4 \cdot cr_{i,t} + \alpha_5 \cdot ro_{i,t} \qquad (7.3)$$

The regression was based on equation (7.3), with the addition of a constant term, time dummies for the periods 1975–80 and 1980–85, and the stochastic error. The results are presented in Table 7.1 and are consistent with the conclusions from the theoretical analysis.[3]

The variation in time of the agricultural area (proxy for deforestation) is positively related to the change in time of agricultural prices, credit, road building and land prices, and inversely related to the variation of rural wages. Both time dummies are positively related to deforestation, suggesting that there were other factors contributing to deforestation in the 1975–80 and 1980–85 periods which were not captured by the model. All results are significative at the 5 per cent level of confidence.

7.4   CONCLUSION

The empirical exercise confirms that the relationship between deforestation and the objectives of structural adjustment and stabilisation is not straightforward. Table 7.2 summarises the inferred linkages between both: there are pros and cons.

Table 7.2   Public policies and deforestation

Policies which favoured deforestation	Policies which discouraged deforestation
• Appreciation of agricultural prices	• Reduction of subsidised agricultural credit
• Depreciation of the real minimum wages and other policies aimed at the reduction of labour costs	• Reduction of road building
• Export and other incentives which led to land price appreciation	

It is very difficult to deduce from quantitative analysis the total 'net' impact of such policies because there is no overwhelming support for the hypothesis that adjustment programmes tend to favour natural resource conservation, or the other way round. Perhaps a better way to conclude this chapter is through a qualitative interpretation of the deforestation problem, focusing the debate on the policymakers' perspective over the Amazon.

The nature and motivations behind the occupation of the Amazon are not static but change over time. The importance of government intervention that directly favoured settlements, such as subsidies and infrastructure facilities, gradually decreased. Instead, the interference became more indirect but no less important: the economic incentives posed by the rent-seeking possibilities were enough to dispense with the direct facilities structure elaborated in the early years of the military regime. Empirical studies clearly indicated that cultivation, ranching and logging activities became far more profitable than usually thought (for a review see Young and Fausto, 1998).

The problem is that this shift in the orientation of public policies has not reverted the mechanisms that lead to the land-clearing process. In that sense, despite the differences between them, both the market-oriented policies adopted since the 1980s and the previous interventionist policies can be considered responsible for setting up economic motivations that intrinsically favour deforestation.

To understand this apparent paradox, it is important to highlight the role of institutional failures. There has been some improvement in the environmental legislation, mainly caused by the 1988 Brazilian Constitution, and the increasing domestic and international awareness with environmental issues reached its peak during the 1992 Rio Summit (see Seroa da Motta, 1993). Legislation concerning land taxation has been modified, in order to accept forest areas as productive land, reducing the respective tax rate. The concession of fiscal incentives has been altered by the introduction of a new law in 1991, which restricts the application of the remaining incentives to areas approved by the ecological–economic zoning, and under the consent of IBAMA, the National Indian Foundation (FUNAI) and other federal agencies. The ecological–economic zoning is a (federal) constitutional requirement to discriminate areas to be devoted to preservation or to sustainable economic use. The zoning is intended to orient the application of incentives and public investment in the region, harmonising the government actions concerning the Amazon. The zoning procedure would provide detailed assessment of selected regions, where land uses are to be defined, and present corrective actions designed to protect specific areas under critical pressure.

Nevertheless, given the interests involved, it is not surprising that the conclusion of the ecological–economic zoning is well behind schedule. The delay in the completion of the zoning and many bureaucratic problems have resulted in the persistence of the concessions on an *ad hoc* basis to ranching and sawmill activities. Moreover, it is important to consider that most of these advances refer to the federal government, which lacks the capacity or will to enforce them. State and municipal governments are much slower in terms of incorporating considerations about the environment and indigenous population, and even less concerned about the effective application of the new legislation.

Another important point that has yet to be properly addressed refers to legal enforcement. In legal terms, there is no open access land in the Amazonian territory. However, the government practice of land concessions and the widespread corruption and falsification of land titles resulted in a situation of 'quasi-open' access land. This uncertainty about land rights is repeatedly referred to as a main contributor to deforestation. When land rights are not well defined, the time horizon of the farmer is reduced considerably. The capital losses caused by the 'mining' of natural resources are not incorporated as profit losses, and the deforestation cost is reduced only to short-term expenditures that assume monetary values. Long-term losses and non-market values are ignored in this equation.

The conclusion is that institutional reforms are essential to correct this failure. The concession of land to large projects should be stopped, and only the entitlement of small farmers should continue, but with mechanisms to reduce turnover and speculative claims on land. This would contribute to the slowing down of deforestation and the promotion of social justice if the conditions are provided to agriculture to perform better than land speculation. Promoting agriculture in the old frontiers, through improving transportation, commercialisation and other infrastructure investments, should be combined with direct measures against deforestation and land speculation. Taxation of the capital gains on land transactions, higher stumpage fees, levying fines and other measures would provide a mix of economic and legal discouragement to speculative land clearing.

Another suggestion in favour of forest conservation is the introduction of payments for carbon sequestration and biodiversity preservation, in a way that the international community compensates local farmers for the benefits which are globally captured. If compensation is paid to landowners who decide to preserve forested areas, the foregone revenues with deforestation are increased. The user cost of deforestation becomes higher, thus establishing more incentive to reduce land clearing. However, this system can only operate properly if the issue of land rights is clearly settled.

NOTES

*   This article is based on part of my Ph.D. Dissertation 'Economic adjustment policies and the environment: a case study for Brazil', with the financial support of CAPES. This work was only possible thanks to the helpful comments by my supervisor, Professor David Pearce, and all the other friends that helped me during my stay at the University College London.
1.   An indirect indication that small-scale agricultural production has been successful in the

Amazon relatively to other regions is the fact that the Gini coefficient for land concentration in the North region is smaller than the Brazilian average, and fell systematically between 1975 and 1985 (Schneider, 1994).
2. After their partition, it was considered the average value between Mato Grosso and Mato Grosso do Sul, and Goiás and Tocantins.
3. Because of heteroscedasticity problems, White's method was used to produce robust standard errors (Greene, 1993). This made possible appropriate inferences based on the results of least squares without actually specifying the type of heteroscedasticity. If the ordinary standard errors, the coefficient estimates would be the same, but the confidence level would be slightly different: 10 per cent for rural wages, and 5 per cent to all other variables. For methodological details, see Young (1997).

BIBLIOGRAPHY

Almeida, A.L. Ozório de (1992), *The Colonisation of* the *Amazon*, Austin: University of Texas Press.

Almeida, A.L. Ozório de and Campari, J. (1994), *Sustainable Settlement in the Amazon*, Washington, DC: The World Bank (Education and Social Policy Department Discussion Paper, n.26).

Binswanger, H.P. (1989), *Brazilian Policies that Encourage Deforestation in the Amazon*, Washington, DC: World Bank (Environment Department Working Paper, n.16).

Browder, J. (1985), *Subsidies, Deforestation, and the Forest Sector of the Brazilian Amazon*, Washington, DC: World Resources Institute.

Brown, K. and Pearce, D. (eds) (1994), *The Causes of Tropical Deforestation*, London: University College London Press.

FAO/UNDP/MARA (1992), *Principais Indicadores Sócio-econômicos dos Assentamentos de Reforma Agrária*, Brasília: FAO/PNUD/MARA, Projeto BRA-87/022.

Fearnside, P.M. (1993a), 'Deforestation in Brazilian Amazonia: the effect of population and land tenure', *Ambio*, **22** (8), 537–45.

Fearnside, P.M. (1993b), 'Desmatamento na Amazonia: quem tem razão nos cálculos – O INPE ou a Nasa?', *Ciência Hoje*, **16** (96), 6–8.

Greene, W.H. (1993), *Econometric Analysis*, New York: Macmillan.

Mahar, D. (1988), *Government Policies and Deforestation in Brazil's Amazon Region*, Washington, DC: The World Bank. (Environment Department Working Paper, n.7).

Mahar, D. (1992), *Government Policies and Deforestation in Brazil's Amazon Region*, Washington, DC: The World Bank.

Mahar, D. and Schneider, R. (1994), 'Incentives for Tropical Deforestation: some Examples from Latin America', in: K. Brown and D. Pearce (eds), *The Causes of Tropical Deforestation*, London: University College London Press.

Mueller, B., Alston, L., Libecap, G.D. and Schneider, R. (1994), 'Land, property rights and privatization in Brazil', *Quarterly Review of Economics and Finance*, 34, (summer), 261–80, special issue.

Redwood III, J. (1993), *World Bank Approaches to the Environment: in Brazil a Review of Selected Projects*, Washington, DC: The World Bank, Operations Evaluation Department Study.

Reis, E.J. and Guzmán, R. (1994), 'An Econometric Model of Amazon Deforestation', in: K. Brown and D.W. Pearce (eds), *The Causes of Tropical Deforestation*, London: University College London Press.

Reis, E.J. and Margulis, S. (1991), 'Economic perspectives on deforestation in Brazilian Amazon', Paper presented at the Annual Meeting of the EARE, Stockholm, June 10–14, 1991.

Schneider, R. (1994), *Government: and the Economy on the Amazon Frontier*, Washington, DC: The World Bank (LAC Regional Studies Program, Report n.34).

Seroa da Motta R. (1993), *Policy Issues concerning Tropical Deforestation in Brazil*, Rio de Janeiro: IPEA.

Seroa da Motta R. da and May, P.H. (1992), *Loss in Forest Resource Values due to Agricultural Land Conversion in Brazil*, Rio de Janeiro: IPEA (Discussion Paper, n.248).

Southgate, D. (1990), 'The causes of land degradation along "spontaneously" expanding agricultural frontiers in the Third World', *Land Economics*, **66** (1), 93–101.

Southgate, D. and Pearce, D.W. (1988), *Agricultural Colonisation and Environmental Degradation in Frontier Developing Economies*, Washington, DC: World Bank. (Environment Department, Working Paper n.9).

Wilson, J.F and Alicbusan-Schwab, A. (1991), *Development Policies and Health: Farmers, Goldminers and Slums in the Brazilian Amazon*, Washington, DC: World Bank (Environment Department, Working Paper n.18).

World Bank (1992), Brazil: an Analysis of *Environmental Problems in* the *Amazon*, Washington, DC: World Bank. (Report n.9104-BR).

Young, C.E.F. (1997), *Economic Adjustment Policies and the Environment: a Case Study of Brazil*, London: University College London, PhD Dissertation.

Young, C.E.F. and Fausto, J.R.B. (1998), 'Valoração de Recursos Naturais como Instrumento de Análise da Expansão da Fronteira Agrícola', in: IPEA (ed.), *A Economia Brasileira em Perspectiva 1998*, Rio de Janeiro: IPEA, vol. 2, pp.793–822.

8. Technology, climate change, productivity and land use in Brazilian agriculture

Robert E. Evenson and Denisard C.O. Alves

8.1 INTRODUCTION

The 'Ricardian' model of land productivity has been applied to Brazil by Sanghi et al. (1997) and Sanghi and Mendelsohn (2000). Since land productivity is associated with land use (that is, the use of land for crops, pasture and forestry) there is a natural extension for the Ricardian model to a land use analysis.[1]

The original application of the Ricardian model to land productivity did not explicitly consider spatial differences in technology. Implicitly the climate change estimates obtained assumed that the technology available to farmers at the time of the census observations would continue to be available during the climate change simulation period. Sanghi et al. (1997) and Sanghi and Mendelsohn (2000) examine how climate in different places of Brazil affects the net rent or value of farm land. Doing so enables them to account for both the direct impacts of climate on yields of different crops as well as the indirect substitution of different activities, introduction of different activities, and other potential adaptation to different climates. Using Brazilian municipio level data they estimate the effect of climatic variables and a variety of geographical, soil, economic and demographic factors to determine the intrinsic value of climate on farmland. Their analysis suggests that climate has a systematic impact upon agricultural rents and thus costs through temperature and precipitation. They also suggest that these effects tend to be very non-linear and quite different by season. Studies of agricultural productivity in Brazil (Avila and Evenson, 1995, and da Cruz, et al., 1995) have developed procedures for associating agricultural productivity with investments in both public and private sector R&D, with extension program investments and with infrastructure investments.

In this chapter we report two extensions to the original Ricardian studies. The first is to combine the methodology of the agricultural productivity studies with the Ricardian methodology to achieve dynamic estimates of climate change impacts on agricultural productivity in Brazil. The second extension is to bring both the Ricardian and the productivity methodologies into a land use analysis. It is very important to understand how climate change will affect farmland value or productivity as well as to estimate the possible effect on land use and more specifically on the natural forest share on total agricultural land in Brazil. Not less important is to shed some light on the relation between climate change and technological change. Technological change is affected by private as well as by public resources allocation. These extensions enable us to examine climate–technology interactions and to assess the prospects for offsetting climate change impacts through investments in research and extension. The estimates are based on farm data from the 1975, 1980 and 1985 Brazilian Censuses of Agriculture, supplemented by climate, institutional and technological data.

This project was financed by CNPq's PRONEX project Nemesis of the Ministério de Ciência e Tecnologia of Brazil.

In Section 8.2 we review the methods underlying our empirical specifications. In Section 8.3 we describe our data and variables. Section 8.4 reports our estimates. Section 8.5 reports computations of climate, technological and infrastructural change on land use on farms in Brazil. Section 8.6 reports estimates of climate, technological and infrastructural change on farm land productivity. In the concluding section we discuss the policy implications of our estimates.

8.2   METHODOLOGY

We describe production options for each land use with a general transformation function:

$$F_i(Y_i, X_i, L_i, C, G, E, T, I, W), i = 1, \dots, 6 \tag{8.1}$$

where:

i is land use
Y_i is a vector of outputs produced on land use i
X_i is a vector of variable inputs used on land use i
L_i is land area in land use i
C is a vector of normal or expected climate variables (temperature, rainfall, and so on)
G is a vector of geographic variables (altitude, and so on)
E is a vector of edaphic variables measuring soil characteristics

T is a vector describing available technology
I is a vector describing market infrastructure

The maximized profits function associated with (8.1) for each land use category is

$$\Pi_i = \sum P_{yi}Y_i - \sum P_{xi}X_i = \Pi_i(P_y, P_x, L_i, C, G, E, T, I, W) \qquad (8.2)$$

and the system of product supply and factor demand equations is[2]

$$\partial \Pi_i^* / \partial P_{yi} = Y_i = Y_i(P_y, P_{xi}, L_i, C, G, E, T, I, W)$$
$$\partial \Pi_i^* / \partial P_{xi} = X_{ij} = X_{ij}(P_{yi}, P_{xi}, L_i, C, G, E, T, I, W) \qquad (8.3)$$

Note that expressions (8.2) and (8.3) state that farmers choose profit maximising output and input combinations in response to climate (and other variables).

We define land use categories as follows:

APC: Area in perennial crops
AAC: Area in annual crops
ANP: Area in natural pasture
APP: Area in planted pasture
ANF: Area in natural forests
APF: Area in plantation forests

Within each of these land use categories we argue that farmers can change areas planted to particular crops or type of pasture and forests at low cost. Significant investments are required, however, to convert land from one of these categories to another.[3]

Total land in farms in a Brazilian municipio is relatively fixed and determined by past road building investments, industrial development and infrastructure. A considerable amount of Brazilian land in farms is actually in the forest use categories (see below). Total land in farms also includes fallow land and unproductive land. These uses are treated as the residual category in our empirical work.

Land use investments will be based on expected profits for each type of land (as noted in (8.2)). Expected profits are governed by the C, G, E, T and I vectors as well as relative prices. Using the argument that total land in farms in a municipio is relatively fixed, we argue that land use shares in each municipio are related to the C, G, E, T and I variables.

$$S_i = S_i(C, G, E, T, I) \qquad (8.4)$$

where S_i is the share of total land in farms in land use category i. We also use the argument that relative price differentials between regions are effectively determined by the C, G, E, T and I variables and can be eliminated from (8.4). In the next section we define the variables that we use to estimate (8.4). We note here that while, in principle, there are cross-equation restrictions associated with commodity prices and with investment goods prices, we have not utilised them because of the price endogeniety argument.[4]

The relationship between land productivity and climate, technology and infrastructure is essentially based on the same arguments. The average profits per hectare of land will be reflected by (8.2) in the short run for each land use. In the longer run, land use will respond to changes in technology, climate and infrastructure. Potential buyers and sellers of land will capitalise expected future profits from the most valuable land use and we thus expect land values in a cross-section to be related to the C, G, E, T and I variables

$$\text{Value/Hectare} = V_L(C, G, E, T, I) \tag{8.5}$$

We argue, as did Mendelsohn et al. (1994), that cross-section (or multiple cross-section) differences in land use and land values can be utilised to estimate (8.4) and (8.5) and identify the effects of climate on land use and land values enabling us to compute the following expressions:

$$\partial S_i / \partial C, \partial S_i / \partial T \text{ and } \partial^2 S_L / \partial C \partial T \tag{8.6}$$

and

$$\partial V_L / \partial C, \partial V_L / \partial T \text{ and } \partial^2 V_L / \partial C \partial T \tag{8.7}$$

Expression (8.6) shows the impact of climate and technology on land use shares. It also shows the interactive effect of technology on the climate impact. (These computations are reported in Section 8.5.) Expression (8.7) shows the impacts of climate and technology on land values and indirectly on land productivity. (These computations are reported in Section 8.6.)

Expressions (8.4) and (8.5) allow for farmer adaptation in Y and X to climate change and to technical change. This adaptation includes investments in farm level irrigation and drainage and in farm practices. There is, however, potential adaptation by the organisations producing technology and infrastructure for farmers to be considered and these create technology–climate interactions. The technology and infrastructure organisations include private firms who conduct R&D to develop improved factors to be supplied to the agricultural sector and the public sector agricultural research and extension organisations who also develop improved technology for agriculture. They also include public sector units providing for and maintaining infrastructure.

We know that researchers do consider climate conditions in their research programming. Plant breeders are continually seeking genetic traits to change the length of growing seasons and to endow plants with 'host plant tolerance' to cold and warm temperatures, to drought and flood stresses, and related climate effects. Their motivation for seeking to incorporate these traits in crop varieties is to allow superior genetic material (for example, the semi-dwarf wheat and rice varieties) to overcome climate and edaphic barriers to their 'migration', to new areas. This cross-section motive is likely to be good proxy for a time series motive, that is, to respond to increases in temperature.[5]

Implicitly, this suggests that there may be important 'expected' $C \times T$ and $C \times I$ interactions in (8.4) and (8.5). It may be argued that since climate has changed little over the past 25 years or so, the developers of technology (both public and private) and investors in infrastructure have not responded to climate change. However, the underlying premise of the estimates obtained from cross-section data in the Ricardian model where C varies over locations, is that these do measure farmers' responses to C. Similarly one can argue that T and I reflect responses to C and that $C \times T$ and $C \times I$ interactions in (8.4) and (8.5) provide estimates of future net effects of climate on land use and productivity.

Suppose, for example, that we have two regions (1 and 2) which differ in temperature (t_1 and t_2), and edaphic factors (E_1 and E_2). Suppose that a rise in temperature damages crops in both regions if crops do not migrate from one region to the other. If t_1 rises to the former level of t_2, region 1 can escape this damage if the crops suited to region 2 migrate to region 1. This migration will be affected by edaphic barriers. Plant breeders engage in host plant tolerance breeding for edaphic stresses to facilitate this migration (see Avila and Evenson, 1995).

Brazil has a large public sector system of agricultural research centres. It also has industrial R&D where technology is produced to be used in the agricultural sector. Avila and Evenson (1995) and da Cruz et al. (1995) have undertaken productivity studies of both the public and private sector research systems. The public system consists of state research centres and experiment stations and a federal system, EMBRAPA. In these prior studies, research 'stock' variables were constructed to reflect the regional and timing dimensions of this research. Private sector R&D stocks were constructed from invention data (see da Cruz et al., 1995, and the Appendix for more details). These technology variables are suited not only to the productivity analyses conducted by da Cruz et al. (1995), but they are also suited to the present study.[6]

8.3   DATA

Table 8.1 provides an overview of the data on which the study is based (see the Appendix for more detail).

Table 8.1   Variables description and means, 1985

	Description	Means
I. Endogenous variables		
AAC/LIF	Acreage in annual crops	0.07
ARC/LIF	Acreage in perennial crops	0.22
ANP/LIF	Acreage in natural pasture	0.30
APP/LIF	Acreage in planted pasture	0.19
ANF/LIF	Acreage in natural forests	0.17
APF/LIF	Acreage in planted forests	0.02

LIF = APC + AAC + ANP + APP + ANF + APF areas in fallow + areas unsuited to production VLNA = VLAND/LIF

II. Exogenous variables		
(A) Climate (*C*)		
RN DEC	Normal December rainfall	172.9
RN JUN	Normal June rainfall	73.6
RN MAR	Normal March rainfall	173.1
RN SEP	Normal September rainfall	64.5
TC DEC	Normal December temperature	24.4
TN JUN	Normal June temperature	20.0
TN MAR	Normal March temperature	24.3
TN SEP	Normal September temperature	22.2

Note: Squared values and rain and temperature interactions are included in the estimation.

(B) Geographic Variables (*G*)		
ERS1* – ERSS*	Dummy variables for the two dummy predisposition to erosion indexes in the municipios	
ALT'M	Altitude in metres	428.9
LATMN	Latitude in degrees	−16.2
DSEAM	Distance from sea	230.9
(C) Edaphic variables (*E*)		
SCCB*– STBR*	Dummy variables for two dominant soil types in the municipios	
DCATION	Dummy if cation soil restriction	0.93

Table 8.1   continued

		Description	Means
	DORG	Dummy if organic matter restriction	0.45
	DSAL	Dummy if salinity restriction	0.30
	DTEXT	Dummy if soil texture restriction	0.78
(D)	Technology variables (*T*)		
	S-R	Public sector research stock	
	S-RSC	Public research stock times state size	
	PRIVT	Private sector research stock (relevant to agriculture)	352.6
(E)	Infrastructure variables (*I*)		
	POP_ARE*	1980 population/square km	128.20
	POPSQ*	POP_ARE squared	–
	URB_TOT*	1980 Urban Population/Total Population	0.37
	POPDEN85	1980 Rural Population/Total Farm land area	0.37
	ROADS70*	Km of roads (1970)/total farm land area 1970	0.02
(F)	Interactions		
	C × *G*	ERS1TEMD – +	
		ERS5TEMP, ERS1RAIN –	
		ERS5PAIN	
	C × *E*	TEMPSCrB – TEMPSTBR,	
		PAINSCrB – – – RAIN STBR	
	C × *T*	ST_RDEC2 – ST_RSE02,	
		ST_TDEEC2 – – –	
		ST_TDEC2(Public research)	
		PRTRDEC2 – PRTRSEP2,	
		PRTTDEC2 PRTTDEC2	
		(Private Research)	
	T × *G*	STATERS1 – – STATERSS,	
		PRTERS1 – – PRTERS5	
	T × *E*	STATSCCB – – STaTSTBR,	
		PRTSCCB – – PRTSTBR	

Note: *C* – *XG*, *C* × *E* with average of four months rainfall and temperature *C* × *T* with squared values of monthly rainfall and temperature

Data from three census cross-sections (1975, 1980 and 1985) were utilised in the analyses. The dependent variables include the land use shares and the farmer-based estimates of land value in each municipio (municipality).

We estimate a jointly determined system of land use shares and land values based on (8.4) and (8.5). Thus we have six land use equations and one land value equation. We used OLS procedures since we have a common set of erogenous variables for the land share equations. The regression estimates are weighted by total land in farms.

Exogenous variables include climate, geographic, edaphic, technology and infrastructure variables. The climate, geographic and edaphic variables are the same as used in the original Ricardian analysis (Sanghi et al., 1997). Climate was measured by normal (30 year mean) levels of rainfall and temperature. These measures were available for weather stations and pre-dicted for each municipio (see Sanghi et al., 1997). This enabled non-linearities, squared values of each rainfall and temperature and rainfall–temperature interaction variables to be included.

Edaphic variables were obtained from several sources. These variables capture physical properties of soil, aquifers and topography. One of the major challenges in studies of this type is to distinguish the effects of climate on land values from edaphic effects. It is also important that these edaphic variables are not climate (or hidden climate) variables.[7]

The technology variables include a public sector research 'stock' variable and a private sector research stock variable. These variables are constructed in such a way as to be consistent with the 'service flow' concept associated with capital variables in production studies. The effects of investment in research have both time and spatial dimensions. Investments in time t have effects distributed through future years. Consequently a research stock asso-ciated with a productivity index in a given period is based on investments in previous periods (that are having effects in the current period). The research stock variable is thus constructed using estimated timing weights for past investments (and allowing for depreciation).

The spatial dimension is similar. Research conducted in one location af-fects productivity in other locations. This spatial 'spillover' of research effects requires that spatial weights be estimated allowing for the research stock variable for a given location to include past investments made in other loca-tions (see the Appendix and da Cruz et al., 1995, for more details).

Infrastructure is proxied by population density, urbanisation and road density.[8] Table 8.1 also describes the interaction variables used in the study. Note that we define $C \times G$, $C \times E$ and $C \times T$ interactions as well as $T \times G$ and $T \times E$ interactions. We do this to capture crop 'migration' effects. As climate change occurs, these interactions will limit the movement of crops from one region to another.

8.4   ESTIMATES

Evenson and Alves (1997) reports estimated coefficients and heteroscedasticity corrected standard errors for all the six land use share equations (note that fallow and unproductive land is the residual share) and the land value equations.

All equations have good statistical fits as indicated by 'F' tests. All clusters of climate, geographic and edaphic variables are jointly significant in all equations. All clusters of interaction terms are also significant in all equations. Because of the large number of interaction variables it is difficult to place interpretations on any single coefficient. In the sections to follow we report 'partial' effects of key variables evaluated for each data point and summarized in tables for all of Brazil and in map form for regions within Brazil.

8.5   COMPUTED ESTIMATES OF CLIMATE AND TECHNOLOGY ON LAND USE

We report computed partial effects of climate change (rainfall and temperature) and technology (public sector and private sector R&D) on land use shares in this section.

These effects are computed as follows. The partial derivatives (equation (8.6)) from the estimates are evaluated for each municipio utilising municipio level values for all interaction terms. The national mean effects are summarised in Table 8.2.

These partial effects can be interpreted as simulations. The partial effect of a one degree temperature rise is the change in the dependent variable that would occur if all temperature variables in the estimated equations were increased by one degree Celsius. Thus in Table 8.2 the national mean effect (over all municipios) of a rise in temperature by 1°C on the annual crop land use share is 0.50. This means that the annual crop share would rise from 22 per cent to 22.5 per cent. This effect takes into account all estimated coefficients on temperature variables.

For climate effects we compute both rainfall and temperature change effects. For rainfall we compute the effects of increasing each of the four monthly rainfall variables by 3 per cent (that is, 3 per cent of the normal monthly rainfall in the municipio). For temperature effects we compute the effects of a rise in normal temperature by 1°C in each month in all municipios. These computations are thus for relatively modest climate changes.

For the R&D effects we compute the effects of a doubling of the investments in both private and public sector R&D. Given the relatively low level

Table 8.2 Estimated partial effects of climate and technological change

	Crop land		Pasture land		Forest land	
	Annual	Perennial	Natural	Planted	Natural	Plantation
1985 Shares (Per cent)	22	7	30	19	17	2
Climate effects						
3% increase in rainfall	0.35	−0.09	−0.78	0.33	0.14	−0.04
1°C increase in temperature	0.5	0.17	3.54	−1.07	−1.98	−0.14
Combined increases in rainfall and temperature	0.85	0.08	2.76	−0.73	−1.84	−0.18
Technology effects						
Doubling private R&D	0.04	0.07	−0.006	−0.002	−0.1	−0.01
Doubling public R&D	0.22	0.08	−0.55	0.07	0.14	−0.01
Combined doubling of private and public R&D	0.26	0.15	−0.56	0.07	0.04	−0.02
Secondary effects of technology on climate effects						
3% increase in rainfall	−0.0019	0.0062	−0.0088	0.0031	0.0018	−0.0024
1°C increase in temperature	−0.001	−0.0153	0.0152	0.0338	−0.0037	0.0058
Combined increases in rainfall and temperature	−0.0029	−0.0091	0.0064	0.0369	−0.0019	0.0034

of R&D investment in Brazil this calculation presumes that Brazil will expand its R&D investments to approximately the levels of North America.

We turn first to the national mean level effects summarized in Table 8.2. Note that we have estimated six land use share equations. The residual land use category accounting for 3 per cent of land in farms is fallow land and land considered to be unproductive. The first row in Table 8.2 reports land use shares for the six classes of land. Subsequent rows report the partial effects of changes in climate or technology on land use shares. (Since these changes sum to zero the effects on the residual category can be inferred from the estimated effects.)

We begin by noting that the term 'land in farms' in Brazil has a broader scope than in many other countries. It covers cropland, pasture land and forest land. The 19 per cent in forests constitutes a significant part of the forest land in Brazil and represents the forest land that is threatened by cropland and pastureland expansion. (Non-farm forest land is threatened by logging and industrial and urban uses.)

We first consider the effect of a 3 per cent rainfall increase on land use shares. The mean effects for Brazil are shown in Table 8.2 (row 2). A rainfall increase is calculated to lead to an increase in land in annual crops of 0.35 and a decrease in land in perennial crops of 0.09, but a net increase in the cropland shares (from 29 per cent to 29.26 per cent). A rainfall increase will lead to a decrease in natural pasture of 0.78, an increase in planted pasture of 0.33 and a net decrease in pasture land shares (from 49 to 48.55 per cent). A rainfall increase will lead to an increase in land in forest uses (from 19 per cent to 19.1 per cent). These rainfall effects can be considered to be modest in magnitude and they do not imply a threat to forest habitat.

The same cannot be said for the computed effects of a 1°C temperature rise (row 3). A temperature rise is projected to lead to an increase in both the annual and perennial cropland shares. The largest effect is for pasture land where the natural pasture land share is projected to increase from 30 per cent to 33.5 per cent. This is only partially offset by the projected decrease in the planted pasture share. The temperature-induced increase in cropland and pasture land comes at the expense of forest land. Both natural and plantation forest shares decline and the total forest landshare is projected to decline from 19 per cent of land to less than 17 per cent. This estimated temperature effect does raise concerns about biodiversity and habitat loss associated with the conversion of farm forest land to pasture and cropland.

The combined rainfall and temperature effects are dominated by the temperature effects. The modest climate change associated with a 3 per cent rainfall increase and/or 1°C temperature rise is projected to raise the cropland shares from 29 per cent to 30 per cent. This climate change will also raise pasture shares from 49 to 51 per cent. Forest shares will decline from 19 per cent to a little over 17 per cent. (The geographic and regional dimensions of these effects are discussed below.)

Next we consider the technology effects on land use. These can be summarised as follows:

1. Private R&D effects are smaller than public R&D effects. Both public and private sector R&D effects are positive on cropland shares. Since much public sector R&D is directed toward crop (especially annual crop) improvement, this is as expected.
2. Private sector R&D has minimal effects on pasture shares. Public sector R&D leads to a lower natural pasture share and a higher planted pasture share.
3. R&D effects on forest land are small.
4. Private sector R&D has a negative effect. Public sector R&D has a positive effect. Neither has an effect on plantation forests.

The general impact of expanded investment in agricultural R&D is to increase the cropland shares largely at the expense of natural pasture. Improved agricultural technology is thus expected to expand the climate change effects on cropland with both climate and technological change. The cropland shares will increase from 29 to 31.4 per cent. Improved agricultural technology will be counter to the climate effects on pasture land. Technology favours planted pastures and counters the climate-induced conversion of natural forest land to natural pasture land. Technology has small positive effects on natural forest land use. Neither climate change nor technological change favours plantation forestry.

The third set of calculations in Table 8.2 reports the secondary or interaction effects between climate change and technology change. They can be interpreted as the modification to the climate effects that would occur if both climate and technology change occurred. These are generally small except for the temperature effects on pasture land shares. The largest effect is on planted pasture where technology is friendly to planted pasture.

The spatial dimensions of climate-induced land use changes differ across regions. These results are reported in Evenson and Alves, 1998. Recall that the effects of a 3 per cent increase in rainfall were positive on annual crops for all of Brazil. These effects were not uniform spatially. The effects were negative in many municipios including municipios in the southern region where cropping intensity is highest. The spatial effects of rainfall on perennial crops were negative for all Brazil, but there were important and large positive effects in municipios in the Cerrado region.

Rainfall effects were negative for natural pastures and positive for planted pastures. We note, however, that in many municipios the natural pasture effects were positive. Most municipios did show a positive planted pasture effect for rainfall.

Rainfall effects on natural forests were generally positive and inversely related to rainfall levels. That is, municipios in low rainfall areas tend to have positive effects while those in high rainfall areas had negative effects. Similar effects on plantation forests are shown.

As noted in Table 8.2, the mean effects of temperature for Brazil were quite strong. A rise in temperature induces increases in annual crop shares. The spatial dimensions of these effects are quite uneven, with many municipios with significant annual cropped areas showing negative effects. The temperature effects on perennial crops shares were positive for all Brazil, but there were strong regional effects. See Evenson and Alves (1998). We observe some response to an extension of the frost-free zone southward, but for most regions with significant cropped area we observe a negative effect.

Among the largest impacts of a temperature rise for the Brazil means computations were a positive increase in natural pasture shares and a decrease in planted shares. The strong impacts were regional, with the expansion of natural pasture areas being relatively low in the southern states. Similarly, planted pasture shares were positive in many municipios in the Centre and South.

We also noted that a temperature rise had a negative impact on both planted and natural forests. The 'on-farm deforesting' effect is strongest in the North. It is negative in most municipios in the Centre-East and South and is positive in parts of the Cerrado and the Northeast.

It is not possible with the methodology used in this study to identify trade-offs in land use where it can be said that an increase in one reduces another. Some insights can be gained from the spatial correlations, however. Perhaps the strongest of these is the correlation between the increased natural pasture shares and the decreased natural forest shares.

8.6   COMPUTED ESTIMATES OF CLIMATE AND TECHNOLOGICAL CHANGE ON LAND VALUES AND LAND PRODUCTIVITY

We now turn to the estimated effects of climate and technical change on land values. These are summarised in Table 8.3. These estimates are roughly comparable to the climate change estimates reported in Sanghi et al. (1997).

As noted in Table 8.3, the estimated rainfall and temperature effects on land values are substantial for all the Brazil means. We estimate that a 3 per

Table 8.3   Estimated partial effects of climate and technological change on farm land values in Brazil (expressed in percentages)

Climate effects	
3% increase in rainfall	4.59
1°C increase in temperature	−5.36
Combined increase in rainfall and temperature	−1.23
Technology effects	
Doubling private R&D	1.40
Doubling public R&D	1.58
Combined doubling of private and public R&D	3.98
Secondary effects of technology on climate effects	
3% increase in rainfall	0.01
1°C increase in temperature	0.001
Combined increase in rainfall and temperature	0.011

cent increase in rainfall would have a positive 4.59 per cent impact on land values. A 1°C increase in normal temperature would have a negative 5.36 per cent effect on land values. The combined rainfall–temperature effect is a negative 1.23 per cent. (Note that since variable inputs account for roughly half of the costs of production for agricultural commodities in Brazil, the implied effect of climate change on land productivity is roughly half of the estimated effect on land values.)

Before turning to an assessment of the spatial or regional dimensions of the climate change effects we will discuss the technology change effects on land values. These are positive for both public and private R&D. It is difficult to relate these effects to absolute changes in productivity because the coefficient estimates are based on relative differences in land values (as in the case for climate change). Since equilibrium prices are affected by technological (and climate) change these estimates understated the actual effects of technological change on TFP (see da Cruz et al. (1995) for estimates of R&D on TFP). Since both climate and technological change have similar price effects we can compare the 2.98 per cent increase in land values for technical change with the 1.23 per cent decrease for climate change. It appears that the negative effects of climate change can be and will be offset by technological change in Brazilian agriculture.

We note further from Table 8.3 that technological change is 'friendly' to both rainfall and temperature change in that these effects are made more positive by technical change.

Rainfall effects, while positive for Brazil as a whole, are actually negative for many municipios in Brazil. The net positive effect for all Brazil is the result of relatively high positive impacts in a few municipios and relatively low negative impacts in many municipios.

Temperature effects also have very strong spatial or regional effects. They are strongly negative throughout the North, Northeast and much of the Centre-West. They are positive in much of the Centre-East (especially Minas Gerais) and the South.

The combined rainfall and temperature effects and the combined effects of public and private R&D on land values are largely negative in the North and Northeast regions. Much of the Centre–East and most of the South benefit from climate change. We also note that technological change is positive in most municipios and that its spatial pattern is inversely correlated with the spatial pattern for climate change. This inverse correlation further supports the suggestion that the positive effects of technological change are likely to compensate for the negative effects of climate change.

8.7   IMPLICATIONS FOR POLICY

Two sets of implications for policy emerge from the estimates of climate and technological change for Brazilian agriculture. The first set is indirect regarding the urgency and importance of policies designed to slow climate change. The second set is direct regarding policies to compensate for and ameliorate climate change.

Regarding the first set of implications for policies to slow global climate change, our estimates do not have implications for achieving the most cost-effective slowing of climate change. They do, however, have implications for income distribution and related equity considerations and for environmental concerns.

The income distribution and regional equity implications emerge from our land value effects estimates. These estimates show that climate change will have significant negative impacts on a large part of Brazil notably most of the North and Northeast and part of the Centre-West. These parts of Brazil are currently generally 'disadvantaged' in terms of soil resources, rainfall and temperature. They are also disadvantaged in terms of per capita income.

By contrast, many municipios in the Centre-East, South and Coastal regions will benefit from climate change. These regions are currently advantaged regions in terms of soils, climate and income.

The fact that there are gains from climate change probably reduces the urgency of policies slowing climate change for much of Brazil. The fact that climate change will exacerbate existing income distributional inequities should result in an increase in the urgency for and support of policies slowing climate change.

The second set of policy implications are more direct. They speak largely to agricultural technology policy in Brazil (and also to schooling, migration and infrastructure policy). Our finding that technological change is not only positive but compensatory is important. Our estimates show that if Brazil brings its investment levels in both public-sector and private-sector research relevant to agriculture up to developed country standards, productivity change can largely prevent climate change losses from occurring in most regions (and many regions will benefit from both technical and climate change).

Investments in schooling, retraining and infrastructure to reduce regional inequities have been given high importance in recent years. Our estimates call for maintaining these policies.

Finally, our land use estimates have implications for both sets of policy concerns. Many policymakers will find the land use implications of climate change (especially warming) alarming. The conversion of forest land to pasture and crop land will be of particular concern to those who wish to protect biodiversity habitats. This will increase the urgency and support for policies slowing climate warming.

Our estimate regarding the compensatory potential of technical change are similar, but of lessor magnitude. Higher investments in private sector R&D, and especially in public sector R&D, will modify and reduce the estimated 'deforestation' effect of climate change. Our estimates do not suggest that technological change can actually prevent this deforestation effect, although they do suggest a positive effect of technology on natural forest land use. In conclusion we can say that R&D does not harm natural forests and may slow down the rate of deforestation.

NOTES

1. Land use is implicit in the product supply and factor demand systems. That is, the choice of output supplies and inputs implies a land use allocation. See Merrick (1978) for an early land use study in Brazil.
2. Land use is implicit in the product supply and factor demand systems. That is, the choice of output: supplies and inputs implies a land use allocation. See Merrick (1978) for an early land use study in Brazil.
3. We are thus acknowledging that within each land use class farmers shift between different: crops from year to year.
4. The profits function system (8.3) has cross-equation price terms.
5. These motives are not necessarily the same as those that would be generated by an explicit recognition that temperatures were rising and that growing seasons were changing, but the research techniques for developing heat tolerant cultivars, and so on would be similar to those employed for crop migration motives.
6. The actual variables are 'capital stock', variables constructed to reflect the productivity contributions in each region.
7. Variables that reflect climate may be highly correlated with actual climate variables and create biased estimates of climate effects.

8. These variables were developed for the productivity studies of da Cruz et al. (1997).

APPENDIX 8A: AGRICULTURAL RESEARCH STOCK VARIABLES

Brazil has a complex system of public sector research institutions. Appendix 8B lists the Federal EMBPAPA research units and State research units. The State research variable $S - R$ (Appendix 8B.2) was constructed as follows:

Each municipio, i, in period, t, was assigned a State research stock variable of the following form:

$$S\_R_{it} = \sum_{t,j} W_t' S_{ij} R_{cj} \qquad (8A.1)$$

where

W_t' is a set of time shape weights
S_{ij} is a set of spatial weights, and
R_{tj} is research spending (in constant currency units) in region j, time t.

There is a time lag between the conduct of research activities and the development of improved technology. Experiments require time and evaluation and sequences of experiments and tests must be designed before new technology is developed. Then the technology must be diffused to farmers. Some of this diffusion requires embodiment in farm inputs (seeds) and some is diffused as information (improved practices). Farmers must experiment and evaluate as they adopt technology and modify it for their farm conditions.

The 'time-shape' of these lags is thus similar to the classic technology diffusion lag with a period of little research impact after investment, rising to a peak some years later. However, a second factor, depreciation, plays a role in the time-shape also. It is important to distinguish between depreciation and obsolescence in this regard. Technological obsolescence occurs when new technology (say a variety of rice) is superior to an existing technology and displaces it. If the new technology was developed as an extension of existing technology (that is, it was an 'add-on' to an existing technology) then the investments associated with the development of the existing technology did not depreciate even though the technology becomes obsolete.

Depreciation occurs (a) when there is incomplete additivity in technology development and (b) when there are 'exposure' effects to reduce the value of technology after it has been exposed to use. Host plant genetic resistance to plant insects and diseases is often reduced by use exposure and this is an example of depreciation. Changes in prices can reduce (or enhance) the value of technology and this is a source of depreciation as well (for example, a rise in energy prices may reduce the value of technology that is highly dependent on energy).

The formula used to build the research stocks in this study is:

$$S_t R_t = (ExpRE_{t-4} \cdot 0.2) + (ExpRE_{t-5} \cdot 0.4) + (ExpRE_{t-6} \cdot 0.6)$$
$$+ (ExpRE_{t-7} \cdot 0.8) + \sum_{t=8} (ExpRE_{t-2} \cdot 1.0) \qquad (8A.2)$$

where $ExpRE_{t-4}$ is spending in year $t-4$, and so on.

We built in a time lag of four years between the initial investment in agricultural research (first year of the research project) and the impact on agricultural production at the farm level. The full impact is realised after eight years. Given the relatively recent development of ENBRAPA research we did not built in a depreciation component. These estimates are based on previous studies (Evenson and da Cruz, 1989).

Research conducted in one location will produce technology that is useful in other locations. But it is not necessarily equally useful in all other locations. We know that plant and animal performance is sensitive to climate and soil factors. The natural selection model of Darwin tells us that genetic diversity is associated with a high degree of location specificity of plants and animals to environmental niches. Modern plant and animal breeding programmes have only partially overcome this 'Darwinian' phenomenon. Research systems in Brazil have incorporated Darwinian targeting into their structure.

The problem that we face in this study is to assign the research stocks from the National Centers, Regional Centers and State Programs to specific micro-regions and municipios (our unit of analysis). In practice, there are two methods for doing this. One is the technology distance method where research conducted in region 'I' is assigned to region 'i' in proportion to a technology distance index between them. Technology distance indexes are measures of the relative performance of regions i's best technology in region i relative to region i's best technology in region i.

The second method, used in this study, is to 'test' alternative assignments of research based on geo-climate and priority zone evidence. For example, in the work reported below we construct three alternative assignments for EMBRAPA National Program research. They are:

1.   Assignment 1 where all micro-regions in the country are assigned the National Program research stock. This is consistent with complete full

'spillover' of National Program research from the National Product Center to other locations.

2. Assignment 2 where National Program research is assigned to 'Priority Zones' as identified by National Product Center staff. This is a sub-set of the 92 agro-ecological zones (on average 40 per cent). This assignment is consistent with spillovers limited to these priority zones.

3. Assignment 3 where National Program research is assigned only to micro-regions in the Agro-ecological zone in which the National Research Center Program is located. This is consistent with very limited spillover of research benefits.

A similar procedure is applied to EMBRAPA Regional Center Research where a test is made between assignment to the region as defined by EMBRAPA and assignment 3.

Mean square error tests are performed to select the assignment most consistent with the data. As we note below, these tests show that assignment 1 was best for National Program livestock research. Assignment 2 was best for crop and agricultural research generally. For Regional Center research, assignment to the region was best. State research assignment to all micro-regions in the State was best.

APPENDIX 8B: BRAZILIAN AGRICULTURAL RESEARCH SYSTEM

8B.1   EMBRAPA Decentralised Units

(a)   Agroforestry or Agricultural Ecoregional Research Centers

CPAA – Agroforestry Research Center for Western Amazonia
CPATU – Agroforestry Research Center for Western Amazonia
CPAC – Cerrados Agricultural Research Center
CPAF-AC – Agroforestry Research Center of Acre
CPAF-RO – Agroforestry Research Center of Rondônia
CPAF-RR – Agroforestry Research Center of Roraima
CPAF-AP – Agroforestry Research Center of Amapa
CPAP – Pantanal Agricultural Research Center
CPAMN – Center for Agricultural Research in the Mid-North
CPAO – Center for Agricultural Research in the Mid-West
CPATC – Center for Agricultural Research in the Coastal Tablelands
CPACT – Agricultural Research Center for Temperate Climate
CPATSA – Semi-arid Agricultural Research Center
CPPSE – Center for Research on Cattle Raising in the Southeast

CPASUL – Center for Research on Cattle Raising in the Southern Fields

(b)   National Commodity Centers
CNPA – National Research Center for Oleaginous and Fibrous Plants
CNPAF – National Rice and Beans Research Center
CNPC – National Goat Research Center
CNPF – National Forestry Research Center
CNPGC – National Beef Cattle Research Center
CNPGL – National Dairy Cattle Research Center
CNPH – National Vegetable Crop Research Center
CNPMF – National Cassava and Tropical Fruit Research Center
CNPMS – National Corn and Sorghum Research Center
CNPSO – National Soybean Research Center
CNPT – National Wheat Research Center
CNPSA – National Pig and Poultry Research Center
CNPUV – National Grape and Wine Research Center

(c)   Basic Theme Research Centers
CENARGEN – National Genetic Resource and Biotechnology Research Center
CNPAB – National Agro-biology Research Center
CNPAT – National Research Center for Tropical Agro-industry
CNPDIA – National Center for Research and Development of Agricultural Instrumentation
CNPMA – National Research Center for Monitoring and Assessment of Environmental Impact
CNPS – National Soil Research Center
CNPTIA – National Center for Technological Research on Information in Agriculture
CTAA – National Agro-industrial Food Technology Center

(d)   Special Services
SPI – Informational Production Service
SPSB – Basic Seed Production Service
NMA – Nucleus for Satellite Monitoring of Environment and Natural Resources

8B.2   State Research Institutions

(a)   South Region
IPAGRO – Agricultural Research Institute, RS State
IRGA – Rio Grande do Sul Institute of Rice, RS State
FUNDACEP – Agricultural Research Center Foundation, RS State

EPAGRI – Agricultural Corporation for Research and Development, SC State
IAPAR – Agricultural Research Institute of Parana, PR State
OCEPAR – Cooperative Organization of Parana (Agriculture Research Units), PR State

(b)   Southeast Region
IAC – Agronomic Institute of Campinas, SP State
IB – Biological Institute, SP State
IZ – Zootecnical Institute, SP State
PESAGRO – Agricultural Research Corporation of Rio de Janeiro, RJ State
EMCAPA – Corporation of Espirito Santo for Agricultural Research, ES State
EPAMIG – Corporation for Agricultural Research of Minas Gerais, MG State

(c)   Northeast Region
EBDA – Agricultural Research and Development Corporation of Bahia, BA State
EMDAGRO – Corporation for Agricultural Development, SE State
EPEAL – Corporation for Agricultural Research of Alagoas, AL State
IPA – Agricultural Research Corporation of Pernambuco, PE State
EMPAR – Agricultural Research Corporation of Rio Grande do Norte, RN State
EMEPA – Corporation of Parafba for Agricultural Research, PB State
EPACE – Corporation of Ceara for Agricultural Research, CE State
EMAPA – Corporation of Maranhao for Agricultural Research, MA State

(d)   North Region
The states in this region do not develop agricultural research. EMBRAPA Research Centers are responsible for the agricultural research.

(e)   Centre-West Region
EMGOPA – Agricultural Research Corporation of Goias, GO State
EMPAER/MT – Corporation for Agricultural Research and Rural Extension of Mato Grosso, MT State
EMPAER – Corporation for Agricultural Research and Rural Extension of Mato G. do Sul, MS State

BIBLIOGRAPHY

Adams, Richard, Rosenzweig, Cyntha, Pearl, Robert, Ritchie, McCarl, Joe Bruce, Glyer, David, Curry, Bruce, Jones, James, Boote, Kenneth and Hartwell, Allen

(1990), 'Global climate change and U.S. agriculture', *Nature*, **345** (6272), (May), 17, 219–24.

Avila, Antonio Flavio Dias and Evenson, Robert E. (1995), 'Research and productivity growth in the Brazilian grain sector', *Revista de Economia Rural*, SOBER.

Cline, William (1952), *The Economics of Global Warming*, Washington, DC: Institute of International Economics.

Cruz, Elmer Rodrigues da, Avila, Antonio Flavio Dias and Evenson, R.E. (1995), 'Research and productivity growth in the Brazilian grain sector', *Revista de Economia Rural*, SOBER, July.

Evenson, R.E. and Alves, Denisard (1997), 'Climate change and technology change effects on land use and land productivity in Brazilian agriculture', Economic Growth Center, Yale University, July.

Evenson, R.E. and Alves, Denisard (1998), 'Technology, Climate Change, Productivity and Land Use in Brazilian Agriculture', *Planejamento e Politicas Públicas*, **18**, December, 223–58.

Evenson, R. and da Cruz, E.R. (1989), 'Returns to Research: A Comparative Study of National and International Programs (with special reference to the PROCISUR Program)', Discussion Paper no. 588, Economic Growth Center, Yale University.

Mendelsohn, Robert, Nordhaus, William D. and Shaw, Daige (1994), 'The impact of global warming on agriculture: a Ricardian analysis', *American Economic Review*, **84** (4), 88:753–71.

Merrick, T. (1978), 'Fertility and land availability in rural Brazil', *Demography*, **15** (3), 321–36.

Sanghi, A. and Mendelsohn, R. (2000), 'The climatic sensitivity of Indian and Brazilian agriculture', submitted to *Climatic Change*.

Sanghi, Apurva, Alves, Denisard, Evenson, Robert and Mendelsohn, Robert (1997), 'Global warming impacts on Brazilian agriculture: estimates of the Ricardian model', *Economia Aplicada*, **1** (1).

9. Economic incentives and forest concessions in Brazil

Claudio Ferraz and Ronaldo Seroa da Motta

9.1 INTRODUCTION

The deforestation process in Brazil, mainly in frontier areas, is a result of economic and social factors, along with institutional failures. In the past, structural problems, such as highly concentrated income distribution and land tenure, worked in conjunction with policy failures, such as favourable credit and fiscal systems to agricultural activities and regional development programmes in frontier areas, to create a deforestation process driven mainly by the synergy between agricultural and logging activities.

The association between these activities plays a crucial role in the deforestation trend by financing land clearing for agricultural purposes in exchange for timber extraction. Economic agents move to the frontier, clear the land, sell the timber and start an agricultural or cattle-raising activity expecting to get the title for the land. Such an exploitation pattern, identified as typical dynamic behaviour in open access areas, is a direct consequence of the lack of perception of scarcity associated with the forest value. Consequently, the privatisation of the forest and its land through the assignment of private individual rights, has been very harmful for sustainable purposes in the region.[1]

Some of these factors cannot be easily reverted since it would require long-term structural adjustments to alleviate social inequalities, accomplish a satisfactory land reform, create the proper incentives and enhance the planning capacity of human resources in governmental agencies.

Because of these failures, regulation on sustainable logging practices and economic instruments such as funding mechanisms, forestry taxes and fiscal incentives did not succeed in promoting sustainable extraction practices in the Amazon.

A promising alternative policy that is being discussed and implemented in Brazil is a system of public concessions in National Forests (FLONA), where long-term leasing contracts of large tracts of forests are made with private corporations, by international auction, with clauses specifying accepted conditions on the sustainable use of land and natural resources. Non-compliance with sustainable practices defined in concession licensing would be subject to sanctions and concession termination. Additionally, supervision and monitoring costs could be decreased if monitoring could be shared with NGOs and communities. Such a scheme is particularly feasible, for example, in the Amazon where there is still a large availability of unclaimed areas.

Nevertheless, the need for sustainable logging practices in these concessions, together with the prevailing pattern of timber extraction in the Amazon, raises some issues related to the financial viability of these concession schemes. Sustainable logging will represent higher average costs if compared to the actual pattern of production. These additional costs are mainly associated with:

a.   Selective extraction has to reckon on rotation practices. Considering the variety of species in the Amazon, and its density, the area used for sustainable logging would have to be larger if compared to the actual pattern of exploitation.
b.   Sustainable logging is going to be more intensive in capital and advanced technology. This could create productivity gains, but will also create additional costs and will increase the need for skilled labour.
c.   The necessity of post logging care in order to decrease waste.
d.   Efficient infrastructure for transportation and costs associated with auditing, certification and administration needed in order to attend rules and norms imposed on the concession.

Consequently, for the logging concession system to work, given the market structure, some compensation is going to be needed for this additional higher unit average cost. The price charged for this sustainable log will therefore have to be higher. Nonetheless, this will only be financially sustainable if either the sustainable product could be differentiated from the open access extraction, or the supply of illegal logging is decreased.

In addition to the feasibility problem, the use of a concession system implies the replication of a pattern of logging that is known to have not worked properly in many other countries.

Bearing in mind the current deforestation and logging patterns taking place in the Amazon, this chapter is going to address some of the determinants that are needed to be taken into account to foster an efficient system of concessional forests in the region. These determinants are going to be analysed using the following classification:

a.   auction procedures for concession allocation;
b.   payment instruments;
c.   regulation and monitoring aspects;
d.   industrial structure and competition on timber markets.

This analysis, instead of proposing normative recommendations, will try to draw attention to some issues that are in general not explicitly mentioned in the literature and are fundamental for the attainment of the objective proposed by the Brazilian government in promoting sustainable logging extraction in concessional forests.

Section 9.2 presents some characteristics of the deforestation process in Brazil. Section 9.3 analyses the international experience on concessional forests. Section 9.4 identifies the main conditions for sustainable logging under concession in Brazil. The last section presents the conclusion and recommendations.

9.2   FOREST CONVERSION AND DEFORESTATION IN BRAZIL

To understand the context in which the creation of national forests and their utilisation for private logging took place, it is fundamental to comprehend the process of forest extraction and deforestation in Brazil. There is a wide array of work done on the causes of deforestation in Brazil.[2] Nevertheless, the geography of deforestation and its causes have changed substantially during the years. Nowadays, the main causes of deforestation are less associated with cheap credit from the government and road building, and more related to the link between agriculture conversion and timber extraction.[3]

The Deforestation Process

The expansion of the agricultural frontier took place in the last 20 years, following the same development model adopted in the southern regions. The movement occurred from south to north into the Central and North regions of the country where the Cerrados and Amazonian Forests are respectively located. Moreover, the occupation of these regions was determined by ambitious regional development programmes and this expansion resulted in large areas of forest conversion.

Furthermore, regional development programmes were accompanied by an important migration process, which was accentuated by the income and land inequality in Brazil along with the need to incorporate higher productive areas for the development of agriculture activities. EMBRAPA (1991) classified areas in Brazil according to their appropriate use, namely: crops, livestock and extractivism/preservation.[4] According to its results, less than 10 per cent of the total area in the Amazon is suitable for crops/agriculture and livestock while this proportion is over 90 per cent in Southern regions. Secondly, it can be seen that livestock activities in the country as a whole exceed the area suitable for them by about 800 000 km^2. Furthermore, more than 90 per cent of this excess takes place in the North and Central Regions where most recent deforestation is occurring. Consequently, low productivity cattle raising is occupying non-appropriate areas in the Amazon region. This activity expansion takes place after the soil is exhausted for agricultural activity causing the conversion of fragile ecosystems and pushing crops towards inadequate areas.

On the other hand, land areas suitable for crops are still available with the impressive figure of about 1.6 million km^2 for the country as a whole. Thus the expansion of agricultural activities towards the Amazon, taking into account agroecological features, cannot be recommended.

So why does it occur? Timber exploitation in the Amazon takes advantage of legal land clearing for agriculture which gives right to deforestation. Timber sale based on this licence creates an opportunity for making up-front capital for full clearing afterwards and to bear later costs of securing property rights. Timber exploitation, in fact, acts in some areas as inducing factors for land conversion.

Apart from the general weak capacity of public agencies in a country where public deficit cuts are erratic and, sometimes, drastic, institutional performance in such a large and remote area is likely to be fragile and creates more room for illegal logging at the top of the clearing licence loophole.

As said before, a very minor fraction of forestland in the Amazonian region is suitable for cropping and cleared soil ends up eventually in extensive cattle raising in order to secure property rights. Once the soil is degraded the movement for new areas of forestland continues. In a simple way, that has been the land conversion pattern elsewhere, but in the case of the Amazon there is still time and opportunity to make better use of forestland.

Deforestation in the Amazon should not be measured on the remaining area basis because it is a recent frontier region covering almost 50 per cent of the country area. In 1978–79 when recent occupation was at the peak, annual deforestation was 0.54 per cent or an equivalent area of 21 000 ha. The forest would be totally deforested in 130 years if this rate was kept up. During the 1980s, economic recession and the consequent lack of public and private resources to maintain the costly and ambitious development programmes, associated with increasing monitoring forced by external pressure, can explain the decreasing deforestation rates estimated for the following years. In 1991, the deforestation rate fell to 0.30 per cent or less than 11 000 ha (see Seroa da Motta, 1996).

After the 1994 stabilisation plan, the deforestation rate increased substantially. The 1994/1995 rate was the highest ever reaching 0.81 per cent which represented an average gross deforestation of 29 059 km²/year. This rate decreased in 1995/1996 to 0.51 per cent representing 18 161 km²/year.[5]

Although total deforested area is still no more than 10 per cent of total original area, the recent increasing of deforestation rates in inner regions may indicate that new frontier advance fronts are being opened.

Timber Activity Expansion

The fraction of the Brazilian timber production that has its origin in the Amazon (Northern region) increased from 9.2 per cent in 1980 to 23.1 per cent in 1991. This substantial increment represents the increasing importance of Amazonian timber species in the national timber activity.

The timber production coming from the Amazon region has increased dramatically in the last decades, if measured as effective production, as shown in Table 9.1. It also presents, for several periods of time, estimates of the potential commercial volume of timber which could be extracted from cleared areas due to agriculture expansion. Comparing these figures with the timber output values which were effectively produced in the region, one can estimate the fraction corresponding to the relative amount that is utilized for commercial purposes from the timber that is cut for agriculture purposes.

From Table 9.1, one can observe from the total amount of potential timber available in the opening of the frontier process that in 1975/78 only 13 per cent was sold as commercial timber. This result contrasts enormously with

Table 9.1 *Volume of timber available from deforested areas and the effective production of logs in the Northern region, 1975–90*

Period	Average area deforested per year (ha.)	(A) Commercial volume available from deforestation (1000 m³)	(B) Effective production of logs (1000 m³)	Fraction (B)/(A)
1975/78	1 619 300	32 386	4 064	0.13
1978/80	2 323 550	46 471	11 476	0.25
1980/88	5 940 987	118 820	19 539	0.16
1989/91	2 064 600	41 292	39 087	0.95

Source: Prado (1995).

the result in 1989/91 where 95 per cent of the timber stock cleared in the advancement of the frontier was used for commercial purposes. This pattern change through time confirms that the product from the timber extraction activity is increasingly financing the deforestation since legal licences for the agriculture expansion in the frontier legalise the timber extraction activity. This synergy generates a much higher private economic value from the deforested land areas than the one that could be obtained with a sustainable logging activity.

Seroa da Motta et al. (2000) present some estimates of the rates of return for the sustainable logging activities developed in the traditional areas of the Amazon. They estimated financial rates of return lower than 1 per cent. This implies that sawmills in the Amazon can count on an illegal supply of timber (sometimes legalised through deforestation licences for agriculture purposes) at very low cost. This allows high rates of return with which the sustainable timber production can hardly compete.

Summing up, the agricultural expansion in Brazil has to be reoriented in terms of its spatial dimension regarding soil suitability. Moreover, logging activities have to take place based on a distinct land property right system if ecosystems are to be preserved.

9.3   INTERNATIONAL EXPERIENCE WITH CONCESSION SYSTEMS

A forest concession system is a contractual arrangement where the rights of exploitation of the natural resources from a government-owned area are given to a private user. This mechanism was created as an alternative to the sale of public land for private exploitation. Concession schemes are common, as an alternative to privatisation, in many types of markets characterised by natural monopolies with high sunk costs. Nevertheless, the use of concessions in forestry is not associated with the monopoly characteristic, but is related to two other factors: the capture of rent and the sustainability issue. On the one hand, there is a need for the government, as the resource owner, to capture part of the rent generated from the logging process. On the other hand, there is also a need to regulate the extraction process in order to preserve other socially valuable services associated with the forest existence.

In the past, the establishment of concession systems was mainly motivated by revenue-raising aims from user charges, royalties and fees for forestry exploitation. The basic concession scheme had, on one hand, logging companies trying to maximise profits, and on the other hand, the government trying to maximise rent capture. Both economic agents, the companies and the government, were mainly interested in the type and quantity of timber extracted without paying any attention to the sustainability of the harvesting process.[6]

This logging behaviour has motivated the depletion of vast areas of Southeast Asian tropical forests. Furthermore, as the timber stock diminished considerably, Southeast Asian companies looked for forest areas in other geographical locations, and Latin America was a natural destiny due to its forest richness.

Nevertheless, if the pattern of harvesting used in Southeast Asian countries is simply repeated in the Amazon, appended with the institutional and structural failures in the region, the deforestation process can be encouraged faster than it has been occurring. Consequently, it is mandatory for the government to implement sustainable logging practices through stringent regulatory practices. In this perspective, the initiative of using national forest areas for implementing concession schemes for sustainable logging has to take place in a planned and gradual way, accounting for all the cares needed, particularly on the monitoring and regulatory aspects.

International experiences have shown that concessions were not fully successful in attaining its objectives. In most cases, logging followed an unsustainable pattern with overexploitation. Furthermore, governments were not able to capture the rents associated with the natural resource being exploited.[7] The problems associated with concession systems worldwide can be divided in two types of failures: design failures and implementation failures.

Design Failures

Design failures are related to the formulation of the concession system. They occur when the government creates concession systems that are not compatible with sustainable logging practices. Concession periods that are too short and logging areas that are too large are known to create negative incentives for sustainable logging practices.[8] Short periods do not allow the concessionaire to obtain benefits with second growth forest creating an incentive to harvest as much as possible in the present concession period.[9] The size of concessions is also important. Large areas decrease the perception of scarcity considerably, creating a perverse incentive for overexploitation.

Additionally, the method used to allocate concessions and the mechanism used to collect rents are an important source of design failure. Concessions that are awarded in an *ad hoc* way[10] create negative incentives for sustainable management since the concessionaire does not necessarily have the highest willingness to pay for that forest area. Consequently, the company will harvest as much as possible since the forest area was obtained at free cost.

Likewise, the government has to establish in the concession contract the type of fee that is going to be charged. If the fee is not well designed, it could increase the incentive for over harvesting. A fee that is established too low will create an incentive to harvest above the optimal level.[11] On the other hand, a fee that is established too high could increase the incentive for illegal logging.

Although it is important to take into account all the previous design problems, it is also important to mention that the institutional aspect is fundamental for the incentive of sustainable logging behaviour. Uncertainty about the validity of the contract in the future creates an incentive for the logging company to extract as much as possible in the present. Thus, smaller areas and longer concession periods can be necessary conditions for a sustainable pattern of harvesting, but these are not sufficient conditions to guarantee sustainable logging behaviour.

Implementation Failures

Although the contract establishing the concession system is sometimes wrongly designed for sustainable purposes, the main source of inefficiency in the timber harvesting activity is also associated with implementation failures. Most countries that utilise concession systems have problems in monitoring and regulating concessions, as well as charging the fees associated with the harvesting.

Along with monitoring problems, governments in developing countries suffer, in general, from lack of enforcement power. Due to local political power and strong economic interests, logging companies are able to impose their will through strong power bargaining and rent-seeking behaviour. Moreover, the government faces strong difficulties in collecting adequate fees from logging activities, mainly because of poorly structured collection systems, but also because of corruption. Adequate monitoring is costly and, along with political will, it requires a strong organisational structure. Problems with corruption are commonly due to geographical isolation and low wages paid to monitoring workers. Furthermore, sometimes governments lack adequate technology for monitoring vast areas.[12]

All the previous failures are attenuated by the lack of credibility on government sanctions. Consequently, even when non-compliance is detected, this does not guarantee that a sanction is imposed due to the possibility of bribery and political arrangements between companies and fiscal authorities.

9.4   CONDITIONINGS FOR THE BRAZILIAN CONCESSION SYSTEM

Although the analysis of international experiences with concession systems is crucial for Brazil to avoid repeating mistakes that occurred elsewhere, specific characteristics exist for the Brazilian case that need to be understood in order to implement a successful concession system in national forest areas. Furthermore, the use of concessions in the Amazon has to be planned as a gradual path in order to observe outcomes and problems to revise and enhance the system before fully applying it to the whole region.

The elements that are important to be analysed, prior to the full implementation of the concession allocation, can be classified in four broad categories. Although some of these aspects are relevant not only for Brazil, some of them are not widely discussed in the related literature in other countries. The categories specified are related to each step of the concession progress, namely, allocation of the concession, fees collection by the government, regulation and monitoring and evolution of the market structure.

Allocation of Concessions

The establishment of auctions for the allocation of concessions has great advantages. Transaction costs are lowered since there is no need to previously select the company that is going to take the concession. The company with the highest willingness to pay (reflecting its productivity and expected profit) would make the highest bid and take the concession. Moreover, the auction generates additional revenue for the government.[13]

Nevertheless, some important elements have to be accounted for in order to allocate the concession in an efficient way. First, there is an element that relates to participation in the auction. Given the need for sustainable forest logging, participation in the auction should be restricted to companies that are likely to explore the forest area in a sustainable basin. The government could use a series of characteristics to approve the participation of a specific company in an auction. Gray (1997) proposes this approval to take place based mainly on the company's financial situation, environmental performance records and previous experiences with forest management and its plans for utilisation of the concession area.

Nevertheless, it can be difficult for the government to obtain some of this information and, if the companies are asked directly, they are not likely to tell the truth. This is a typical case of adverse selection[14] where the companies have private information that is not known by the government. There are possible solutions to this problem. The government could propose a kind of contract that would separate the companies between environmentally and non-environmentally correct. This could be done using a random auditing of the company's history and forcing the company to pay a penalty for falsified information.

Secondly, beyond the participation problem, there are two additional aspects that are fundamental for an efficient auction design: (i) the revenue generated for the government should be the maximum to capture part of the rents associated with the concession area, and (ii) it is necessary that the concession should be attributed to the company with the highest valuation for the forest area.

The maximum revenue for the auctioneer (the government) would not depend, in theory, on the type of auction used.[15] Nevertheless, in practice, due to the possibilities of failures in the basic assumptions, different types of auction could yield different results.

The two main failures that are likely to occur are the low number of participants and the low bid values offered by participants. The first problem generates a lower revenue for the auctioneer since the larger the number of participants in the auction, the higher, on average, will be the revenue for the seller.[16] The low bid problem could be solved with the imposition of a minimum price which would, on average, increase the price paid for the concession.[17]

Payment instruments on Concession Allocation

Theoretically, the most efficient way to make sure that the concession is given to the highest valuation bidder is the government trying to extract the maximum amount of information from the bidder. Given the nature of asymmetric information, one way of doing this is to condition the payment for the concession on information that affects the bidder's valuation for the good. This could be done if the government could observe *ex post* the amount of timber extracted. It could charge a multiple part tariff, a combination of an initial fee plus a royalty on the timber extracted.[18]

In practice, it would be very difficult for the government to control the exact amount of logs harvested. The companies, on the other hand, will not have any incentives to tell the truth since they would end up paying higher royalties. Consequently this type of two-part tariff would be, in practice, hardly feasible.

Other types of charges could be used by the government to collect the rent. First, it is possible to charge concession fees in the beginning of the concession period in order to generate revenue for control and monitoring and, at the same time, decrease speculation behaviour in the auction process. Some alternative measures for charging the logging company are annual charges based on areas and minimal stumpage prices based on the concession area.[19]

Regulation and Monitoring Issues

Once concessions are allocated, the government needs to function as a regulator if it wishes to create incentives for logging companies to harvest in a sustainable pattern. Nevertheless, this regulatory process is characterised by incomplete information and limited observation. If, on the one hand, the government does not have perfect information on the amount of timber harvested in the concession, on the other, monitoring is limited due to high costs. Thus, one may define two regulatory tasks for the government: one consisting of the design of a regulatory mechanism compatible with the sustainable forestry objective and the second consisting of monitoring mechanisms for this objective to be met.

As previously said, the government regulation over the logging company suffers from the classical problem of asymmetric information. The government does not know what is going to be the quantity of timber harvested after the contract is signed, a situation known in the literature as moral hazard.[20] Without any regulation from the government, the logging company will have an incentive to overextract. Since it is very costly for the government to set up a complete monitoring system, it will have to use some alternative instruments in order to create the right incentive for the firm to approach the desirable logging outcome.

There are basically two types of mechanisms that the government could use to create incentives for sustainable management. It could impose command and control methods or, alternatively, economic instruments can be used for creating incentives for sustainable management.[21]

Under the command and control approach, the regulatory agency would fix the maximum amount of timber that could be extracted from the concession area per period of time. The company exceeding this limit would pay a fixed monetary penalty. This penalty has to be sufficiently high to create the appropriate incentive for the company and, at the same time, the government enforcement power has to be sufficiently strong in order for the penalty to be credible.

Market-based instruments to control the amount of timber extracted from the concession can be applied as taxes, and royalties as previously identified for the capture of rent associated with the resource extraction. Furthermore, taxes and royalties on the quantity extracted also impose an additional variable cost to logging companies creating an incentive for lower logging levels. Nevertheless, as was already mentioned, levies on the quantity extracted suffer from the problem of monitoring and observation of the quantity extracted.

An alternative for this is the utilisation of performance bonds. This instrument consists of collecting a penalty bond associated with the non-compliance of the sustainable management contract. This bond would be returned to the company if its exploitation pattern complied with all the pre-established harvesting conditions. Additionally, a relationship that returns part of the bonus could also be employed. This function, relating the bonus to the type of environmental degradation, should be defined a priori in order for the incentives to be as clear as possible and to avoid rent-seeking behaviour (see Kahn et al., 1998)

No matter what type of incentive is used, command and control or market-based instruments, the participation of a regulatory agency is necessary in order to monitor the logging companies. Consequently, the institutional capacity strength of the regulatory environmental agency in charge of the system is crucial in order to increase its efficiency and decrease the incentives to destructive logging. Besides, it is important to include communities and NGOs in the monitoring and auditing process to reduce transaction costs associated with the monitoring process and give it an international credibility.

Industrial Structure and Competition on Timber Markets

It is plausible to expect that the concession of national forest for timber extraction can produce a transformation of the pattern of timber exploitation in the Amazonian region. That change could occur in relation to three basic aspects: change in the technological profile; change in the industrial concentration; and change of the deforestation geography.

There is a current trend of vertical integration between the extraction and processing activities in the Brazilian Amazon (see Stone, 1998). This tendency has a direct influence on the technological profile being used in the region. Additionally, this trend could be reinforced if the companies taking the concessions are processing sawmills already operating in the region.

Furthermore, the requirement of sustainable logging would also transform the technological profile of the companies in the region. This type of exploitation requires a more advanced technology, relatively more capital-intensive and, moreover, a significant investment in research, inventory planning and management plans in order to reduce the negative environmental impacts of extraction.

One possible problem associated with this technological change would be the change in the composition of the labour demand in the region. Due to the potential decrease in the utilisation of labour in relation to capital and knowledge could create a change towards the demand for skilled labour. This increase in the average qualification needed could bring negative impacts to income distribution in the region. Moreover, a more advanced technology and the need for a knowledge-intensive pattern of exploitation (selective logging, GIS and other techniques) will affect the comparative advantage between national and international companies. This could serve as an entrance barrier for national companies and firms with experience in other countries would dominate the market.

Secondly, it is important to take into account the possible change in market concentration levels. If firms that win the concession are vertically integrated and are already producing in the Amazon area, there will be a trend towards the concentration of the productive capacity in the region. Furthermore, it is possible that large companies with economies of scale expel small firms from the market, concentrating the timber activity in fewer hands.

Nevertheless, this phenomenon will only occur if the government can deter illegal logging. If the present possibilities for illegal logging along the frontier continue, small companies will always be able to survive since they can harvest the timber from open access areas at very low cost and sell it in local markets. Moreover, with the existence of this dual market and the difficulties with monitoring, there exists the possibility that companies working with concessions will harvest applying sustainable techniques in their concession area, but participate in the illegal market buying logs from nearby locations at lower prices.

One way to avoid this is to segment the markets (illegal and legal) by applying certification schemes to the timber extracted from concessions in a sustainable pattern. Nevertheless, as long as the frontier is still open access, it will be very hard for the certified timber to compete with lower prices from unsustainable extraction. Moreover, the national market will be very reluctant to pay a higher price for the certified product.[22]

A third consequence of concessions in national forests is the potential change in the geography of deforestation. Once the raw material in the main traditional logging areas is exhausted, logging firms will have to move on the frontier.[23] If the illegal logging process is not curbed, logging agents will have the incentive to move near concession areas, cut the logs and sell them to the concessionaire companies. The lack of monitoring and penalties, and the construction of new roads can create new agglomeration economies for logging and sawmill activities near concession areas.

9.5 CONCLUSIONS AND RECOMMENDATIONS

The creation of concession areas in the national forests (FLONAS) and their private exploitation consists, theoretically, in a solution to the problem of deforestation associated with timber exploitation in the Brazilian Amazon. Nevertheless, if this system is designed and applied without careful analysis of the failures that occurred in similar experiences in other countries and accounting for institutional and economic barriers found in the region, the outcome will not be, even in the short run, the control of the deforestation process in the region. This is because such processes are a consequence of the rational reaction of economic agents to the prevailing institutional context, that is, weakly-defined property rights, lack of credit, concentration of land and income, lack of monitoring and punishment. As we have tried to point out, the national forest system offers very effective economic incentives to counteract these deforestation trends and creates room for making sustainable logging a viable alternative for the use of forestland in the Amazon.

In such a manner, we can summarise the main conditions and cares needed for the establishment of forest concessions in the Brazilian Amazon:

- Concessions should be designed taking into consideration the size and the time needed in order to develop a sustainable logging process and, at the same time, making it financially viable and attractive.
- Concessions should be established using a first price sealed bid auction based on minimum price criteria clearly established with the participation of many bidders to assure fair levels of competition, although restricted only to environmentally sound companies.
- An efficient and credible system of monitoring and sanction fees should be established. Fees should be a function of the non-compliance level and a performance bond may be an interesting option to create this kind of incentive.
- There is a need for the participation of civil society through NGOs and local communities, including the monitoring and auditing phases in order to reduce transaction costs and increase credibility.
- Monitoring is crucial to control the existence of a dual logging market where illegal logging supply from agriculture clearing will reduce the market options of timber supply from concession areas.
- It is paramount to act on the demand side in order to create incentives for the purchase of timber with a sustainable management origin. This should be done not only through marketing and environmental education, but also through direct instruments as certification.
- The relative intensity of capital in the sustainable management forest industry will increase the need for more qualified labour supply in the region. Consequently, that will require labour and income policies related to job qualification and training with active community participation.

In sum, even taking into account the points presented above, it is mandatory to close the frontier in order to create a scarcity value related to forestland.[24] This structural change will take time to be implemented due to national social pressures associated with the need for agrarian reform and the opposition of political groups that benefit from the deforestation process.

Consequently, other types of measures are going to be needed in the short run to ensure the survival of companies that would enter into the forest concession exploitation. One possibility would be for the government to give a subsidy for sustainable logging in national forest concession areas. Alternatively, if the national market does not have the demand for sustainable timber, the solution would be to increase activities on exporting markets, although the international market is limited and a subsidy may still be needed in the initial phase. Note, however, that subsidy instruments, although attractive in theory, may also be difficult to implement due to the current fiscal crisis.

Another option could be the capturing of indirect values of the forest associated with carbon sequestration and biodiversity conservation.[25] Taking advantage of the recent proposals of the Clean Development Mechanism in the Climate Change Convention. Brazil could use its areas of national forest to sequester carbon and sell its credits in the international market. This could serve as a compensation for the sustainable forest management method employed, helping to finance the concession system.

Whatever the incentives, instruments and mechanisms to be adopted, the social question in the Amazon region has to be accounted for. Due to the large size necessary for the sustainable logging exploitation, land conflicts can arise due to the current need for agrarian reform actions in Brazil. Thus, the participation of local communities in the timber extraction and processing activities is crucial to deal with this equity issue.

It is also important to give priority to the institutional capacity of regulatory and monitoring agencies related to the system. The government has to establish a sound reputation and credibility for the sanctions and penalties imposed on non-compliance. This is a basic condition for the security of property rights and the development of efficient incentives which are needed to accomplish the economic and environmental aims of this promising concessional forest system in the Amazon.

Additionally, it is important to emphasise that concessions should be allocated gradually in order to make possible the revision and improvement of the system according to the existing institutional capacity.

We can conclude, therefore, that the implementation of large concessions in national forests with the adequate contract design is a necessary, albeit insufficient, condition to guarantee the sustainable timber exploitation in the region. Political will, the resolution of persistent social problems and the implementation of policies that create the land scarcity perception in the region are fundamental conditions to assure that timber exploitation in the Amazon forest can be compatible with the possibilities of sustainable development in Brazil.

NOTES

1. See Schneider (1995) and Seroa da Motta (1993) for a more detailed analysis of this process.

2. See for example Mahar (1986), Seroa da Motta (1993), Ozório de Almeida and Campari (1995) and Young (1996).
3. This process was accentuated with the entrance of Southeast Asian companies in Brazil.
4. In fact, the classification is broader but it was aggregated here to allow for calculations.
5. Deforestation data are based on official figures from INPE (1998).
6. Sustainability in the extraction process consists, on one hand, in allowing for the natural growth of new trees in the harvested areas and, on the other hand, in maintaining the environmental services of the forest such as soil preservation, regulating the water cycle and recycling nutrients. For a detailed analysis of the environmental services of the forest: see Myers (1997).
7. In the Philippines and Indonesia, for example, the government collected only 16.5 per cent and 38 per cent respectively, of the rents associated with timber harvesting (Repetto, 1988).
8. See Gillis (1992) and Gray (1997) for details on size and length of concession in different countries.
9. This will also depend on the possibility of renewable contracts. Nevertheless, great uncertainty in many developing countries creates myopic behaviour in terms of extraction.
10. Many concessions in the past were awarded on political power base and bargaining creating high incentives for corruption and rent-seeking behaviour.
11. See Repetto and Gillis (1988) and Gillis (1992) for examples of countries that established royalties that were too low.
12. In some African countries, for example, the lack of capacity of governments to measure and classify logs led them to permit companies to present their own data (Gray, 1997).
13. Although the auction system is the most efficient way to allocate concessions, it: has rarely been utilised in the past. This was specially true in Asian and African countries where the allocation of concessions has a direct relationship with rent-seeking behaviour. For details on the allocation mechanism in a diverse number of countries see Gray (1997).
14. The term 'adverse selection', is used to designate a relationship between two or more economic agents where the characteristics of the agent (the company) cannot be perfectly observed by the principal (the government).
15. In theory, based on basic assumptions, different types of auctions would yield, on average, the same expected payoff for the auctioneer. This result is known as the revenue equivalence theorem and it was first proved by Vickrey (1961).
16. See McAfee and McMillan (1987) for a review of auction theory. See Brannman et al. (1987) for an econometric test of this result for forest services' auctions in the United States.
17. See McAfee and McMillan (1987) for a proof for this proposition. Note, however, that, although this minimum price would include the value associated with the timber in the forest, it would put aside other kinds of environmental values associated with indirect and non-use values.
18. See Ramsey (1980) for an example of this mechanism for an oil concession.
19. For more details on charging mechanisms see Gray (1997).
20. A situation of moral hazard occurs when there is a relationship between two (or more) economic agents, usually known as principal and agent, and (i) the agent makes a decision that affects his utility and the principal's utility; (ii) the principal can only observe the final result of the action and this final result is an imperfect signal of the action taken; (iii) the action that the agent would chose spontaneously would not be optimal. For additional examples of principal–agent relationships see Salanié (1997) and Macho-Stadler and Pérez-Castrillo (1997). For an example of moral hazard and environmental regulation see Laffont (1995).
21. For a review on environmental regulation see Cropper and Oates (1992). For a definition of economic instrument and some examples for Latin America see Serôa da Motta et al. (1999).
22. It is important to mention that approximately 90 per cent of the timber extracted in Brazil goes to the national market.
23. See Stone (1998) for a description of this process in the Brazilian Amazon.

24. See Seroa da Motta and Ferraz (2000) for an example of the low value associated with the scarcity rent of timber in the Amazonian region.
25. See Fearnside (1997) for a proposal similar to this one.

REFERENCES

Brannman, L. et al. (1987), 'The price effects of increased competition in auction markets', *The Review of Economics and Statistics*, **69** (1).

Cropper, M.L. and Oates, W.E. (1992), 'Environmental economics: a survey', *Journal of Economic Literature*, **xxx** (2), 675–740.

EMBRAPA (1991), *Delineamento Macroecológico do Brasil*, Rio de Janeiro: Serviço Nacional de Levantamento e Conservação de Solos, EMBRAPA.

Fearnside, P.M. (1997), 'Environmental services as a strategy for sustainable development in Rural Amazonia', *Ecological Economics*, 20.

Gillis, M. (1992), 'Forest Concessions Management and Revenue Policies', in: Narendra Sharma (ed.), *Managing the World's Forests: Looking for Balance between Conservation and Development*, Dubuque, Iowa: Kendall-Hunt Publishing.

Gray, J.A. (1997), 'Forest concession policies and sustainable forest management of tropical forests', Proceedings of the Workshop of Forest Policies and Sustainable Development in the Amazon, Rio de Janeiro.

INPE (1998), *Desflorestamento na Amazônia 1995–1997*.

Kahn, J.R., McCormick, F. and Nogueira, V.P.Q. (1998), 'Integrating ecological complexity into economic incentives for sustainable use of Amazonian rainforests', Proceedings of the Southern Economic Association, November 1997.

Laffont, J.J. (1995), 'Regulation, moral hazard and insurance of environmental risks', *Journal of Public Economics*, **58** (3).

Macho-Stadler, I. and Pérez-Castrillo, D. (1997), *An Introduction to the Economics of Information: Incentives and Contracts*, Oxford: Oxford University Press.

Mahar, D.J. (1986), *Government Policies and Deforestation in Brazil's Amazon Region*, Washington, DC: The World Bank.

McAfee, R.P. and McMillan, J. (1987), 'Auctions and bidding', *Journal of Economic Literature*, **xxv**, (June) 699–738.

Myers, N. (1997), 'The World's Forests and their Ecosystem Services', in: G.C. Daily (ed.), *Nature's Services: Societal Dependence on Natural Ecosystems*, Washington, DC: Island Press.

Ozório de Almeida, L. and Campari, J.S. (1995), *Sustainable Settlement in the Brazilian Amazon*, New York: Oxford University Press.

Prado, A.C. (1995), *Exploração Florestal Madeireira*, Brasília: FUNATURA.

Ramsey, J.B. (1980), *Bidding and Oil Leases*, Greenwich, CT: JAI Press.

Repetto, R. (1988), *The Forest for the Trees? Government Policies and the Misuse of Forest Resources*, Washington, DC: World Resource Institute.

Repetto, R. and Gillis, M. (1988), *Public Policies and the Misuse of Forest Resources*, Cambridge: Cambridge University Press.

Salanié, B. (1997), *The Economics of Contracts*, Cambridge MA: MIT Press.

Schneider, R.R. (1995), *Government and the Economy on the Amazon Frontier*, Washington: The World Bank (World Bank Environment Paper, n.11).

Seroa da Motta, R. (1993), 'Past and current policy issues concerning tropical deforestation in Brazil', The Kiel Institute of World Economics, Kiel Working Paper 566.

Seroa da Motta, R. (1996), *Indicadores Ambientais: Aspectos Ecológicos, de Eficiência e Distributivos*, Rio de Janeiro: IPEA (Texto para Discussão, n.399).

Seroa da Motta, R. and Ferraz, C. (2000), 'Estimating timber depreciation in the Brazilian Amazon', *Journal of Environment and Development Economics*, **5**, (1&2).

Seroa da Motta, R., Huber, R. and Ruintenbeek, J. (1999), 'Market based instruments for environmental policymaking in Latin America and the Caribbean: lessons from eleven countries', *Environment and Development Economics*, **4** (2).

Seroa da Motta, R., Ferraz, C. and Young, C.E.F. (2000), 'Brazil: CDM Opportunities and Benefits', in: D. Austin and P. Faeth (eds), *Financing Sustainable Development with the Clean Development Mechanism*, Washington, DC: World Resources Institute.

Stone, S. (1998), 'Evolution of the timber industry along an aging frontier: evidence from the Eastern Amazon', *World Development*, **26** (3).

Vickrey, W. (1961), 'Counterspeculation, auctions and competitive sealed tenders', *Journal of Finance*, 16, March.

Young, C.E.F. (1996), 'Economic adjustment policies and the environment: a case study of Brazil', University College London, PhD Dissertation.

Index